JACK DRYDEN

MADE IN LONDON

A DOG CALLED HORSE

The amazing true story of the extraordinary
life of Paul Henry Jarvis né Byfield

SOLIS
WEBER

Solis Weber
An independent publication

This paperback edition published in United Kingdom in 2018

Copyright © Jack Dryden 2018

Jack Dryden asserts the moral right to
be identified as the author of this work

Typeset in Garamond

Printed and bound in United Kingdom

The majority of the names and places described in this
book are genuine. However, to protect the anonymity of
certain individuals, some of the names have been changed.

Acknowledgements

First of all, I'd like to thank the biographer of this book who is like a brother to me. He knows more about me than my own family and has always been there for me, along with his lovely wife and children.

I have visited Ireland many times in the last three years to stay with them and work on this book, and professionally and leisurely, nothing was ever a problem for them. Everything would be planned out, allowing them to be the brilliant parents they are, while juggling me around the running of their family and I never wanted for anything.

I love you all, my Irish family. Thank you, as without your support, guidance, professionalism and loyalty, this book would never have been written.

I would also like to thank everyone that contributed to the book in one way or another - Sean McGuigan (the love of my life), Sue Gomer Bennett, Laura Jarvis, Linda Brown, Leigh Brown, Michael Patterson, Karen Flynn, Norah Roberts, Iwona Joanna, Paul Hennen, Horse, Chase - and to thank everyone that has been in my life and with me on my journey.

I thank you all.

Paul Henry Jarvis

Contents

Prologue

I first met Paul in 1993 when I moved to London to attend South Bank University. I was a fresh-faced teenager, new to the wonders of seemingly endless metropolitan jungles like London, having been brought up in primitive Donegal, on the rural West Coast of Ireland.

For my first year at university, I lived with my sister, Michaela, in Olympia, West Kensington. During this period in her life she was very much the urban socialite and had many friends and acquaintances that I found to be both fascinating and disconcerting in equal measure.

The most memorable of all the people I met during this part of my life was, without doubt, Paul Henry Byfield, as he was known to me at the time. Paul was just eight years my senior but seemed to have lived a whole lifetime more than me. He was clearly unhinged, utterly hilarious and, it would seem, driven solely by the want to party, to drink to excess and to experiment with every vice known to man.

I have seen Paul clear a nightclub dance floor in a matter of seconds with his flailing, spinning moves. I have been at parties where Paul has left at 4am and shaken the host's hand while unsuccessfully trying to hide a box of wine that he has just stolen from the kitchen. I have seen Paul in so many states where the simple act of speech has long since left him. I have been with Paul while he was in the depths of depression and in the peaks of ecstasy. And I have frequently experienced first-hand the madness that often consumes Paul's everyday life.

But I have also seen another side to Paul, one that he reserves for only his closest family and friends. It takes much loyalty, many acts of forgiving and an unerring faith in him as a person to get close enough for him to reveal all of his true self. What lies beneath is the most sensitive, beautiful and intriguing human being imaginable. Fatally flawed no doubt, but one of the most genuine, honest and special people I have ever had the pleasure to meet.

I visited Paul in the early winter of 2014, using the lure of England v San Marino at Wembley as an excuse to spend time with my old friend. Over a pint of lager in The White Horse pub in Shepherd's Bush, Paul told me that he had always wanted to write the story of his life but felt he didn't have the know-how to do it. I told him I had always wanted to write a book but couldn't think of a good enough story. By the time we had finished our pints, we determined that together we would write this book.

What you have in your hands isn't intended to win the Booker Prize or to find itself in the window display of Waterstones. This book is simply one friend helping another friend to put down in words the remarkable tale of the ability of one man to have lived an ordinary life in an extraordinary way.

We hope you enjoy it.

Chapter 1 - Made in London

Paul Henry Byfield was born on 23rd July 1967 in Burdett Road, East London, not far from Mile End and coincidentally, within a few hundred yards of St Paul's Church in Bow Common. Paul was being born into a new era of 'Swinging London', with a hedonistic mix of music, discotheques, fashion, sexual promiscuity and an upsurge in the availability of drugs and other risky experiences. All of these things Paul would embrace and take to an extreme as his life unfolded.

Hip and fashionable London had entered a new era of optimism. The capital was on the crest of a wave having survived the German onslaught during the blitz that had ravaged much of the city during the early 1940's and then, less than a year before Paul's birth, enjoying the success of the national team when England once again triumphed over the old enemy, this time at football, at a venue less than ten miles from where Paul would spend his formative years.

Into this new positive vibe was born the baby Paul. London, like many sprawling metropolises, sat uncomfortably balanced between the lights, the glitz and the glamour along with an equally potent underbelly of crime, addiction and sexual deviancy which would draw Paul in as the years progressed. Why Paul became ensnared in this dark world is open to interpretation. Maybe it was through desire, perhaps it was simply fate, or most probably, it was a combination of both.

Before Paul was born, his mum, Linda, was married to Mr Byfield, who she had seven children with. The Byfield children were all very close together in birth ages and it seems that Linda had very little time when she wasn't either pregnant or having recently given birth.

The family lived together in Hackney, and during this time a good friend of Linda's became homeless. Linda said she could stay with them for a while until she got back on her feet. Extending the arm of friendship to an ally in need was very noble of the young woman, but she was soon to realise that the huge favour wasn't to be reciprocated. In fact the opposite was to unfold as Linda's 'friend' was soon to embark on an affair with Mr Byfield.

As the situation worsened and Linda found it more and more

difficult to cope, she confronted her husband with the dire state of their marital situation but, instead of being understanding and attempting to help, Mr Byfield retaliated initially with anger and then with physical violence. Left with little hope for her marriage and with the likelihood that her husband would only become increasingly aggressive towards her, and possibly the children, if she stayed, Linda fled the house leaving a very young brood of babies in nappies and cots. She was left to hope that having lost her husband and her home, that at least her young children would be cared for.

Linda Byfield fled to Burdett Road where she would go on to live for many years and where she would give birth to four more children, two boys and a girl, and then latterly, Paul. Linda was white and Paul's father was black, of Caribbean descent, hence the mixed-race colour that Paul was born with. His siblings are also all mixed-race, and although it is obvious this was because each sibling's respective father was black as well, what is not so clear is whether it was the same man, or a series of different lovers that Linda had.

The man Paul knows to be his father is Johnny Brown, or Johnny Brown the Banana Man as he was most commonly known on account of his arrival on a Jamaican Windrush 'banana boat' that made its way from Jamaica to London and back. HMT Empire Windrush had been a German passenger liner and cruise ship during the 1930's and then during World War II, the German navy used her as a troopship. She was acquired by the United Kingdom as a prize of war at the end of World War II and renamed Empire Windrush.

The ship was then used to transport people and goods across the globe and is best remembered today for bringing one of the first large groups of post-war West Indian immigrants to the United Kingdom. She carried four-hundred and ninety-two passengers and one stowaway on a voyage from Jamaica to London in 1948 including, it would seem, Paul's future father.

Among the other passengers was Sam Beaver King who went on to become the first black Mayor of Southwark. There were also the calypso musicians Lord Kitchener, Lord Beginner, Lord Woodbine and Mona

Baptiste, alongside various other regular West Indians looking for work and a decent wage in England.

The arrivals were temporarily housed in the Clapham South Deep Shelter in south-west London, less than a mile away from the Coldharbour Lane Employment Exchange in Brixton, where some sought work. Many only intended to stay for a few years, and although a number returned, the majority remained to settle permanently as was the case with Johnny Brown.

When Paul was just a few months old, Linda moved him, his two older brothers, and older sister, from Burdett Road to Matilda House, off Thomas More Street, Wapping, East London. Their new residence was a stone's throw from Tower Bridge and less than fifty metres from the banks of the River Thames. Paul was to stay here for several years and the ground floor flat at Matilda House is the first place that he remembers as 'home'.

Paul's earliest memories are what would seem, by today's standards, incredibly chaotic and overcrowded. There were two new arrivals in the shape of younger brothers and Paul slept in one bed along with the older of the two babies, one of his older brothers and his older sister. There was little in the way of home comforts for the children but Paul and his siblings knew little else, and were content to be safe and cared for by their mother, and also by Linda's mum, or nanny May, as she was known by all the family.

Nanny May lived with the clan for some time in Matilda House where she had her own room. She helped out with raising the children when she could and would go on to become a very important influence on young Paul as he grew up.

Nanny May's close bond with the children may well have stemmed from her appreciation of their vulnerability, something that she understood from her own experiences. Paul's great-grandmother had died prematurely and his nan had been brought up by her father - Paul's great-grandfather - who went on to remarry and had several more children. The new step-mum singled out Paul's nan, severely bullying her and he remembers being told this on many occasions by his grandmother.

His mum was commonly known as Linda and although her name was actually Ivy, which was the official name on the Family Allowance Book, she chose to call herself Linda and that's the name everyone knew her by.

Before Paul was born, his eldest brother, Peter, had been raised for some time by nanny May and his granddad on his mum's side, Henry Jarvis, who later died of a brain haemorrhage. Granddad Henry had passed away just before Paul was born and that is why he was named Paul Henry Byfield, after the grandfather he never actually met.

Peter was a young adult by the time Paul was born, and had returned to live with his mother following the care provided by his grandparents. He had his own room in the house, despite the fact that he wasn't around very often, due to either being out doing his things or, as was probably more often the case, being incarcerated for various misdemeanours. Peter had served several terms in borstals for crimes committed, though none of them particularly nasty or violent, more the 'normal' offences and prosecutions that prevailed among young black males in 1960's London.

With Linda's previous family and the one now homed in Matilda House, Linda had given birth to thirteen children in total, with Paul being the eleventh child. For the young Paul growing up in Matilda House, his immediate family was Peter, the eldest, sister Elaine, John, then Paul himself, and after that, Gary and Wayne. Paul knew them simply as his brothers and sisters, but he would never know his half-brothers and half-sisters from the time his mum fled from Hackney, save for a strange and brief encounter with one of them later on in his life. It wasn't until much further into adulthood that Paul would find out more about his actual family history and it was then that he would begin to use the terms 'half-brother' and 'half-sister'.

The accommodation in Matilda House which the family shared was a three-bedroom ground floor flat with a communal courtyard. There were several stories to the overall House and residents could go to the upstairs levels via stairwells and onto landings. The top floor properties weren't yet furnished as habitable accommodation so the locals would hang their laundry up on clothes lines on the otherwise derelict floor.

Matilda House is still there today although it has now been divided into luxury flats and sits in an exclusive area of East London. The value of the flat where Paul lived was about £5,000 in 1967 but to buy it today would require upwards of £800,000 which gives an indication of how sought after the area has become.

In the late 1960's, East London felt very safe to Paul and he didn't experience any fear. This would change due to a catalogue of unsavoury incidents and accidents that would befall him in the following years but for now it was as safe as London probably ever has been, or was before. People left their front doors open, neighbours openly trusted each other and everyone kept an eye on each other's children without needing to be asked. As a toddler, Paul spent lots of time at the front of the flats in the courtyard area which he remembers as a large square where he and other children from the surrounding houses would congregate and play together.

As Paul grew older, the playground that was London became more and more enticing and as his years progressed, so did the places he would frequent to find amusement, company and sometimes, danger.

Matilda House is very close to St Katharine Docks which, at the time, housed big rag warehouses containing massive bundles of clothes, compacted and strapped together. These bundles, collected by the merchants and earmarked for onward journey were so large it took heavy machinery to lift and move them around. As children, Paul and his siblings would go and play in the big warehouses although they knew they weren't supposed to. As they skipped out the door, their mum would often shout after them, "when you fall down and break your legs, don't come running to me!" Paul was fascinated by the size and noise of the docks and would spend many an hour playing in amongst the machinery and clothing bundles, despite the obvious dangers.

A short walk from Matilda House, over the Thames by St Katharine's Way, the children also played in a big fountain outside The Tower Hotel which is still there to this day - the 'Girl with a Dolphin Fountain'. The fountain depicts a dolphin with a child hanging on to its fin. Into the fountain, tourists, many of them Americans attracted by the lure of 'Swinging London', threw money in to make a wish. Paul and his siblings would then reach in and grab the pennies and half pennies and, if they were really lucky the two penny pieces, out of the pond until they were shushed away by the hotel staff, who were keen to keep the grounds clear of the little, local urchins.

Past Traitor's Gate and the Tower of London, at Tower Hill Station, Paul has a vivid recollection of the Tube Station escalators and how he and his siblings, along with other children from the nearby estates, would ride up the staircase, gripping on to the black handrail. At the time he didn't realise but looking back he muses that they must have looked like little marmoset monkeys, particularly him, being very young and with his big afro hair which was all the rage among black children back then. Paul's hair was particularly wild coming as he did from a white mother who didn't have much knowledge of how to look after black hair, or indeed black skin.

Tourists at Tower Hill Tube Station would frequently take pictures of them and it would seem that these little marmosets would form part of a collage of slide shows upon their return to the States or Canada or Western Europe or wherever they had originated. One can only imagine the joy that the passing tourists felt when, as part of their hedonistic escape to late 1960's London, they happened upon the pure photographic opportunity of genuine London street kids with their crazy afros and smiling faces, revelling in the fun that a tube station escalator handrail had to offer. What is harder to imagine perhaps, is whether any of the tourists stopped to consider the hardships and enduring difficulties that lay behind the smiles of these little marmosets?

Not many people came to Matilda House as there was often no electricity and most times things were done by candlelight or the coal fire. This was because Linda was very poor. These were difficult times for a single mother trying to raise and support six children on her own and Linda's situation wasn't helped by the fact that she was very bad at money management. She wasn't a drinker or a gambler, but life was tough and she had to constantly try to make ends meet wherever she could.

In addition to her promiscuity that had brought into the world a large number of children whom she could barely support, Linda's other main vice was that she was a smoker, although Paul recalls that she could retain throughout her life the ability to stop and start smoking, seemingly as she pleased.

In Matilda House, they had baths in a tin in front of the fire and it wasn't necessarily because that's what families did in those days. It was more because there was either no gas or because there was a problem with the bathroom. Paul remembers clothes were on a drier in the bathroom and that the bath was never actually used. There was nearly always a problem with the water heating and it was never fixed, simply because there was never any money for repairs. Often times in the flat, the children would have gone for long periods suffering with no heating, huddled together in their one bed, trying to keep warm.

Paul has no early memories of their father as he wasn't around and to make matters worse, he didn't contribute financially in any way to support Linda. She instead survived on Child Benefits to support the children and would get Family Child Allowance on a Monday - that was the day she would go shopping for provisions for the week and the children would usually get a little treat.

The norm was very much a case of limited cash coming in, and then quickly going out again. Throughout his own life, Paul has followed this trend and has found it difficult to manage his money. Indeed, like his mum, he has always been able to find ways to get cash to come in but has always been equally adept at letting it go freely.

There were also additional residents in the Matilda House home. Paul's nan had lots of dogs - he remembers Lassie, Sally and Ringo, among others - and they were all inbred, all related in one way or another as he recalls. His nan's bedroom window looked directly out from the front of the house and when somebody knocked on the door, all the dogs would go crazy and start jumping up and down. Newspaper covered much of the windows so when people walked past the house, they may not have noticed the passive dogs. But whenever there was a caller or any kind of noise outside, the dogs would bounce up and down and start barking and could just be seen over the top of the paper from anyone looking in from outside. Onlookers would have seen the hilarious circus with various deranged dogs leaping above the line of newspaper and creating the most deafening racket.

There was also a terrible smell of dog urine from the room, and Paul, perhaps not surprisingly, rarely went in there. Apart from the stench, there was also the risk that when he opened the door the dogs would try and escape and get out, running amok all over the flat, or worse still, managing to get outside. Even if he managed to keep them all in the room, there was still the hazard of newspaper strewn across the floor with various dog's waste all over it. Looking back, Paul describes his nan as eccentric and a bit crazy. She must have been, he reflects, to live in such close proximity to all these demented dogs and their unrelenting smell of urine.

In addition to nanny May's room, the other bedroom in the flat housed the five children, including Paul. The youngest, Wayne, slept in a cot and the other four children shared a bed. As well as the crazed menagerie of dogs next door, Paul vividly recalls many a night where he and his siblings could hear mice or rats scurrying about the flat. Because of the closeness to the dockyards, rodents were common-place and they'd hear noises outside and in the room from the scampering animals, probably attracted by the environment of the flat with the unkempt dogs. Although Paul can't remember seeing rats and mice that often, he had no doubt they were definitely there and he remembers it being talked about as the scared children huddled under their blankets in the bed.

Linda slept in the living room and there was also older brother Peter's bedroom. Paul wasn't really allowed in Peter's room and although Linda may have stayed in the room occasionally when Peter was away, it was generally 'out of bounds'. This is a further display of the generosity and kindness of a mother who would sleep on a sofa so that her children and mother could have a bed and the eldest child could have his own room, even though he wasn't even there much of the time.

Despite it being forbidden, Paul does remember the odd occurrence when he would go and snoop around Peter's room, and on one of these secret missions he hit the jackpot when he found a little book with pages that you could flick through with your fingers. The flicking pages showed images quickly changing, like a real life film in your hands, a mild form of pornographic imagery of a woman getting undressed. Paul remembers it being amazing, as much for his first proper sight of a naked lady as for how new it was, having the sensation of appearing to see a little film right before his eyes.

With the relentless chaos that seemed to shape her existence it is not surprising that Linda didn't want people coming round as she was most likely consistently embarrassed about having no electricity or gas, the smell and noise of the crazy dogs, or perhaps simply having so many young children living under the one roof.

But regardless of how it appears looking back, to Paul it was the place where he felt safe and secure and loved. It was his home and where the little boy's discovery of the disjointed world he was about to inhabit began.

Chapter 2 – He's Such a Good Boy

Paul recalls being a very shy and withdrawn child. Everyone would always praise him for his good behaviour and comment on his angelic good looks. But beneath the beauty and serenity of the infant Paul, something more sinister and evil lurked within. Something that Paul, to this day, has struggled to come to terms with. He didn't talk much as a child, communicating instead by facial expressions and body language. The reason for this still bothers him and when he thinks about it he becomes upset.

He recalls being constantly aware of adults around him saying things like "isn't he a good boy?" and "isn't he quiet?" as if making noise or asking for anything like sweets or new shoes was seen as something incredibly bad and naughty for a young child to do. Paul was always praised for never asking for anything or demanding things as many young children naturally do. He was regularly complimented by those around him for being so placid and this form of behaviour was always very much verbally promoted.

The young boy would often hear such things being said about him as "Isn't Paul good?...he's such a well-behaved child...he's got good manners...he's never any trouble." As a result of this, Paul always felt under pressure to maintain his status as the impeccably behaved child and this may go a long way to explaining why he found it so difficult to come out of himself as a youngster.

Paul was also an extremely attractive child. A lot of people thought he was actually a girl at the time and not because of how he was dressed but because of his angelic features and his soft, candy-floss afro hairstyle.

When they lived in Wapping, Paul's mum, Linda, would sometimes meet men outside their home, under the archway where the stairwell led up to the other flats. Most Fridays she would meet one of these men, 'The Fish Man', a black man who worked in Billingsgate Fish Market. He would bring fish to Linda nearly every week and was talked about as an 'uncle' but he wasn't really an uncle - he was really just somebody that Linda would see most Fridays. Paul was allowed to follow his mum and hang around on the stairwell and he would watch, silently and perfectly behaved, as Paul's mum and the Fish Man would talk and kiss. Paul would just stand there in his own little world, oblivious to his surroundings, yet feeling safe being close, as he always was, to his mother.

Of all these encounters, Paul remembers one most vividly. The Fish Man had a big watch which he showed to Paul. To the young child's eyes, it seemed huge and as The Fish Man gave him the watch to look at, Paul was enthralled by the big blue face, the silver metal strap and the heavy weight of it. Paul held it to his ear and heard it tick like a big, bold heartbeat. He held it and listened to the ticking for a very long time. The Fish Man smiled and told Paul he could keep the watch. This was so exciting for the young boy, holding in his tiny hands the huge watch with the big heartbeat. Later, Paul would listen to the deep sounds of the ticking watch over and over again, locked away in his own fantasy world.

When his mum would meet her new men, her boyfriends, occasional flings or 'uncles' as they were often called, Paul would invariably be allowed to hang around in the shadows. But it was only ever allowed to be little Paul, not the others, and it was always on the hush-hush – he was on strict instructions not to mention these encounters to anyone. This wasn't a problem for the angelic, well behaved, young child. He was told to pretend he was going out to play but was really under direction to meet his mother at a certain place. This would happen quite a lot and Paul would tell his brothers and sister that he was going away to play somewhere, but then go around the corner to his mum.

Paul wonders why his mum behaved like this. Was it simply as cover as she didn't want people knowing her business or was it more of a safety issue? It was unlikely that the men in question would do anything untoward if she had a child in tow. Or was it maybe just because Paul was her favourite and she liked to have him around?

Paul knows he was treated differently to his other brothers and sister and it still baffles him to this day exactly why this was. He was special, he was quiet, he wasn't a problem-child. But why exactly was he singled out for this special treatment, to be sneaky and to be encouraged to tell lies to his siblings? He doesn't really know, but can only think it may have been because he was the favourite one and his mum would rather have him with her whenever she could.

However, while Paul undoubtedly felt loved and wanted by his mother, the isolation from the people much closer to his own age, his siblings, left him with feelings and emotions that would follow him well into adulthood. From as early as he could remember Paul felt socially inadequate, that he didn't fit in and carried with him a sense of being perpetually lost in the world of others which constantly left him feeling very lonely. As a young child, through his teens and early adolescence, these were his prevalent emotions which perhaps goes a long way to explaining his soon-to-be-developed coping mechanisms.

Sometimes Linda would take Paul to go and see a woman who was referred to as Paul's 'aunt Betty'. Aunt Betty, a white woman, lived in Plaistow and was married to a big stocky black man called Al who was completely blind. Paul never remembers seeing a guide dog or anything else that would suggest Al was blind but he knew he was. He also knew that Al was a solid bloke and he recalls that at the time aunt Betty was his mum's best friend. They would call to Betty and Al's for hours at a time or even on occasion, for a couple of days.

Paul enjoyed these excursions but always remembers it was just him and his mum, once again isolated from the rest of his siblings. Sometimes though, Paul's mum would do a 'disappearing act' without taking him with her and be gone for several days without warning. Paul recalls her doing this several times when he was very young and although the children were never definitively told where she was, Paul thinks she was probably either staying with her best friend and seeing men at Betty's or perhaps staying at the man's place. When she was gone for days, nan would look after Paul and the rest of the children.

Given the choice what would Paul rather have been doing? Did he want to be at home playing with his siblings or was he happy enough to be away with his mum most of the times? The answer is that Paul didn't actually care either way. As a young child, he never felt that anyone really understood him, and the affection and attention he was given transferred to his own sense of worth in quite the opposite way to how it was most probably intended. Paul felt pitiful, paranoid, desperate and not liked.

Looking back he feels it's easy to see why these were his over-riding emotions. Despite the positive words, these were all learnt behaviours he witnessed every day from the two greatest influences in his life, his mother and his nan. Spending so much time with his mother meant, without realising it until he was much older, that she projected, and he adopted, many of her traits. Isolation, misery, a sense of being attacked, persecuted and not being liked were the feelings that formed in Paul's head and these were the things that would haunt him throughout his life.

He can't really remember playing with his siblings much and recalls spending most of the time in his own little world. There wasn't a lot he had in common with his younger siblings as, although Paul was still very young, his brother Gary was two years younger than him and Wayne was four years younger than him, so really they were just babies. Paul remembers more times spent with his sister, particularly when she was left in charge when Paul's mum and nan would go shopping on their own, often for hours on end. But other times, Paul felt he was bullied by his siblings, most probably because they were jealous of how their mother and nan doted on him.

It wasn't just his mother who enjoyed his company. Paul remembers that he used to hang around with one of the other kids on the estate. His friend's mum had a three-wheeler disability scooter with a handlebar steering wheel. She would use this to go shopping and Paul and his friend would often accompany her and sit on the floor while she went out and about. Paul also visited his friend at his house, moving seamlessly between flats and houses as was the norm of the day.

But it wasn't always just innocent fun, as Paul was soon to discover. On one occasion, Paul, just six years old, went round to play at his friend's house and a man was there in the living room. Paul assumes it was his friend's father although this was never actually mentioned - it may have been his friend's mum's boyfriend at the time or perhaps a friend of the family. The man had Paul on his lap and was jigging him up and down and being very pleasant. Paul had shorts on and could feel the material of the man's trousers which were itchy to the touch, like heavy wool on bare skin. The feeling of the fabric against his legs was unfamiliar to Paul and he was about to feel another new sensation when he became aware of the man's erect penis bouncing against his small virginal bottom. As Paul bounced up and down on the man's knee, he didn't know exactly what was going on but was aware enough to know that it was wrong. He didn't yet possess the life experience to really know why it shouldn't be happening and moreover wasn't aware of how he should deal with it then or in the future.

It's hard to know where to rank this act, especially in light of the exposure of the rampant paedophilia of the time but it is clear that regardless of what happened, it left an indelible mark on Paul insomuch as his later understanding of his ability to give his body for the sexual gratification of others, whether for money, for love or for attention.

When Paul recalls his childhood and always being talked of as a "good, quiet kid", he gets very tearful and emotional. Paul feels that, although he admits he could be wrong, his family are very good at keeping secrets and not telling the truth about things so there may be something that he should know about but doesn't.

He thinks partly he was singled out for being 'angelic-looking' but when he delves deeper he also feels that there is some trauma lurking in his past, something that happened that was never spoken of again but that left an unerasable stain on Paul's mind and an emptiness in his soul.

Something happened to Paul in his very early years that affected him to such an extent that he barely spoke or made any noise, communicating nearly exclusively through facial expressions, behaving impeccably as a young child and continuing like this for many years.

At least that's what Paul thinks happened. The reality is he simply cannot remember. The only tell-tale sign that Paul can link this to is that he has a slightly deformed finger on his right hand and has a vague recollection of having it shut in a door with a lingering darkness that it had something to do with his dad. Although Paul can't remember the exact specifics of any incidents, he knows that there was something that caused him to lock himself away in his own childhood world, where little plastic farm animals were a greater source of comfort to him than the adults that were supposed to be there to care for him.

Later in his adult life Paul sought solace from his multitude of issues by going into rehab and it was here that he started to become aware of this hidden secret from his past, this trauma that was always there, yet never was? He had genuinely forgotten or managed to find a way to temporarily forget through his later childhood and teenage years and it was only when he received specialised support and help as an adult that the memories began to come back, though never fully.

Could it have been that his assumed father, in a cruel fit of rage, had deliberately trapped the baby Paul's fingers in a door? Surely not? The thought left him as soon as he had imagined it. But maybe? Or could it have been something less sinister, an accident that shouldn't have happened. Surely he should have been better protected and saved from such dangers?

There was also talk of him having had an operation as a child but again he can't fully recall the details and doesn't know if this was a routine procedure or if it was something more serious.

It may have been that his withdrawn shyness wasn't simply through choice, but perhaps was related to a physical condition that required medical intervention.

He cannot fully remember and probably never will. But despite the vagueness and the confusion, it undoubtedly affected his early years and the not knowing has lingered with him since then.

When his mother passed away several years ago, perhaps with her went the final chance Paul had of ever finding out the truth behind his childhood trauma.

Chapter 3 – A Cat of Nine Lives

Those who know Paul will testify to the fact that he is a bit of a cat, not only in his feline mannerisms and his ability to always seemingly land on his feet, but also for the fact that throughout his life he would appear to have had, and used up, quite a few of his nine lives. There have been various near-death experiences and close-shaves both in childhood and throughout his adult life, many of which would have consumed a lesser mortal, but each time Paul survived and came out stronger on the other side, eager to tell the tale. He attributes much of this luck to his nan and latterly to his mother who he believes are looking down on him from their elevated perches in heaven. After all, a creature with nine lives can afford to take risks.

One of the first times that Paul cheated death was when both his nanny May and mum were still very much of this world. Paul had found a box of matches whilst out rummaging through the old warehouses and, being too scared to light one of them where he had found them, had returned to the sanctuary of Matilda House to try out his new-found hoard. After lighting several matches and being encapsulated by the small flames, Paul had sought a more exciting, larger thrill – this was the feeling of always wanting a bit more, something more adventurous, which would become his hallmark – and lit a tissue which he had found on the kitchen table.

In the blink of an eye, the kitchen at Matilda House went on fire, so much so that the Fire Brigade had to be called to put it out. Despite it being very apparent that it was Paul who had caused the fire, he received no punishment other than a stern verbal warning. The fact that he didn't even receive a slap for doing it, instead of making him think he had got away with it, simply strengthened the respect he had for his compassionate and understanding mother. Paul didn't need to receive physical punishment for this act anyway. Standing in the kitchen with the walls covered in black soot and scorch marks everywhere was punishment enough and even at this young age, Paul realised how close he had come to causing a major disaster, not just for himself, but moreover for his beloved mother and nan.

Paul and his siblings found much entertainment not far from where they lived. Much of their time would be spent playing about the St

Katharine Docks, at Tower Bridge and around the River Thames. There would always be a variety of little boats moored up on pontoons running the length of the Thames. As children, they would sometimes take one of the boats out for a brief voyage on the river, but Paul knew they should only do this when they had older children with them to prevent them from getting into difficulty.

On one particular occasion Paul went with Elaine, his elder sister, to the river and recalls an older black girl, one of his sister's friends, accompanying them. It was early winter and the air was cold. Paul was wearing a blue coat with a fake sheepskin collar and lining which provided warmth on this chilly day but that weighed down on his little frame. They found a small rowing boat which was moored up and decided to take it out onto the river.

The children often played a game where if one of them was sitting on a wall, another child would come up behind them and give them a little push, before grabbing them again and saying "saved your life!" Once out on the river, Paul sat facing the two girls in the boat and they played the same game by gently pushing Paul backwards before pulling him forward, and each time crying out "saved your life!" Elaine's friend then pushed Paul backwards a bit more firmly and tried to grab him but she was too late and he toppled over. She tried desperately to grab him once more but she missed him again and he fell backwards out of the boat and into the murky waters of the Thames.

These were the days before compulsory school swimming lessons or the weekend family trip to the pools. Paul had no experience of deep water and felt himself going down, further and further into the dark depths of the Thames, and not aided by the heavy coat that had been his warmth and protection only seconds earlier.

It was the darkest place Paul had ever been and in that moment, he thought he would never see light again. Near the top, the river was dark green in colour but as he went down it became blacker and blacker. He began desperately flailing his arms and legs to find some direction, to try to negotiate his way back to the surface. All around him was complete darkness and he struggled to see anything that he could recognise as normal, like plants or fish, as he experienced the gut-wrenching feeling of going further and further down into the black void.

The small boy went down for what seemed like an eternity and then, resigned to his fate, he closed his eyes tight against the harsh blackness and tried desperately not to open his mouth to breathe as he knew that the water that was consuming him would simply flow into his tiny body and leave him with no chance of survival.

Then, as quickly as he had gone under and with an almighty rush of air, Paul felt hands on him and he was dragged from the surface of the water and desperately hauled back into the safety of the little rowing boat by his sister and her friend.

With the drama of what had just occurred and with the weight of the coat soaked with water and now feeling like it weighed a ton, Paul lay sobbing, curled up in the bottom of the boat. He tried desperately to come to terms with what had just happened but was relieved nevertheless to at least still be alive.

As well as the trauma of that day, Paul vividly remembers the blue coat he was wearing on the day he nearly died. Each year, during the summer months, he and his sister, Elaine, would go and stay with rich 'foster-parents' to give his mum a bit of respite over the school holidays. These trips were to support the less-well-off and to give poor kids a special break. The host families would offer these needy children a holiday free-of-charge and presumably thought they were doing their bit to help the impoverished youth of London. The reality however wasn't always so cheerful and sometimes the families they would end up staying with felt strange and alien to the visiting children.

On these excursions, Paul would find himself in places like Guernsey, Jersey or The Isle of Wight for respite holidays where the children would stay with their host families for a week or sometimes a two-week break. Paul would always travel with Elaine and then they would usually be separated and placed with different families for the duration of the holiday. He recalls how, after being sent away on one of these excursions, he was to come by the coat which very nearly contributed to his downfall.

This experience began with Paul travelling to Guernsey on a boat along with Elaine and some other children. Paul was violently seasick because of the motions of the ferry on the choppy seas and Elaine, being five years older than Paul, was made to mop it up. When they arrived at their destination, as usual, the children were all split up and taken off to their respective families.

Paul ended up staying on his own with a family who had a child of a similar age. This child had a go-kart and Paul got into a dispute because he had a turn in the go-kart for too long. As a punishment, the foster family took the lamp from the bedroom where Paul was sleeping that night and left him in the dark. Although lonely and missing his sister, this penalty didn't bother Paul as much as it might have done as he had spent many a long night in the dark in Matilda House without electricity or gas so he was well used to darkness.

Paul had been punished for his actions but the grandmother of the family he was staying with took pity on him and bought him the sheepskin coat that he was wearing when he almost drowned in the Thames. She had felt sorry for him, being a small child chastised on his first night for simply enjoying the thrill of the go-kart, and had taken him to a shop on the island and let him pick the coat he wanted. Paul doesn't remember the old lady just for this though, more for her being one of only a handful of genuinely loving adults in his young life.

As well as the coat, she also bought him a watch – a Timex watch which wasn't flash or big or heavy like the one The Fish Man, his alleged uncle, had given him – this was a basic 1-12 numbered child's watch, but Paul loved it, and her, all the same.

Apart from the episode with the go-kart and the ensuing punishment, Paul's experiences of his time as a poor child cared for and spoilt by the well-to-do of the day were largely positive and he was glad of the respite from the daily grind of the everyday of London life, as no doubt was his long-suffering mother.

Back home, it was clear that this was a dangerous time in London, despite the feelings that Paul presented as it being a safe time for children in the area. On reflection, it was an era rife with the potential dangers of blatant paedophilia, children running amok in the streets or warehouses and being left pretty much to their own devices most of the time.

Shortly after their return from Guernsey, Paul was out playing in the park with his sister when they were approached by a man with white curly hair who said that he had lost his puppy. The man asked if they could help him find the dog. At the time it seemed quite innocent and it was only much later on that Paul realised that what the man was really trying to do was get hold of Paul's sister, clearly for sinister means.

These London kids, through no fault of their own, were left wide open to a large degree of danger. This took a variety of forms including being exposed to unsavoury individuals, playing around on escalators, bouncing off huge piles of fabric in the warehouses, hanging around by the river, or a new risk of frequenting the local pubs and encountering the Travellers that were usually drinking there – Paul's sister was very friendly with many of these local Travellers, although Paul always viewed them with a justifiable suspicion as they were most times up to no good.

But, despite all these imminent dangers and near-misses, Paul survived and the experiences merely served to strengthen his resolve and his ability to cope with whatever life was to throw at him.

This resilience and strength of character would serve Paul well as he moved into his formative years, against the harsh backdrop of 1970's London.

Chapter 4 – Primarily Non-Educated & the Man in the Forest

Paul's first memories of school were of St Paul's Primary School, formerly on Wapping High Street and now relocated to Tower Hamlets, E1. Throughout his first year, Paul's mum would bring the children down to the school, transporting the babies in the 'original people-carrier' - a silver-cross pram with big springs, wheels and spokes - and with Paul always walking beside her.

As Paul moved into his second year at primary school, his attendance became more sporadic. There were two entrances to the school and each day his mum would leave him off at the main entrance, give him a kiss and wave him goodbye. When the coast was clear, Paul would often sneak out the other entrance and slowly follow his mum back up the road to their house, maintaining a safe distance so as not to be seen and sent back to school. Once back home, Paul's mum would keep him with her rather than making the troublesome walk back to the school.

This became a regular habit although it was never deemed to be too big a deal as these were the days when truanting wasn't really seen as a major crime and if a child wanted to find a way to flaunt the system, he was generally left to his own devices. A few times Paul did actually stay in school but he remembers the norm as being him briefly entering the school from one entrance before swiftly departing from the other.

Other times, when clean clothes were deemed to be a higher priority than schooling, Elaine would pack the old pram with black bin bags full of dirty clothes and drag Paul along the long stretch of Thomas More Street to the launderette at the very end of the road. Once there, they would spend half a day just washing and drying clothes and folding them up. Sheets would be folded with Elaine at one end and Paul at the other and they would "fold it, shake it, fold it, shake it". Sometimes, as a joke, she would yank the sheet clean out of Paul's hands and then they'd have to start all over again. It didn't matter as it broke the monotony of the ritual and, anyway, they had plenty of time to kill while they waited for the rest of the laundry to finish. It never seemed to matter that Paul would be sent along with Elaine to do the laundry when he was really meant to be at primary school.

As well as school, another part of Paul's life which he would have only a fleeting engagement with was his relationship with his brother John, or Johnny Brown as he was known to his friends. He was several years older than Paul and his next sibling up. Paul remembers being an infant and then a young boy and Johnny living with them during this period. But that all changed when Johnny was about ten or eleven and all of a sudden Paul, who would've been seven or eight at the time, remembers him not being around – he'd simply disappeared. Paul had no idea why his older brother had suddenly left or where he had gone to. It later transpired that their dad had taken Johnny to live with him, but at the time the young Paul was left wondering why he had suffered this loss and why no-one had explained to him what had happened.

It is this confusion, the fragility of family ties, and the ease with which loved ones seemed to come and go in his life which has had a profound effect on Paul and could well explain why he struggles with issues of trust and building long-term relationships. From a very young age, he saw that kinships could be fleeting and could be ripped away in the blink of an eye.

What made the incident with Paul's brother disappearing overnight even harder to take was it became apparent that their father saw John as his son, accepted him and was therefore happy to take him on. But The Banana Man would go on to deny the other children were ever his, leaving the rest of the siblings confused as to who their father was and as to why no-one had ever come for them, the way someone had for young John.

Who Paul's father was has always remained unclear and to this day, Paul refers to his father as his 'alleged' dad. However, Paul does have some memories of seeing him from time to time. This was very infrequent though as Johnny Senior worked as a chef on boats and oil rigs, or at least that's what Paul was told as he was growing up. He doesn't know if this was actually true or if it was used as the reason why his father was never around. There was also the rumour that those who 'worked on oil rigs' were actually spending their time a lot closer to home but equally as cut-off as those miles out to sea, and in reality serving a term in Her Majesty's Prisons.

Paul knows that his dad was actually a chef by trade and does recall that he would go away for long periods on end, so has come to accept that it probably was true that he was working on boats. This was the reason why, when Paul tracked him down much later on in life, his 'father' told him that Paul could not possibly have been his as he was not around at the time Paul would've been conceived.

It must have been hard for Paul and Elaine to be told on one hand that they and John were fathered by Johnny Brown but to have their father reject them, whilst taking on the care of their brother. Despite welcoming John as his own, the man continued to deny that Paul or Elaine were his.

What had made things so much more difficult was that John left literally overnight without saying a proper goodbye and as it would unfold, Paul would not see his older brother again until much later on in his adult life. Paul would hear John mentioned in conversations over the years, but always carried the sadness of the memory of the brother who was snatched from him at such an early age, without so much as a "cheerio".

Shortly after the departure of his brother, Paul and his family left Wapping for good. The reason they moved was due to a large scale redevelopment of the area, or more accurately, a redeployment of the poor away from the area, including the working class families and residents of Matilda House.

They were moved wholesale out of the Wapping flats and the area underwent a major financial investment, to be regenerated and turned into an upmarket domain for the rich elite of London's Docklands. No longer would the area be the one of poverty that Paul experienced as a child. Still to this day, the area is one of London's most sought after residential zones, with luxury two-bedroom flats now commanding anything up to a dizzying £1.9m purchase price.

As part of the redevelopments, the family were moved to Stanford Road, East Ham, and in tow came the few dogs that they could realistically accommodate in their new abode. This was just a sample of their canine collection and three of them were the lucky ones – Sally, nan's dog, Lassie, a mongrel-bitch of ginger-colour that belonged to Peter, and Ringo, the family favourite. The selected few accompanied their owners to the new house and all the other dogs went to farm, or at least that's what Paul was told (only later would he discover that this actually meant they were all destroyed). There were somewhere in the region of ten other dogs, all related, and all sadly put to sleep.

Paul's early love of animals came from the weird and wonderful collection of dogs in Matilda House and, in particular, these lucky ones that followed them to East Ham. Paul's nan was obsessed with dogs and with Paul being very close to her, he developed an equal affection for the animals – he became fascinated with their characteristics and understanding the difficult life they had led, which he felt was similar to his own upbringing and character in many ways. This exceptionally strong bond has stayed with Paul throughout his life and where he has often found it hard to make and maintain permanent relationships with humans, he has never had any trouble doing this with his canine friends. Could it be the unerring similarities he shares with the dogs in his life? The desperate need for attention, the urgent longing for true companionship, the faithful loyalty to another, the protection, warmth and trust of the relationship, the vulnerability of the animal and the need, most of all, to experience unconditional love.

In later life, Paul also liked the responsibility that came with owning an animal where you agree to nurture, to love and to protect it. The animals give him so much and ask for so little in return. Recalling the many dogs Paul has had leaves him emotional, a clear indication of just how important these 'pets' have been to him throughout his life.

Paul's early memories as a child are heavily linked to animals and he remembers having a little farmyard set with horses, pigs, cows and green plastic fencing. He would play with the set, totally contented for many hours, and always by himself, lost in his own little dreamland of creatures that wouldn't ask him awkward questions, would show him the utmost respect and perhaps most importantly, allow him to be unequivocally in control.

In East Ham, the family were moved into a nice big house with a large living and dining room area separated by fold-up, dividing doors. Paul remembers much of it as being in want of repair but still, it suited the family's needs and they felt spoiled as their new home also had a conservatory and outside there was a garden with a little pond.

The house felt like a proper home to them and was airy, clean and bigger and brighter than their previous residence. It had the bonus of the front garden, and a little back garden too, and although the property wasn't new, its brightness was notable compared to Matilda House where everything, apart from the coal fire, was enveloped in darkness.

Paul had many good times in East Ham although he recalls some trepidation as the end of the garden featured a high brick wall with broken glass cemented into the top. On the other side of the wall there was a cemetery and it was spooky for a child, imagining the proximity of all those dead bodies so close by at the end of their garden. Paul wasn't allowed in to the cemetery and doesn't have too many memories of it but he does remember occasionally going there with friends, via a side gate down the street, but always in the daytime, too scared, as they were, to visit in the dead of night.

During this time in East Ham, Paul got his first-ever job, helping out on a milk round. There was a Unigate Milk Dairy not far from their home and Paul found gainful employment as a milkman's assistant. When the milkman would go to deliver the milk up into the flats, he would leave Paul minding the milk float. In the float, the milkman kept a tin money box and sometimes there were bank notes which weren't pushed all the way in. Paul would take a couple of them out and when he got home, he would tell his mum who would keep most of it and then give him some small change back.

If Paul ever had any pang of guilt or remorse about his wrongdoings, his mum did little to dissuade him, and was in fact encouraging of his thieving by always moaning about money. "I don't have enough for the gas...the electric...I've no money for cigarettes", she would frequently say. He feels, looking back, that she was always manipulating him, and Paul, ever eager to please, would often say, "Oh don't worry, mum, I've got three pounds", or whatever he had procured after working on the milk round.

This system of finding ways to top up his legitimate work roles with cunning ways of adding to the weekly income is one that Paul would employ throughout his various jobs as time went on, always finding a way to get more than what he was actually paid. The ease with which Paul was able to generate additional income through these dodgy means helped mould his criminal tendencies and would lead directly to his later ability to engage in a range of illegal schemes in order to achieve his needs.

When he wasn't out working, Paul enjoyed making use of the extra space the family were experiencing in the new house. The conservatory, which wasn't without its problems (the glass roof had lots of leaks), was however also home to a secret space that Paul made his own.

There were twins that lived on Paul's road, Russell and Stephen, and soon after moving in, Paul befriended them. He used to go with them to Epping Forest, near the Wanstead Flats, in the six-week summer school holidays.

In those days, children could use The Red Bus Rover where they'd buy a ticket and then just jump on and off buses and tubes as they pleased. Paul and his new friends would use the Rover ticket to go to the forest and look for frogspawn and newts. When they found these creatures they'd capture them and bring them back to Paul's house, where he would keep them in little containers in the conservatory which housed a built-in wardrobe. Paul would climb up the wardrobe and right at the top, there was a tiny little space where he kept all his secret containers.

These holiday excursions didn't always end so happily though. One time a group of the children went over to the forest. There was Paul, his younger brother Gary, the twins and a couple of other local children. Again they were looking for frogspawn but this time, as they were going through the woods, they encountered a man who started talking to them and asking if they wanted some money. The stranger in the forest had shorts on and started putting paper bank notes down his shorts and getting the children to take the money out, which they did, unaware of the sinister intent behind the man's actions.

The children felt like millionaires with all this new-found money and shortly afterwards, they made their way back home. On their return journey the children went into their local corner shop and bought big lollies and masks and felt as though they had plenty to spend as it was a lot of money to them at the time.

What they didn't pay as much attention to, although they couldn't help but notice it, was the fact that the man had masturbated and come. Although he didn't touch the children while doing this, they were all around as it happened, and it was only later when Paul reflected on the incident that he became aware that the man they had met in the woods was clearly a paedophile.

When they got back home, the twins told their mum and dad what had happened in the forest. The twins' parents then went round and told Paul's mum what had gone on. Immediately the police were called and not long after, a man was arrested. Paul and the other children had to go and identify him in an identity parade. The children went in individually and they all picked out the same culprit so it was clearly the man that they had met that day. Promptly the man was prosecuted, and was soon safely behind bars.

The whole unsavoury affair troubled Paul for many years, not so much for what had occurred in the woods that day, but more for what would happen when the man was released from prison, and the fear that he would then come looking for them.

Although the identity parade was conducted from behind a one-way screen, the man had obviously seen Paul and the other children when the incident originally occurred and Paul had many fearful moments that the man would try to come after them when he was freed. It later transpired that the offender had actually been sentenced for a number of different crimes so it could have been that this was something he had done many times and therefore would have had difficulty recalling all the children he had encountered and subsequently abused. Still, the fear lingered with Paul that somehow the man would know who he was and would come and find him for reporting him to the police and the identification in the line-up.

But, regardless of this clearly unsavoury incident, Paul's overall memories of the house in East Ham were largely favourable. However, it wouldn't last long as the house was slowly falling apart at the seams and after a few years, Paul's favourite place - the conservatory - was nearly uninhabitable.

So now, after several years of relative happiness, the house was no longer fit for purpose and once more, the family found themselves on the verge of yet another move.

Chapter 5 – Black Kid, White World

With the house in East Ham collapsing around them, the family were moved to 13 Haskard Road, Dagenham in Essex. Along with his mum and siblings, a new member of the family was added, Jasper, the dog Paul recalls as being his first proper family pet. The dog was golden-coloured and was half-Golden Labrador and half-Whippet with a Whippet's body but something of a Labrador-shaped head.

When he lived in East Ham, Paul has only vague memories of going to primary school, and probably because he was rarely there. In Dagenham, Paul did attend Southwood Primary School more frequently, albeit for only eight weeks because then it was the summer holidays.

After this it was time for Paul to enter secondary school and he was enrolled in Erkenwald Comprehensive School, on Marlborough Road in Dagenham. In 1990, Erkenwald would amalgamate with Parsloes Manor School and Mayesbrook Secondary School to create Sydney Russell Comprehensive School which is now rated as outstanding by Ofsted and is one of the top three schools in the local authority.

But at the time when Paul enrolled, Erkenwald was a very run-down school. Often the pupils would be sent home because the heating wasn't working and broken windows were commonplace, even in the classrooms. The toilets were all located outside and originally these were covered with old corrugated plastic but this hadn't been there for a while so if it was raining and you were in the toilets, you'd end up getting soaked! It is no surprise that the school has long since been condemned to the annals of history but back then, it was 'big school' for the young Paul.

These were the days when successive governments turned a blind eye to the standard of educational facilities for the very poor. Erkenwald Comprehensive, housing mostly young people from the surrounding estates, was rarely considered for investment. Nowadays all pupils, regardless of background, are entitled to and usually get a decent standard of education along with respectable physical buildings and resources but Paul's school still operated in that generation where the gap between the 'haves' and the 'have-nots' was vastly unfair.

In addition to the disgraceful state of repair of the school, Paul also suffered from bullying in his early time there and always felt picked on, though not just by his fellow pupils. A theme throughout his education, Paul also felt constantly singled out and treated unfairly by his teachers.

He remembers shortly before he left primary school when he was in the playground during P.E. The children were playing rounders and Paul politely asked the teacher if he could go to the toilet. She told him he wasn't allowed and he ended up wetting himself and had to stay in the same clothes for the rest of the day, including going back and sitting in the classroom, soaking and smelling of urine. When he went home, he told his mum and nan to which the old lady responded "if she ever tells you can't go to the toilet again, you just go in the corner and piss there and tell her that your nan said you could!"

The thought of progression to secondary school had filled Paul with a tremendous sense of dread and his overwhelming emotions were of complete fear of what lay ahead. He had heard the tales of first year pupils regularly having their heads flushed down the toilets. This, mixed with his already apprehensive nature and the knowledge that as a mixed-race child he would be very much in the minority, led him to be massively anxious about his next transition.

But, whilst it wasn't all plain sailing and despite some initial troubles that he encountered, Paul managed to make it through his first year at Erkenwald.

There then followed an eight week summer holiday, during which time he was to begin dabbling with his sexuality. By now he was twelve but he looked more like nine. Perhaps due to his childish looks, he found it easier to make friends with younger children and Paul had become pals with a local boy, Andrew Juffs, who was a year and a half his junior.

Andrew lived nearby and his family were significantly better off than Paul's. Due to their blossoming friendship and to give Andrew's new friend something he would probably never have the opportunity to do otherwise, Andrew's parents arranged to take Paul with them, over the summer months, on their upcoming European coach holiday.

In addition to the holiday, the Juffs bought Paul new clothes as they saw him as being a really good friend, and great company for Andrew. Paul was ecstatic about his impending trip and soon they were off to exciting places like Venice and Rome. Paul recalls they were the only two children on the Thomas Cook coach tour package holiday so it was probably easier for the Juffs to have Paul in tow and besides, the two boys were so well behaved.

As well as his first proper foreign trip, the coach holiday was also memorable for Paul for a completely different reason. They were in a Spanish hotel and there were lots of other children staying there with their parents. One of these was a young girl, also aged twelve, from York, and she and Paul got chatting. In the evening time, they went to the beach.

Legend at Paul's school had it that girls smelt of fishy tuna between their legs, so much so that they had a rhyme to go along with it "oh no, what's that smell, fucking hell". Paul was kissing the girl and giving and getting love bites. He then fingered her vagina and, without her noticing, he put his finger to his nose. He was pleased and interested to note that she didn't smell of tuna after all!

They went back to the hotel and Paul initially managed to hide his love bites from Mr and Mrs Juffs, but got caught out the next day at breakfast. They were a relaxed couple though and just laughed it off.

They were also relaxed about giving the children free reign on the holiday and Paul remembers another night where he was dancing in a nightclub. He recalls being there, although can't quite recollect the facts of how a baby-faced pre-teen was allowed to be on his own, throwing his shapes, in the middle of a foreign discotheque!

Paul would have a third and final holiday with the ever-generous Juffs, spending his 13th birthday with them in Canada, where they stayed for six gloriously fun-filled weeks. While there, they resided with Andrew's aunt. The next door neighbours, a friendly couple with two young daughters, were filthy-rich and took Paul up in their private jet and he remembers them wanting to adopt him!

The couple had already taken an instant liking to the gorgeous, young, mixed-race London boy anyway but Paul really helped his cause when the adults went to the store one afternoon leaving the girls, Paul and

Andrew in the car. Andrew started annoying the young girls and being mean and horrible but Paul defended them and the eldest girl told their mum when she came out and they loved Paul even more as a result. His 13th birthday was also memorable as it was the first cake with candles he ever remembers being given.

Back in Dagenham, Paul's family were the only black children on the street and he can only recall two other black families that he knew in the entire local area. Prevalent in the locality were white punks and skinheads. Just down the road at St Martin's Corner was where the local parade of shops was located and there was a lot of intimidating graffiti proclaiming 'BM' which stood for the British Movement and 'NF' for National Front.

The British Movement was a British neo-Nazi organisation, founded in 1968 by a man called Colin Jordan. It spawned from the National Socialist Movement which had begun six years earlier in 1962. The BM were always on the margins of the British far-right, and the organisation has had a long and chequered history for its association with violence and extremism. Much of this was prevalent on the streets near to where the teenage Paul was living. Nicky Crane was famed as one of the BM's fiercest street fighters, and he had organised and led several violent attacks on non-whites. Following a BM meeting in May 1978, Nicky Crane and other BM members took part in a nasty assault on a black family at a bus stop in Bishopsgate, East London, using broken bottles.

In 1979, Crane and BM members were part of a mob of roughly two hundred skinheads that attacked a group of Asians on Brick Lane, East London.

Crane also led and instigated the infamous Woolwich Odeon attack of 1980. After their intended victims ran inside the Odeon cinema to escape attack, Crane and other BM members started smashing windows and doors, and one Pakistani man was knocked unconscious in the melee.

Crane would finally be jailed in 1981 for his part in an ambush on black youths at Woolwich Arsenal train station. During the trial, the Old Bailey judge described Crane as "worse than an animal" after his part in the May 1978 bus stop attack in Bishopsgate.

Understandably news of these attacks were a constant cause for concern for the young Paul and his family being, as they were, so racially outnumbered in the area.

The National Front had its heyday in the 1970's. Founded by AK Chesterton in 1967, it capitalised on growing public concern, particularly regarding Asian emigration to Britain. As a neo-fascist organisation, its primary ideology was that only white people should be citizens of the United Kingdom. It promoted open racism by demanding an end to non-white migration into the UK, with a call for settled non-white Britons to be stripped of their citizenship and deported from the country.

The Headquarters for both the British Movement and the National Front were on Dagenham Heathway, close to where Paul's family lived. One wonders at the fear of a marginalised family trying to survive in such close proximity to the inordinate far-right and bigoted groupings. Not surprisingly, Dagenham at the time was an overwhelmingly white-populated area and with the encouragement of the BM and NF there were a lot of openly racist people about.

To a certain extent though at least the racists who were obvious and 'in your face' were easy to spot and steer clear of. What was harder to contend with was the greater fear of the unknown, the less blatant but nevertheless dangerous, concealed and hidden racists. These were the ones who acted normal to your face while disguising their real feelings and intentions.

Paul remembers one such individual, an older teenager, who had recently left school and lived next door but one. Paul had previously felt he wouldn't have had cause to worry about the boy but one night while Paul's family were asleep, his neighbour and a friend painted 'National Front' in big capital letters on the Byfields' front door. The door was turquoise blue and the graffiti paint was white in bold letters so it stood out clearly and was very disturbing and threatening to Paul and his family. They felt there was an impending and inescapable witch-hunt against them.

Paul attempted to remove the paint himself but couldn't get it off and remembers it being there for quite a while, until eventually, officials from the local Council came by to paint over it. This kind of act was to happen more than once and would leave the family feeling very alone and alienated in an area dominated by white people, many of whom carried a disproportionate negative view of black families. These hate-crimes were further exacerbated by other incidents of blatant racism for Paul and his siblings which made his early years into adolescence all the more difficult.

Not only did the family struggle because they were black, they also found life a challenge because they were so poor. One of the results of this poverty was that they received grants for school uniform vouchers which meant they could only purchase the required outfits at certain shops. These were basically the worst copy of the uniforms, whereas most of the other local pupils had better quality ones. The grant-provided uniform trousers all had massive flares and Paul recalls hand sewing the legs to make them into the fashionable 'drainpipes' of the day.

This temporarily alleviated his embarrassment until he sat down one day in class and the stitching suddenly came undone at the knees where he had sewn them. He then had to sit there wearing his big flared trousers with his classmates chuckling all around him.

Another time his mum had bought him a pair of cheap, fabric, green trousers for school which were elasticated and although he already hated them, his misery was compounded when a fellow pupil pointed out that they were girl's trousers as they didn't have a zip.

Paul also remembers wearing cheap shoes that were bought in the same discount uniform shop and these had a pointed shape, with a slight heel and gold striping going all round the edges. He wore these shoes when he went to visit Erkenwald with his mum to apply for a place during Open Day. On the way into the school he had to walk past a couple of young males sitting on a nearby fence. They looked like adults to the youthful Paul, but they were probably actually 4th or 5th year pupils. As he approached them, Paul's ankle gave way as would a woman's if she went over wearing high-heeled shoes. Paul wasn't used to wearing shoes like these as the only ones he had worn until then were cheap plimsolls, bought from Woolworths. When he fell over he could hear sniggering from the young people. The embarrassment of having older kids laughing at him was especially hard to bear for someone who was so conscious of his looks and his appearance.

It was one of the few times he remembers his mum coming with him to secondary school which didn't help his attempts to look cool. After that, for any parents' evening or parental occasion, his mum never came along and she never again visited the school. This trend wasn't uncommon though as his mum tended to shy away from these sorts of encounters as much as she could. Paul thinks the reason she didn't take more of an active role in his schooling and upbringing was a generational characteristic where there seemed to be a family trait of avoidance of any kind of authority.

Another reason Paul's mum was often uncomfortable in dealing with outside individuals was because she had a bad left hand. Paul recalls her having this for as long as he can remember and right up until she died, her hand was always bandaged up. Paul was told a story and he can't remember if it is what actually happened or if he has heard it so many times that he actually believes it. The tale was that Paul had given his mum a ring and that once she had put in on her hand she couldn't get it off, and over the years it had caused a number of complaints and issues. Paul's mum and nan were very 'old-school' and they would shy away from doctors and dentists and anything like that so the normal course of action of getting the troublesome hand looked at was ignored. With medical advances, the ring that was stuck on her hand could easily have been cut off without her having any injury.   But at the time, she had no dealings with the medical profession and she hardly ever went to the doctors. It was probably true that she wasn't even registered with any doctor. When she did occasionally go to a practice, if they started prying about her hand and the bandage, she wouldn't let them examine it and would immediately stop going to that particular doctor. Paul remembers that her nails would need cutting from time to time so the bandage would come off and he recalls the distinctive smell of the pink antiseptic cream, Germolene. This had its uses but the hand ended up being deformed over the years by being bandaged up like that for so long.

Owing to her reluctance to attend medical and dental appointments, in the later years before Linda died, she was very gaunt and had most of her teeth missing. She never went to the dentist throughout her adult life and had severe dental problems later on. When she finally went to get the problem sorted out they had no choice but to take out nearly all her teeth. Linda was meant to go back for dentures but never did. Maybe it was because she thought it would be more pain but perhaps she didn't realise that she had already done the hard bit.

Because his mum and her mum before her never went to the doctors or dentists it wasn't common for the children to go either, although Paul does remember going one specific time when as a young child he had a huge thirst problem and was constantly drinking water from the tap. Around this time, he also had the operation at the ear, nose and throat hospital although this was linked to the dark demons from his past that he can't really remember. The only reason he knows anything about it is because he has heard of it since in conversations.

As a result of his mum's hand problem, Paul's sister always did the washing. She also did much of the shopping and the list always started off with the exact same items, "tea, sugar, butter, marg, cooking fat". Without fail, this was always the same and Paul can still rhyme it off like it was yesterday. His sister did the shopping lists, she did the notes for the school absences and she did most of the other normal parental duties. Then, as Paul got older, he took over and he remembers having to then predominantly fulfil this role for him and his younger siblings, hence the photographic memory of the order of the set shopping list.

Elaine went to a secondary school in Green Lanes in Plaistow which was predominantly black whereas the school that Paul went to was predominantly, as much as 98%, white. Aunt Betty lived near the Plaistow School and Betty's daughter, Kim, went there. Elaine was more assertive and had more of a voice about what she did and didn't want so made sure she got to go to the same school as Kim, but Paul, being less forceful, had to go to the other white-dominated school.

As per the norm, this was a further example of him being told what to do rather than him being asked what he wanted. Paul was a bit envious of his sister asserting her rights and she clearly fitted in much better than he ever did at Erkenwald. Within a few weeks, Elaine had lots of black friends and developed some of the clichéd black traits like sucking her teeth and knowing how to cook rice and peas!

Paul, however, didn't just struggle with the logistical transition from primary to secondary school. The physiological and emotional changes from small boy to early pubescence also had a major effect on him. Shortly after he turned thirteen, his emotional state was such that his mother had no choice other than to bring him to the doctor for assessment, a major event given her usual trepidation associated with such occurrences.

At an extraordinarily young age, Paul was diagnosed with depression and though prescribed, this would later be defined as the start of his incessant interest in pill-popping and the ingestion of mood or mind altering substances.

During this time he felt very alone, like he didn't fit in, and he always hung around with the girls at school and definitely didn't want to do anything manly like play football with the boys.

Whilst Linda may have circumvented most dealings with authority and the medical world, what she didn't avoid was her role as the maternal linchpin of the family. Never was this felt more than when tragedy struck when Paul was only thirteen years of age.

His eldest brother, Peter, had by now moved out and had met a slim and beautiful half-Bangladeshi, half-white Irish girl, also called Linda. Immediately, they fell in love, and not long after they got married. The happy couple then gave birth to their first child, a gorgeous baby girl called Laura.

After the birth, Laura's mother fell into a deep bout of post-natal depression. Unable to pull her out of the darkness, Peter was to face the ultimate nightmare when his young wife committed suicide, just seven weeks after giving birth.

Peter, unable to cope with the situation, asked his mother to take care of Laura for him and so young Paul suddenly had a new 'sister' in the home, although he knew she was really his niece. It was initially meant to be a temporary arrangement but the little girl would end up spending the next nine years of her life with her adopted family, before her father felt able to take on the responsibility of looking after her again. During the early stages of little Laura's life, her uncle-brother, Paul, learnt how to change her nappy, how to feed her and how to wind her.

Another regular member of the extended family who lived with them during this time was Paul's beloved nan. Nanny May would be in and out of Paul's family's lives and he now knows that it's because she was usually avoiding people for rent owed and on one occasion, more serious fraud was mentioned as the reason the old lady was lying low with the family.

Paul recollects how his nan would've lived with the family and then suddenly she didn't live with them. During one period when she wasn't there, she had her own flat and Paul remembers going up to the now-empty property with his mum. They brought some black bags of clothes out and that was the last time they ever went there. To the innocent Paul he thought they were just out and about doing errands, but it was to later materialise that his nan was in prison during this period, probably for the fraud or rent avoidance.

This was another generational attitude that he inherited - the negotiating of money and authority and getting what you can, whatever way you can. Paul was brought up with the 'any means necessary' attitude to bringing in money, whether it was legal or illegal. That said, because everything was normalised, the young Paul struggled from an early age to understand what was actually illegal.

One time as a young teenager he had got into trouble as he had been out with some friends who were carrying an air rifle. This was common with young children in those days and air rifles, cap guns and CB radios were the staple of many a group of youngsters on the streets. The kit would usually be bought by an older brother or dad and then passed down to the younger kids. They would use the air rifles to shoot cans in their back yards which wasn't a problem, but it was against the law to transport the guns from one house to another without a proper carry case.

In this instance, not only was the rifle the young people carried in full view, but the lads were also pointing and shooting it at street lights and other 'targets'. A woman living in one of the houses along the way rang the police and reported that they had pointed the gun directly at her, which Paul maintains didn't actually happen. Regardless, the police turned up and they took Paul and his friends to the station before ringing his mum to tell her he had been arrested for firearms offences. He was lucky to escape with just a caution but nevertheless his mum was in a blind panic and rumours quickly spread. When they heard about the offence, friends of his were left wondering how Paul had managed to get hold of an AK-47 or similar kit!

Another criminal activity that Paul honed during his schooling at Dagenham was his penchant for shoplifting. With four or five of his friends, they developed an enterprise utilising stolen goods from the stores in Romford. The gang would get orders from the girls at the school gates for cardigans in their required size and colour. They would then go into Marks & Spencer and visit the ladies section before promptly exiting the store with a selection of burgundy or beige cardigans as was the want of their 'customers' at the school.

This went on for several weeks until they also began to target Debenhams where on the third floor they had rows and rows of Adidas trainers in boxes, right beside a fire exit. The gang would literally walk out the fire escape with boxes of the trainers, which in those days didn't come with a security tag.

They were on a roll for several weeks and thought they were unstoppable. It was a false dawn for the would-be criminal masterminds though, as the long arm of the law was soon to fall on them.

One afternoon in Romford, they were seen shoplifting in Marks & Spencer and tried to make good their escape. Paul sensed that they had been rumbled and immediately made for the exit door where he was quickly grabbed on the arm by a short, stocky lady with high heels, one of the shop staff. Paul managed to shrug her off and ran with the lady in hot pursuit trying to catch him. At school during this phase, he was doing the 100m hurdles so he was in decent physical shape and unsurprisingly, managed to outrun his pursuer.

Not long after, he caught up with his friends who had also managed to scarper and they snaked their way round the back streets to their favourite chip shop near the bus stop where, to celebrate their escape, they had their usual meal of a portion of chips with green liquor and salt & vinegar. The green liquor is a key element of a famous East End dish which is usually a combination of mince pie, mash and the liquor. This is like a green gravy made from water, chopped parsley and cornflour.

As the jovial gang left the chip shop, they were pounced upon by several plain clothes police officers, who arrested them. Not only had they succumbed to the law, but they were also forced to throw their meals into a nearby bin. Paul was placed in the back of a police car and remembers trying to hide some pens that he had also stolen earlier in the day.

Once the thieves had been processed, the Public Prosecution Service decided there was enough evidence and severity of crime to warrant a court hearing, and the wait was something that would hang over Paul for the next number of months.

The turbulent range of emotions he faced as he awaited his fate would be repeated again later in his life but this was the young Paul's first scary experience of the dread and fear that accompanies a criminal as they contemplate the possible sentence that lies ahead of them.

Chapter 6 – Music, Vice & Young Men Nice

The arrest for the shoplifting spree in Romford was the first time that Paul had been brought to book for his crimes. However, he had been given a very early grounding long before that in most things illegal. Paul was encouraged to understand that while certain actions were not necessarily right, they also weren't that wrong, and he was brought up to know that it was acceptable for him and his family to manipulate the system in as many ways as they could to make ends meet.

This wasn't an uncommon theme during these times with role models such as the Kray twins showing the world how easy it was to find money if you were prepared to stray over the line of legality whenever it was needed.

Back during their time in Matilda House, Paul was encouraged by his mum to steal from the TV meter and she would use the money for whatever was required at the time. It was a messy job because the meter had a lock on it but Paul would usually get the cash out and then Linda would later find money to put back in so that when the men came to get the monthly rental for the TV, nine times out of ten, the correct money would be in the box. On the odd occasion that there was no money available to put back in the box, Paul would always be the one sent out to see the TV meter man and he would have to tell him that they had been robbed and all the money taken.

It wasn't just the TV box and Paul was also sometimes encouraged to do likewise with the electricity or gas meter boxes. The money for the gas was housed in a money box, a large black box with a wire seal and a heavy lock and occasionally, Paul would be set to work on it. When the lock and seal were broken, the casing inside exposed the money, the old-style, large fifty-pence pieces. Paul would get a treat of one of the fifty-pence pieces as his reward for carrying out the break in and to him, this seemed like a lot of money and well worth his efforts. When the meter men came calling, the family would have to say that they had been broken into, if they were caught with no money in the box. All three meters were inside the house and Paul, aged just thirteen, was always dealing with the men because his mum would be hiding in one of the rooms saying, "Paul, you go and see them", and Paul would have to say, "yeah, we got burgled again!" The men must have been suspicious that this seemed to happen fairly frequently but Paul always seemed to have the gift of convincing them into believing what he said was true.

Undoubtedly this grounding in petty criminality, lying effectively to authority and being cunning yet charming enough to get away with it, served Paul well throughout his life. On many occasions during his later years, a lesser performance could well have landed Paul in prison or in serious trouble during some of his future criminal activities.

Also, given that Peter, the eldest boy contributed to some of the household outgoings when he could, and that Linda sometimes used some of this money to buy things for Paul, it could have been said that she was literally robbing Peter to pay Paul!

To help him spend his ill-gotten and other gains, an ice cream van would come round, driven by John, whose distinctive face Paul can still remember to this day. As well as the ice lollies and ice cream, John sold things like toilet roll and singles (single cigarettes for 2p each at a time). Linda would ask Paul to go out and John would sell them to him. The reality was the singles Paul bought weren't always all for his mum and it was his dealings with John that started Paul on one of his main life vices – his addiction to tobacco.

Paul started smoking when they lived in Matilda House when he was aged just nine. Before he had the means to buy some for himself, he started by stealing cigarettes from his mum who always had a pack of small Embassy, the ones with the white packaging and the red band, Embassy Six as they were known. He stole some of the cigarettes and hid them under his mattress, and his sister, Elaine, usually got the blame for stealing them. It was pretty obvious someone had done it as there were three missing from a pack of ten, but Paul was happy enough to let his sister take the rap on each occasion.

Like all good Cockney families, the Byfields always celebrated their endeavours by having afternoon tea on a Sunday, no matter how much money they had. It would be things like a trifle with tinned fruit and jelly and sprinkles on it, a Knickerbocker Glory, or if it was a really good Sunday, it could be winkles, cockles, whelks or shrimps as a big treat.

As well as his developing propensity for crime, Paul was also nurturing another of his life traits – the understanding of his homosexual tendencies. When Paul thinks back to when he first started thinking he might be gay, he recounts his mum lying on the sofa, watching TV. Paul would always nestle beside her and he often remembers her saying, "he's handsome," or, "he's cute", and then Paul would repeat it and find himself really thinking it too!

Aged fourteen, as Paul began his fourth year at secondary school, he got really into music in a big way. This was the era of The Human League, Culture Club, Adam Ant, Marilyn, Marc Almond and Soft Cell and Paul embraced this New Romantic era with open arms. It would drag him from the initial depression and awkwardness of his formative teenage years and have an unfathomable defining impact on the man that he later became.

New Romanticism was a largely manufactured scene within London nightclubs which took its form in the early 1980's. Those who embraced this new movement were often the biggest posers within their peer groups. They tended to be the more creative people who had always been more interested in the thrill of dressing up than the anarchic statement of anti-fashion and they were the ones who always looked for new ideas to draw attention to themselves.

Often, there would be adapted factual or fictional themes with vivacious, colourful and dramatic frills and fabrics associated with historical periods or Hollywood motifs. In contrast to the punks that had gone before them, the New Romantics made a big effort to look flamboyant in an attractive, luxuriant, beautiful and narcissistic way.

There was another evolving trend emerging as London nightclubs started to change their standard format of only opening on Friday and Saturday nights for the important music events. Gossips, in Soho, began to do Bowie nights on Tuesdays and then offered other one-night specials for niche tastes. That set the scene for one-off club evenings throughout London.

Suddenly narrow tastes could be catered for and opportunities were in abundance. The former punk posers had taken to glamour and romance in clothing and the club venues offered them a chance to show off their chic styles at dedicated evenings. Theatrical ensembles were worn to selected clubs in London such as Blitz and St. Moritz and these became the recognised venues where the New Romantic movement started.

The Human League were an electronic band from Sheffield who had been formed in 1977 by Martyn Ware and Ian Marsh. Originally called The Future, they changed their name to The Human League in 1978 with the addition of vocalist Phil Oakey and the release of the single, Being Boiled. This original line-up lasted until 1980, after which Ware and Marsh left to form Heaven 17. Oakey kept the band name, added female vocalists and it is this incarnation that gained widespread popularity.

1981 was a huge year for The Human League. Following an unimpressive chart high of forty-eight for Boys and Girls in February of that year, they then roared up the charts with three consecutive top twenty hits with The Sound of the Crowd, Love Action (I Believe in Love) and Open Your Heart. They topped off their phenomenal year when the timeless Don't You Want Me hit the number one spot on 5th December, securing the Christmas Number One for 1981 and staying top of the tree for the next five weeks.

Culture Club was a new wave and pop band from London who would go on to have a string of hits during the 1980's. Their second album, Colour by Numbers, sold more than ten million albums, was ranked in the top one hundred best albums of the 1980's by Rolling Stone, and contained their most famous song, Karma Chameleon. They were formed in 1981, at exactly the same time as the fourteen-year old Paul was discovering this new world, by lead singer Boy George, bassist Mikey Craig, drummer Jon Moss and guitarist Roy Hay. Culture Club was named after the diversity in ethnicity and backgrounds of its members and the areas they represented. They were signed to Virgin records, but what led to their launch into the pop stratosphere was as much about Boy George's androgynous style as their early music. The press were fascinated by his stage persona and his 'genderqueer' image, and this helped propel Boy George and the rest of Culture Club into the mainstream media.

They would go on to sell more than fifty million albums worldwide, and had major international success with songs such as Do You Really Want to Hurt Me?, Time (Clock of the Heart) and I'll Tumble 4 Ya.

Adam and the Ants was an English new wave band, active from 1977 to 1982, and existed in two incarnations, both fronted by Adam Ant. The first, founded in May 1977, achieved considerable cult popularity during the transition from the punk rock era to the post-punk and new wave era and were noted for their highly camp and overtly sexualised stage performances and songs.

The second incarnation of Adam and the Ants featured guitarist Marco Pirroni and drummer-producer Chris Hughes and achieved major commercial success with seven UK top ten hits from 1980 to 1981, including two UK number one singles, Stand and Deliver and Prince Charming.

Adam Ant remains to this day one of the iconic figures of his time, notable for his seminal styles of dress, influenced by classical romantic looks and 16th century pirates, blended with a new wave, punk twist and often a gypsy-like edge to his looks - Adam Ant's maternal grandfather, Walter Albany Smith, was a full-blooded Romanichal gypsy, hence Adam's liking for this particular style aspect.

He also appealed to Paul in another way. Adam had been diagnosed several years earlier with bipolar disorder, so his mental health issues resonated with Paul as much as his music and style did.

Marilyn was another icon of the day. Real name Peter Robinson, he had earned his nickname from a schoolboy fascination with Marilyn Monroe. While the name originated from homophobic bullies at school, Robinson decided to appropriate it to his advantage.

As a teenager, he was a regular nightclub-goer and wanted to look different, so he adopted a Marilyn Monroe image, wearing vintage dresses with bleached blond hair. Marilyn became one of the 'Blitz Kids' regulars at the New Romantic-inspired Blitz nightclub, a highly stylised club in London run by Steve Strange of the pop group, Visage, and a place which spawned many early 1980's pop groups and stars, such as Spandau Ballet.

During this time, Marilyn met Boy George and the pair would later share a squat together. While Boy George went on to form Culture Club in 1981 and secured a recording deal with Virgin Records, Marilyn was still scouting for a recording contract and had relocated to Los Angeles for some time. But after Boy George had made such a massive commercial impact with Culture Club, record companies were looking for other artists with a similar cross-dressing image and so later on, in 1983, following a high profile appearance in the promo video for Eurythmics' hit single, Who's That Girl?, Marilyn signed his own recording contract with Phonogram Records. Marilyn's first chart success came in late 1983 with his debut single, Calling Your Name, which reached the top five in the UK and Australia, and number one in Japan.

Soft Cell was an English synthesizer duo consisting of Marc Almond on vocals and David Ball on synthesizers. Their lyrics often focused on love and romance as well as the darker side of life, with subjects such as kinky sex, transvestism, drugs and murder. They had a huge worldwide hit in 1981 with a cover version of Tainted Love, a northern soul classic originally sung by Gloria Jones, the girlfriend of Marc Bolan.

The music and style helped Paul in many ways and most pertinently, it led him to know for sure that he was gay. It was the time, almost overnight, when it became acceptable for men to do things like wear eyeliner and experiment with cross-dressing and Paul and many of his peers loved the sudden explosion in expressionism. There was one boy in Paul's year at school who had his nipple pierced, following the lead from The Human League's Phil Oakey who, always keen to shock, had posed on one of the band's posters, shirtless with pierced nipples linked together by a gold chain.

The New Romantic days also made it trendy to be bi-sexual and Paul, as well as affirming his interest in boys, also remembers courting girlfriends. His first was Jane Palmer who lived not too far round the corner from him. Shortly afterwards, he had another girlfriend called Tracey Shoots. Tracey had the Phil Oakey hairstyle where one half of her head was shaved and the other side was kept long and swept over. Paul had never seen anyone else with that style except Phil himself. She had obviously copied Oakey's look and Paul loved the rebelliousness and the newness of it all.

As he progressed through fourth year at school, Paul was experimenting with a vast array of styles and concepts, and his favourite for a time was peroxide bleach stained stripes going round his head with little tufts of hair at the front. Given this new outrageous self-expressionism, did Paul define himself at this time as bi-sexual? Possibly, Paul recounts, although he still had so much to discover and was still getting to grips with kissing. He was a long way off sexual intercourse, and certainly not with a male partner.

He also had more immediate concerns as both Jane and Tracey were white. One time he knocked on Tracey's door to take her out but saw her brother approaching instead. Paul knew her brother was a racist and he had to quickly run and hide round the corner until the coast was clear!

Into fifth year, Paul was hardly ever at school and was usually busier in the roles of purchasing necessary shopping from the usual list or looking after the house as his sister was away a lot of the time, often at Blues parties that went on for days on end.

Elaine would stay at a friend's house a lot but would come back home at various unscheduled hours, banging on the doors and climbing in windows. Paul's mum even once made him nail up all the windows to stop her climbing in and there were a couple of times when the police were called and his mum would say, "I've had enough of Elaine – please take her away". Obviously the police couldn't do this as she hadn't actually done anything illegal.

Elaine's late night dalliances and subsequent fallouts were quite a frequent occurrence and Paul remembers it as being a very stressful time, but now realises it was just the classic mother and daughter confrontation of rebelling and growing up that many females face.

Instead of being told to go to school, Paul was encouraged to stay at home. Linda had a habit, which she did in both East Ham and Dagenham, of constantly swapping over the dining room and living room. His mum would quickly get bored of the layout and would change the furniture arrangement. Each time, she would need bits and bobs to complete the look, and Paul would be required to help source the relevant items. Paul also found that the older he got the more his mum was around. She didn't go to pubs or go out with men much anymore, she just stayed about the house and smoked a bit.

Paul would usually help with the general or room change shopping and go out and about with his mum and nan. They would get buses to Shepherd's Bush Market, Petticoat Lane or Romford Market, each with their sprawling stalls full to the brim with every kind of product - fresh produce, foods of every description, clothing, household items, music stands, live animals, pet food and a wide variety of bric-a-brac.

They would invariably make their errands into a full day's activity, always going long distances on an array of different buses and most of the time would be taken up with their travels. They might make various journeys to each of the markets in order to obtain their favourite dog food, compressed sausage meat, horse meat or whatever essential item they deemed necessary. It was a big day out for the simplest purchase, an event in itself! Today, ironically, Paul lives just around the corner from Shepherd's Bush Market where he used to frequently travel to as a child.

But while Paul enjoyed this time being close to his mum and nan and without the pressures of school that face many teenagers, he was still itching for something new, something different.

Unknown to Paul at the time, he was about to embark on another of his lifelong loves, and was soon to become lost in the world of the finest of all animals, the majestic horse.

Chapter 7 – Horsing Around

Paul has always retained a strong attraction to animals and is endlessly drawn to creatures great and small. In addition to the dogs that his nan kept, he can vividly remember Brick Lane and Shepherd's Bush Market with their wild array of various animals for sale.

He loved visiting the pet shops at Shepherd's Bush where they had cages with live animals, like tortoises, for sale. Recently, it has become far harder to buy or own a tortoise owing to their endangered status but back then they were widely available. They also had kittens, cats, hens and other animals in cages, especially down Brick Lane, and it was normal to see a whole menagerie of different animals in the wide variety of local pet shops. These encounters developed Paul's fascination and he also had many early experiences of a very special creature which would later become his driven passion for many years. The Wapping Rag & Bone man would pass by his house every day, collecting scraps of metal, his big Cob horses with their huge bushy legs slowly pulling the cart full of old metal. The Rag & Bone man would call out, "any old iron?", and ring a bell. As various residents came out with their metal and rags, Paul would stand and marvel at these wonderful beasts. The Wapping Rag & Bone man gave him his first exposure to horses and would start his love affair with these proud creatures. This bond would go on to last a lifetime, remaining one of few consistent interests he has maintained.

Realising his fascination for horses was something he wanted to pursue, Paul became aware of some stables called Hooks Hall Riding Centre, which is still in existence, though now called the Eastminster School of Riding at Hooks Hall Farm.

Paul talked about his new interest with his good friend, Andrew Juffs. It turned out Andrew was keen to try horse riding as well and following just a little persuasion, Andrew's parents arranged for the two boys to go to Hooks Hall. Paul absolutely loved the experience and, from that moment on, he had found a new addiction. Paul became a frequent visitor to Hooks Hall over the following months. Sometimes he would pay his own way using the wages from his milk round or with the little extra he might have been able to snaffle.

He had also managed to secure another part-time job, helping out on a market stall selling lamps and lampshades. This job was at Dagenham Heathway Market, which still runs to this day, and was not too far from the Ford Motor Factory, scene of the famous 1968 machinists' strike that led to the demand for equal pay for women across the world. Here, his boss would make the lampshades by piecing them together from a topaz lampshade shell and then Paul would help him sell them at the market to make a few extra pounds for himself.

This job also inadvertently led to Paul's first gay experience. From his lampshade work, he had access to Evo-Stik glue and whenever he could, he would steal some. One time, after Paul had taken a tube of the glue, he went for a ride at Hooks Hall and discovered that there were some gypsies based nearby. They had horses tied up on their site and Paul became friendly with some of the gypsy children, with their common interest in the equine world. After some jovial conversation, one of the gypsies, a tanned young man, encouraged Paul into a secluded wooded area where they did some glue-sniffing and had a bit of glue-induced exploring of each other's bodies!

Paul would use his various sources of income ever increasingly at Hooks Hall and as a regular customer, he would earn a free ride at the weekend from all his paid rides during the week. He soon progressed to helping at the stables by mucking out, grooming and general chores.

Through this work he heard of another opportunity where young lads could get some hands-on experience at Lilliput's Equestrian Centre, beside Upminster, in Hornchurch. Paul got the support of his school as they saw the merit in him gaining practical experience in an area he clearly loved. They helped him follow up on this and soon Paul had been accepted at Lilliput's. Initially aimed as a part-time, temporary arrangement, he had just started his work experience when his school phoned up the secretary at Lilliput's to find out how he was doing. They relayed back that Paul loved it and that he went to the centre every day without fail so the school allowed him not to return, and his unpaid working role at the Lilliput's Centre was extended, which he was over the moon about.

Paul lived at home during his work at Lilliput's but spent all his free time at the Centre. His friend, Andrew, who had helped him get his first ride at Hooks Hall, had asked his parents to buy him his own horse. They decided to buy the boys a horse to share, called My Girl Bonny. She was a skewbald pony which is brown and white, as opposed to piebald which is black and white. Andrew, however, quickly lost interest in his new steed, leaving Paul to have My Girl Bonny all to himself. He had never been as happy in his entire life.

To keep My Girl Bonny was full livery, the cost of which was £55 a week and meant that if Paul couldn't get down any day, the centre workers would muck out the horse, feed her, let her out to the field, bring her in and feed her again. The weekly fee didn't include the saddle, bridle, rugs or the shoeing (depending on how much road work they did, the horses could have needed shoeing every six weeks). It was a lot of money in those days but Paul was lucky to have such well-off friends and they continued to pay, enabling him to own and care for his very own horse.

The experience also enabled Paul to further engage in another of his new loves – sexual encounters with gay men. Paul would have to get two buses to travel from his home in Dagenham to see his horse at the stables in Hornchurch. One of the buses would take him to Roneo Corner, by Grenfell Park near Romford in Essex, and he'd then have to wait to get the next bus to the stables.

There were public lavatories where he waited by the bus stop and he used them the first time legitimately as a toilet. As he entered, there were men at the urinals so Paul went into one of the cubicles and noticed that there were holes cut into the cubicle walls, both to the outside and to the adjoining cubicle. Some of the holes were plugged with toilet tissue but others were open and it was clear that you could see into the next cubicle if you looked through them.

In his subsequent stops at Roneo Corner, Paul became aware of what was potentially or actually happening in the toilets and used these as a means to begin experimenting with his early sexual experiences. During his stop offs, Paul would go into the toilets and wait in a cubicle. Usually it was only a matter of time before a handwritten note would be pushed under the cubicle wall. The note would invariably be enquiring whether he was interested in engaging in some quick and easy sex. Paul was only fifteen at the time but remembers being very promiscuous and curious to find out what it was like to be with an experienced gay man, albeit with the protection of a toilet wall between them.

This was a time when 'cottaging', as it was known, was rife in public toilets. Since then lots of facilities have been closed and the practice isn't so prevalent in modern times. But back then, it was commonplace for Paul to agree to the scribbled notes, and engage in sex. This was usually via men inserting their penis through the holes in the cubicle wall, where Paul would pull or suck them until they came.

On one such encounter, Paul met an older man called Hugh, and had some cottaging fun with him. He would see Hugh many times over the next few months in similar circumstances and Paul had many enjoyable and mutual sexual experiences in the toilets with his new conquest. Paul was chasing a father-figure and he loved the look of Hugh with his big moustache and fatherly looks.

Shortly afterwards, Paul went on holiday with a friend for a few weeks so hadn't seen Hugh for some time. Once home, Paul was walking through Romford Market with his friend, when he suddenly saw Hugh, unmistakable with his butch appearance. Paul began panicking that he would be recognised and that his young friend would find out about his sexual deviancies so he quickly jumped behind a stall and, fortunately, Hugh passed by, oblivious to his presence. Unknown to his straight friends, Paul had got a firm taste for the fun and exciting danger associated with the world of cottaging and would revisit the activity many times during his upcoming, formative years of sexual self-discovery.

Due to his ongoing work with My Girl Bonny, Paul would frequently buy a magazine called Horse & Hound, which is the oldest equestrian weekly magazine in the UK, having been first published in 1884. Paul enjoyed reading through the magazine to make sure he knew everything he should to take the best care of his pony. One day, while flicking through the magazine, Paul's attention was drawn to an ad for an equine scheme called 'Working Pupils'. He was hugely excited about the prospect of furthering his involvement with horses so he contacted the stables who had placed the ad to find out more.

The scheme was for young people who would live on site at the stables and work six days a week. In return, they would get £5-£6 'pocket money' each week from which they'd be expected to buy everything they needed, including toothbrushes, cigarettes, tobacco or any other necessities. To Paul, it seemed like a lot of money to be earning at his age and, as an added bonus, he also got a ride and a lecture a day. The riding lesson and lecture were to build the young pupils up to completing exams that would enable them to become a riding instructor or groom.

To get accepted onto the Working Pupils Scheme, Paul went for an interview at London Weekend Equestrian Centre (LWEC) on Wingletye Lane between Ascot and Windsor – a massive indoor and outdoor riding school, show-jumping and cross-country course. They said yes straight away after he proved he could ride a horse and after a brief chat where it was obvious how much enthusiasm he had for the role. He told them he was sixteen and had already left school and they said he could start with them straight away.

He went home and told his mum he was moving out and would be starting at the centre the very next week. His mum was happy that her son had found something he was so committed to, and the following week he said goodbye to his younger brothers and Laura, now a toddler, and left from Waterloo Station to be met by his new employers at Ascot who took him to LWEC, where he began his life as a working pupil.

In truth, Paul was still fifteen when he attended the LWEC interview and with his sixteenth birthday approaching, he declared to them that he hadn't actually formally left school and was still fifteen but would be turning sixteen within the week. The main reason he had to confess was that every birthday his mum would buy him a massive, oversized card from the same shop in Romford. He knew that his mum would send him one again this year and it would be impossible to hide the fact that it was his birthday! Unperturbed by his little white lie, the management kept him on as he was hard-working and passionate.

Paul was living his dreams but there was still a large black cloud on the horizon. His court case for the Marks and Spencer's theft was due and finally the date arrived. Due in no small part to having completed his work experience and having secured the job at LWEC as a working pupil, he ended up escaping with just a small fine and a two-year suspended sentence. Paul was hugely relieved that the sentence wasn't harsher, although at his age the two year suspension felt like a lifetime.

Just after turning sixteen, Paul returned home and began signing on. From then on his sister would forge his signature when required and every two weeks Paul would return home to Dagenham, collect his dole cheque, give his mum some of the money, and then return to LWEC. This was obviously illegal with Paul claiming he was still unemployed and living at home but it was easy in those days to claim dole money and it was easily accessible to anyone who had turned sixteen so it was pretty clear that Paul would sign up to take his cut, and he did.

During these fortnightly dole collections, Paul would often pay a visit to the toilets at Waterloo Station where he would get the train to his job at Ascot. At the station, there were large toilets with at least ten cubicles in each and, like at Roneo Corner, these were regularly used for quick sexual liaisons. These toilets were rife for sexual activity, especially with businessmen in their suits on a quick train change who wanted the speedy relief of a hand-job. Here people would often see if there was anyone in the adjoining cubicle by standing on the toilets to look over, or by looking under the cubicle wall. If there happened to be a hole in the cubicle wall, they'd look through that. There were holes in walls, notes passed under doors, and illicit activity rife in every cubicle.

Depending on the time of day, there could be any number of sexual exchanges occurring in the cubicles at Waterloo and it wouldn't be uncommon for two people to be in one cubicle at a time, one crouching on the toilet itself while the other stood, so that they wouldn't be caught if anyone in authority came to check what was going on.

One would assume that the activity was so common that the station staff and local police must have been aware of what was taking place, but it may have been simpler for them to turn a blind eye rather than to try and actually address the problem. Occasionally the cleaner put the mop under the door in annoyance, but rarely anything more than that happened as a deterrent.

Though the sex was quick and cheap and throwaway, it was nonetheless exciting and it reaffirmed to Paul that he desired the intimate company of men. He determined that he would embrace everything London's homosexual realm had to offer and these early encounters merely instigated the beginning of his long descent into sexual promiscuity, experimentation and deviancy.

Chapter 8 – Pubs, Clubs & Fresh Meat

While Paul was working at LWEC, the centre manager was replaced by a man called Roy Haggerty. Roy was a good looking man with a proud moustache, and he was to become the latest father figure to the young Paul.

They hit it off almost immediately and Paul was excited to discover that his new boss was also a homosexual. Paul had been having stronger and stronger urges and was in a rush to explore the depths of his sexuality. They were a great match for each other and Roy would soon take Paul to his first gay pub and then, shortly afterwards, to his first gay club.

By this time, Paul was seventeen and, as was the case with all working pupils at LWEC, he had one day off each week. On one of these days, Roy took him to a place called the Queen's Head, off the Kings Road, in Chelsea. Recently, the Queen's Head sadly closed its doors for the last time but had been one of London's most treasured gay pubs and key gay drinking destinations, harking back to the middle of the last century. Situated on the appropriately named Tryon Street, The Queen's Head used to be a safe haven for happy homosexuals and the pub provided a venue for people from all walks of life to meet and chat over a few drinks with the promise of something more exciting to come later in the evening.

Out of necessity, the gay scene in those days was a great social leveller. Modern gay bars and clubs and the gay scene itself have become commercialised and diversified beyond recognition, with big business chasing the pink pound, leading to the decline of the little boozers away from the main drag with their down-to-earth attitude and clientele.

Such was the case for the Queen's Head, probably Britain's oldest gay pub, and in 2016, the inevitable happened. Developers stepped in with plans to convert the building into luxury flats. Suddenly the existing rental was hiked astronomically and the company managing the bar had no choice but to shut up shop. After all, this was Chelsea, a place with some of the most expensive real estate on the planet. Locals were having none of it, gay and straight alike (and those in between). There was a groundswell of opposition supported by a well organised petition but in the end it was fruitless and the iconic bar ceased trading in September 2016.

But back in 1984, it was very much alive and kicking when Paul visited and as the juvenile entered, he felt a lot of eyes on him as he was young and very attractive – fresh meat to the regulars at the Queen's Head. After a few drinks, Paul went to the urinals and while he was in there, another man came in. They got chatting and the man gave Paul his number.

The next week, Paul rang him and arranged to visit him at his address in Putney. Paul went round and found out some things about the attractive stranger he had met the week before – the man's name was Rob and he worked in the theatre, designing scenery and sets for the stage. Rob had a partner, but he worked during the day so they wouldn't be disturbed. Paul found Rob to be very appealing and an intelligent conversationalist and soon they ended up having sex in Rob's bed. Paul very much enjoyed the experience and the following week, he contacted Rob for a repeat performance.

Again Paul called round to Rob's house, but this time the man's partner came home from work unexpectedly. It was a shock to all present but once they had got over the situation, they ended up having a threesome. This would continue for many weeks with Paul coming round on his days off and the three men ending up in bed together. More often than not though, the sex was between Paul and Rob, and Rob's partner was usually left out. Later on in his love life Paul would find out what it was like to be on the other end of group sex where he would be the one left feeling excluded. But during these early liaisons he was just happy to be enjoying the freedom of open gay sex, and worried little about how others on the periphery were feeling.

After being exposed to the dark desires of the Queen's Head and to Roy Haggerty's lifestyle and sexual preferences, Paul firmly established that he was definitely gay, although possibly still somewhat bi-sexual. He was to have the opportunity to fully explore his sexuality over the coming weeks and months and Paul began leading a double life, working for Roy during the week and then becoming his partner at various clubs and pubs at the weekend.

Paul's love of big gay nights was cemented when Roy brought him to his first gay club. Roy also invited a friend of his to meet them, and together they headed off to Heaven, the massive, heaving disco which had opened under the arches at Charing Cross Station in 1979, and was the biggest gay superclub in London at the time.

Paul still remembers what he chose as his fashion statement for that first night in Heaven - a t-shirt with holes cut into it and a little dickey-bow tie. Looking back he was very fresh meat for the regular club-goers and he remembers lots of people looking at him, not in a leering way, more in a 'you're too young and fresh to be in this environment' kind of way.

The club was called Heaven and he felt like he was in heaven! Paul's head was spinning with the occasion of it all – this secret life that he was being ushered in to. He remembers kissing Roy's friend who Roy later pointed out was actually married. By this stage, Paul didn't care and when Roy said he was leaving to drop his friend off at the end of the night, Paul left with the two older men. They travelled in Roy's car and then, when they had arrived at the man's house, Paul was beckoned towards the front door where he shared a long kiss and a grope before the man quietly let himself into his home where his wife and children were sleeping.

The thrill of it all, the lights, the music, the drugs and the alcohol. The new sexual experiences. Paul craved more and more of it and would devote the next period of his life to consuming everything that London's alternative underworld could throw at him.

Chapter 9 – Craving the Buzz

Throughout his life Paul, has had a few constants that have followed him around in some form or another – his affection for animals, his patent sexuality, his near-misses with the law – but perhaps his biggest and most impactful constant is his love of the altered mind.

Alcohol and drugs, both legal and illegal, have played a huge part in much of Paul's life. Sometimes this has manifested in negative ways but often it has resulted in many of the craziest and most hilarious episodes he has experienced.

Paul had got into smoking cigarettes at a ridiculously young age and not too long after, he discovered the delights of smoking the herbal variety. Once he encountered this he was keen to access it from any source possible.

As a young teen, Paul briefly had a job labelling price tags on clothing for Top-Shop and Top-Man in a factory in Liverpool Street. Elaine's friend also worked there and was able to get bags of grass which Paul bought at ten pounds a bag, which, at this early stage of his drug-taking, would usually last him for a whole week.

Around this time, Paul would often accompany his mum to go and see his older brother Peter, now remarried and living in Bow, near the Raymond Road Market. Peter had a globe drinks cabinet and a heavy marble square case on the coffee table where he kept his cigarettes. He would also have a packet of weed in the case and when the coast was clear, Paul would steal some, to take home and smoke.

When he lived in Dagenham, Paul used to hang around with some of the skinheads in skinny jeans and bomber jackets, the more liberal ones who didn't have a problem with his colour or his sexuality. One of the skinheads was a boy called Charlie who was always in the park with a plastic bag or a crisp packet that he used for glue-sniffing. Paul could always tell when Charlie had taken some glue as he'd have his arms up in the air as if he was flying! Paul had tried it a few times with Charlie and was then doing it on his own the odd time with glue stolen from his job on the market.

Another brief job Paul had during this period was making belt eyelets on a machine. This was a really mundane role and to help make the time pass, he was buying regular £10 bags of grass to smoke before, and during, the work.

He was also doing a bit more glue sniffing although he made sure he didn't do too much of it. The effects of the glue lasted for a while and he soon realised that it was best not to do it at home, as he realised it was too easy to get caught. He did it at home once but realised he was probably being too obvious, and then did it outside after that.

What he enjoyed most from these early dabblings in the stimulants was the experimenting and the escapism that it brought him, although he didn't know exactly what he was trying to escape from. He was also fascinated by the curiosity gleaned by watching others, like Charlie, doing it. This was a common feature of Paul's future drug use in that he found it almost impossible not to try something himself when he had seen another person doing any kind of illicit substance.

This early investigation into easily accessible legal and illegal highs was to start a love-hate relationship that would go on to define Paul throughout his life.

At London Weekend Equestrian Centre, there was a livery yard as well as a riding school which meant there were people from the indoor-ménage and outdoor-ménage (indoor school and outdoor school). One of the women who had a horse based there gave him a bag of 5ml yellow valium tablets and 10ml diazepam tablets. There were a couple of handfuls of the drugs in the bags and he remembers distributing them to friends in London on one of the occasions that he went back home.

At the stables, Paul soon found himself to be a male in a very female-orientated environment, but his mentor, Roy, kept pushing and motivating him in his role of 'Head Lad'. He loved it, and the role meant him getting up in the morning, a bit earlier than everyone else, making up all the feeds, then all the other 'Lads' would come out and do their mucking out and preparing feeds.

During his time as head lad, Paul was continuing to develop his other great love - alcohol. The indoor-school at LWEC had a bar and, after shows Paul would be responsible for cleaning up the bar area, putting glasses into the dishwasher and hoovering up. While he worked, he would help himself to gin as he went along. During the summer months he tried Pimms but he always preferred gin.

It started off as a couple of sneaky tipples to help him as he worked but soon he was drinking more and more of the readily available liquor. One time he drank so much gin, he remembers going back to his room and repeatedly headbutting the wall and feeling very down, depressed and sorry for himself. This incident, he recalls, was the drunkest he's ever been.

There was also another activity at LWEC, which honed Paul's love of drinking - horse rides called 'Pub Rides' which were an hour and a half in the saddle to a local pub across private land. Paul would be entrusted with keys for access gates to the land for the trip which often included private, expensive areas of land.

One of the rides, where Queen Anne herself would've rode out and called 'Queen Anne's Ride', would take riders through the expansive lawns of Stag Meadow - a vast parkland dotted with wild flowers, right up to Windsor Castle.

There was another track, 'Windsor Great Park' where riders experienced a landscape featuring a collection of wide paved roads and twisting woodland. At each stage, Paul would have the keys to open the gates to another huge and wealthy area.

Eventually the group would arrive at the pub where there were metal racks filled with hay and metal rings to tie the horses up while all the riders went inside for a pub lunch.

Paul started doing these Pub Rides when he was just sixteen but this didn't stop him drinking during the rides. Also, after the group were finished for the day, Paul would've gone to another pub with the other working pupils. Their favourite was a pub called The Thatched Cottage, a lovely little countryside inn, where Paul's tipple was half pints of lager with lime and a lemonade top.

Although it wasn't the first time he had drunk - he had been drinking a bit before he joined LWEC - it was the first time he recollects drinking regularly and on an increasing scale.

Paul remembers the early days at The Thatched Cottage and the one time when he moved from lager to Pernod and lemonade. He remembers drinking at least three of these and then being violently sick on the way home, with his head hanging out of the window of the car they were getting a lift home in. Over thirty years later he can still remember the sickly sweet smell of aniseed as he retched his way back to the centre!

Rather than dampen his spirits though, it only strengthened his resolve to become a more hardened drinker so that he wouldn't end up in that sorry state again. And so began Paul's endless and fractured relationship with the dreaded hard stuff.

Paul, for the most part, was enjoying his work with horses and he was certainly proving that it was an evolving talent that he was nurturing. During certain phases though he felt like he had had enough of the daily effort and could hear London calling him. At this stage he started going backwards and forwards to and from horses for a couple of weeks at a time. He'd leave his post at LWEC for a short while but then would want to come back, so he'd phone them and they'd allow him to return each time as he was one of their favourites and they understood he was still young and lured by his friends and the bright lights of London.

But as he became a bit older and tasted more of the gay pub and club scene in London, Paul realised he was finding it harder and harder to resist the urge to go back for more.

Paul was conflicted and knew that while he loved the feeling he got when he excelled at his work with horses, on the other hand he felt like he needed something new again. This was to become one of Paul's defining characteristics – he has had a habit of developing life goals and achievements but once he reaches them, he immediately becomes bored and looks for the next challenge.

He decided then that rather than just end his work with horses completely, that maybe it was better to try something different. He sensed the time was right for a move and was afforded the opportunity when he was offered a transfer from LWEC to Priory Equestrian Centre in Frencham, Surrey.

This was a riding school and equestrian centre near the affluent Frencham Ponds, in the heart of beautiful countryside and a very expensive, sought after place to live and to keep horses. He would ride one horse and lead another as part of his new job of exercising the mounts that were homed in the private livery in Frencham.

When he was focused, Paul was very passionate about his work and he was becoming very good at what he was doing. As a result, the senior staff at Priory let Paul take out two polo ponies. These are the Ferraris and Porsches of the horse world and they can go from stationary to a fast gallop in next to no time.

Though called polo ponies, the term pony is purely traditional and the mount is actually a full-sized horse. Originally, a much smaller animal was used and when the sport of Polo originated, Manipuri ponies were preferred as mounts. They stood only thirteen hands or fifty-four inches at the shoulder. The preferred height rose when the game of polo migrated to the west, and height limits were lifted entirely in 1919. Ask any polo player how important their ponies are to them and they'll tell you they account for roughly 80% of their ability to play polo. Physically, they must have speed and endurance along with strong legs capable of carrying riders at full speed and the ability to stop and turn on a dime. There's also a certain amount of heart required for a polo pony.

Paul loved the fact that he was being trusted to take these mighty steeds out for their work. He had learned his initial skills under the watchful eye of Roy and had then improved his technique by taking horses out into the fields and jumping over any obstacle he could find in the open countryside that surrounded the riding schools. He would also merge his love of horses with his love of music and could often be seen riding out with Walkman headphones covering his ears.

Paul's efforts were being appreciated and undoubtedly he loved working with horses and everything that went along with being a head lad. He had got to the stage where he was making a lot of money for the stable owners - Frencham was primarily a buying and selling yard and Paul would go to auctions with the management where they would choose horses that had been broken, meaning they were ridable and groomed but were still very green and needed schooling and trained.

Paul's job with these new horses was to train them to respond and understand the language and commands that they would be given, like "given from your heel, one leg before the girth, inside leg on the girth, outside leg behind the girth" and encouraging the horse to bend round the school ménage, the arena. This would give the horse a sense of balance and understanding of how to be ridden round through rising-trot and sitting down on the trot when the inside foreleg goes forward, and how to go round with balance, supple up, turn left and right in the correct formation and do the transitions from trot to canter, canter to trot to walk. This work was all integral to moving the horses on to the point that they could be sold as show-jumpers or dressage horses.

Paul's early reward for his commitment was to be entered into various show-jumping competitions with his trusted companion, a horse called Irish Lass. The horse belonged to a couple who had bought the horse at the Priory and they let Paul school and ride it for competitions.

Due to his height, weight, and awareness of horses, Paul received another offer and was pushed towards the idea of riding as a jockey in horse racing. But Paul knew he wouldn't have as much time with the horse in the racing world and that, essentially, was what he really loved – the relationship between man and animal. This would have lessened in the fast-moving world of professional horse racing which tends to be mucking out and feeding in the morning, exercising of the horses in the afternoon and then mucking out again in the evening. He liked the interaction of everyday schooling, hacking and developing increasing jumping skills.

But whilst Paul's horsemanship was never in doubt, neither was his pull towards the bright lights and bawdy chaos of the city and the opening that Roy had given him to the pubs and clubs of West End London. Paul found himself increasingly flitting from horses to clubs and back again.

One night the lure was such that Paul and one of the girls at the centre, Cathy, a slim, ginger-haired girl, decided they desperately wanted to go clubbing in London.

Paul and Cathy got on really well, Paul sensing that she perhaps had a bit of Attention Deficit Hyperactivity Disorder as he was sure he had also. They were the same height and expressed roughly the same amount of craziness.

Another girl at the stables, Heather, was learning to drive and she had a Mini parked in the car park. Paul had had his first taste of Heaven when he went with Roy so he jumped at the chance when Cathy suggested that they should take their friend Heather's car and go. They justified it to themselves that it wasn't stealing as she was their friend, more just borrowing it without telling her.

Their plan was to travel to Heaven, about an hour away, and Paul offered to drive, even though he looked like he was about twelve years old. He was used to driving from manoeuvring the dumper truck and tractor as part of his job.

Remarkably, they made it all the way to Heaven without incident, then spent a couple of hours in the club, had a few drinks and then drove back to the stables in the dead of night and put the car back exactly where they had found it. Heather was none the wiser. She was told some time later on but for the time being they had got away with it.

The event was indicative of the contradiction that Paul now found himself living with. On one hand, he was doing something he loved, enjoying the freedom and excitement of his work with horses. But on the other hand, the lure of sex, drugs and music was increasingly becoming too much for the young man to resist.

The Clash had released a famous song a few years earlier entitled London Calling and there wasn't a young person in England to whom the lyrics, "London calling to the underworld. Come out of the cupboard, you boys and girls", weren't more applicable to than Paul with his unfulfilled desires.

Chapter 10 – Goodbye Horse, Hello London

The conflicted Paul finally made his difficult decision and chose to stop working with horses for good. He moved back to his mum's in Dagenham where he would stay for a couple of months.

At first he spent most of his time going clubbing with a friend called Jennifer Ives, still a distant friend to this day, although she lives out in the country now. Paul had first met the young Jennifer many years before when his sister had babysat her, and now the older Jennifer was going through a lesbian phase. She spent much of her time frequenting the London night scene with her friends and Paul would go with them, wearing eye-liner and fully embracing his New Romantic style. They would go out to venues like Heaven, now unashamedly calling itself 'The World's Most Famous Gay Nightclub'. Other favourites included The Bell at King's Cross, a pub where members of the local lesbian, gay, bisexual and transgender (LGBT) community drank and danced until the early hours, and The Scala in King's Cross, a massive old and infamous venue in central London which hosted club nights, live music and cinema nights.

This was a time when places like King's Cross were still rough and ready, before property developers and high-speed rail links brought a veneer of respectability to the area. This was somewhere that many of the LGBT community felt at home, somewhere away from the harsh mainstream, somewhere to party, and somewhere to hide.

After a few months at his mum's place, Paul became aware of a support service called the London Lesbian and Gay Switchboard. This was a helpline primarily for homosexuals, lesbians, transgenders and transvestites who wanted advice and guidance around their sexuality and support issues such as housing and benefits.

Founded in March 1974, the Switchboard would go on to become the main source of help and advice to London's gay community and later would develop into a leading source of information on HIV/AIDS with some of the Switchboard volunteers later forming the Terrence Higgins Trust, a charity that campaigns on and provides services relating to HIV and sexual health.

The Switchboard helped Paul to move out of his mum's place and into a room in a house with other gay people in Oval, not too far from the famous cricket ground. Paul and the men that shared the house with him each had their own lockable bedrooms, alongside a communal kitchen area. However, his new housemates were all a lot older and more mature than Paul and he felt like he didn't really fit in so would only stay in the house in Oval for three months.

At this time, Paul had managed to get a job at the Heaven nightclub which suited him perfectly as he aimed to spend as much time there as possible. Paul's new role at the vast venue was as a bus-boy, collecting glasses and bottles from around the club and then taking them to the washer room to be cleaned, before returning them to the bar. Paul was only seventeen, and legally should have been eighteen to work in a nightclub so he said he was eighteen and gave them a fake National Insurance number. He was also paid cash in hand so he didn't need to go through the formal books.

Paul worked most nights and slept all day and didn't really mix with the other tenants in the Oval house. They worked all day so Paul never really saw them or had any dealings with them. The room was also quite expensive so Paul soon found himself looking for other options.

With the regular nights out with Jennifer in London's clubland, Paul quickly started making new friends and promptly found himself leaving the house in Oval and moving into a squat behind Warren Street Tube Station with some of them. There was Andy, who would become a good friend, along with Liam, David, Lisa, and Michelle. The squat they found was remarkable in that it was a brand new house that went against the conventional view of the dingy and run-down hovels that one might associate with 'a squat'.

Although there had been some squatting in Britain following the first and then second world wars, this tended to be more out of necessity than any particular cause. But on 1st December 1968, a group calling themselves the London Squatters Campaign occupied the rooftop of a luxury block of flats in East London. This small collective of homeless people and libertarian anarchists wanted to protest against the inherent contradiction between London's homeless problem and the local surplus of empty properties. The event became recognised as the start of the UK squatter's movement which gathered momentum and over the next fifteen years became a socialist movement across the nation.

Tens of thousands of people joined the movement, housing themselves in a variety of empty properties up and down the country. The authorities struggled to contain the movement and legislation was always one step behind the radicals involved. This made squatting easy for Paul and his merry bunch, however they did get evicted from the house after only eight weeks, when they were told in no uncertain terms that they had to move on. It was a hurried departure with Paul putting the majority of his belongings in a shopping trolley, before making a hasty exit.

The gang went off looking for a new home and found an alternative squat, this time in Mornington Crescent, a short tube ride or ten minute walk from Camden. This was a very trendy area to be in at the time. The squat was an old three-storied house and the first floor was in a reasonable state but the second floor had no floorboards and the new housemates could literally see right down onto the floor below.

The squat clearly wasn't as good as the new house they had just been evicted from but was still better than some other potential squatting properties in that it did enjoy running cold water and electricity. They got round the issue of no hot water by going to the local swimming pool on regular occasions and having a swim, followed by a warm shower.

On the other side of road from the house where they were squatting was the headquarters of Smash Hits which was the big music and fashion magazine of the era and a publication that would have a significant bearing on Paul's early development.

Smash Hits had been founded in 1978 by Nick Logan, who had previously edited the seminal New Musical Express during one of its most creative periods, and who then went on to create the 1980's fashion bible, The Face. Smash Hits had begun as a test issue in September 1978, with Belgian's Plastic Bertrand on the front and a centre spread of Sham 69.

Following the initial success of the pilot, the first full issue was published in November 1978 with Blondie on the front cover. The publication took off and was soon boasting massive sales which were stable until its later demise. At its peak, the magazine was selling half a million copies every bi-weekly issue and, although it eventually succumbed to the dilution of the printed magazine, the brand survives today with a related spin-off digital television channel, digital radio station and website.

Smash Hits was at its peak in the 1980's, launching the career of many well-known journalists and writers including Heat's editor Mark Frith. Other contributors included Dave Rimmer, Ian Birch and Mark Ellen, who went on to launch Q, Mojo and Word. Neil Tennant of the Pet Shop Boys also worked as a writer and assistant editor, and once said in a later interview that had he not gone on to be a successful pop star, he would have loved to pursue his ambition to become editor of the magazine.

In the 1980's, the magazine appealed to Paul in many ways with its serial publication of 'Top 20' song lyrics and its ability to find the next big thing. During this period, appearing on the cover of Smash Hits was a sign that an act had finally made it, although despite its iconic status, the ethos of the magazine was to stay in control and to never pander to the whims of its associated pop stars.

Paul loved music and as anyone wanting to know anything about pop music during the 1980's usually started with Smash Hits magazine, it was inevitable that the publication would impact on him in a major way, both musically and stylistically. Smash Hits encouraged all young people of the day to express themselves as openly and as loudly as they could.

Paul embraced this and one of his favoured activities during this time was to dress as outrageously as he could. He would often spend hours putting in extensions of fake black hair or trawling the local markets for extravagant outfits that were designed to inspire and excite. Paul loved the alternative look and regularly wore foundation and eyeliner. He often topped this off with a blonde or blue Mohican haircut and dressed in leopard-print and other loud outfits, with every colour imaginable.

The group Paul had become pally with were not shy, they were loud and obvious, they were motivated by being different and they saw themselves very much as part of the 'it crowd'. The friends really came out to play in the nightlife scene and they loved the attention that their big costumes, implausible hair and crazy make up brought them. The brighter the colours, the bigger the hair, the more outlandish the face paints, the more attention they attracted and that's what it was all about for the group - to shock and impress in equal measure.

Smash Hits also had another major influence on Paul as it regularly featured tantalising snippets of all of London's various clubs in the gossip pages section. A club that was regularly promoted and became one of the main outlets for the group's exorbitant expressionism was the nightclub, Maximus, and in particular a weekly gay night run there called Taboo.

Often described as London's weirdest and wildest club night of the 1980's, Taboo attracted an eclectic mix of the bizarre and the wonderful, eccentric queens mixing with suburban-kids-gone-wrong and together making up the cream of the local gay club scene.

It was highly theatrical, unashamedly showy and splashy, and probably the only time it would have been commonplace to see would-be-customers impatiently waiting in the long queue outside sporting lampshades on their heads as if it was the most natural attire in the world. Anyone who managed to be deemed absurd or freakish enough was ushered into the madness that followed and it is somewhat inconceivable that any crazed club-goer who regularly attended Taboo, with its polysexual chaos set against its decadent, rotting club atmosphere, has actually survived to tell the tale.

Taboo wasn't about sexuality, it was about having a certain style or attitude and the same can be true of any great club night which has to have the right blend, as too much of one thing or another just becomes boring.

This weird and alternative outing into the London freak show was hosted by Leigh Bowery, until his untimely death when he would succumb to AIDS-related meningitis on New Year's Eve 1994, aged just thirty-three. When Taboo launched, Bowery was a well-known gay icon and artist, creating and installing fabulous artworks and paintings, and also a significant model for the English painter, Lucian Freud.

Originally from Australia, Bowery was to become widely known in London variously as a performance artist, club promoter and designer. Before leaving home in Australia he began to feel that he didn't fit well with his conservative surroundings and became interested in London and the New Romantic club scene while reading British fashion magazines.

Once established in the more extrovert London he attracted attention by wearing wildly offbeat and creative outfits of his own making. He became friends and room-mates with two others, Guy Barnes (known as Trojan) and David Walls. Bowery created costumes for them to wear, and this trio became known in the clubs as the Three Kings. Bowery was so well-renowned he even had an exhibition at Saatchi and Saatchi, but undoubtedly among his greatest loves was the invention of the bizarre Taboo.

In Taboo, there was a room with a glass fronted window and, each night Bowery would be lying in the space, totally still, wearing really extravagant make up with big circles like exaggerated measles on his face. Bowery's chief aim was to take fashion to places it was never meant to go and to then parade this anti-style for the curiously peculiar visitors to the club. Bowery was undoubtedly immensely talented, but he was equally bitchy, ambitious, charming, and displayed an unerring level of self-loathing – all these things were a microcosm of everything that was good, and bad, about Taboo.

Boy George, fresh from his success with Culture Club, had become a good friend of Bowery after he had first met him in the early 1980's. Boy George would later say in a press interview, "When he was hanging around with his friend Trojan, sporting a look they called Pakis from Outer Space, I thought they were a bit naff. I'd been painting my face blue years ago, darling! But I soon realised Leigh was taking things a lot further. He'd missed out on punk, he'd just missed the Blitz scene, so he knew that he was going to have to be extreme in order to make his mark. Well, he certainly did that!"

With his friendship with Bowery flourishing, Boy George frequented Taboo and quickly became a regular, "Like everything, I saw it, wanted to be part of it, and dived in head first. There were a lot of people hanging around on the periphery of that scene watching, but I was up to my neck." But whilst Taboo fed Boy George's want for the extreme and boosted his underground credentials, it also accelerated his slide into heroin dependency. "There was a lot of self-destructive behaviour", says George. "It was all about extremes, outdoing each other. We tried every drug going, we wore the most bloody silly things. Leigh could be cruel - a lot of people hated him, but admired him too. The downside of Leigh was that he believed in what he wore, that it made him something special. I learned very early in the punk years that clothes are just clothes and that the people underneath them are just people."

In the middle of the dance floor at Taboo was the DJ booth and it was common to have people in the booth snorting lines of coke or 'chasing the dragon' (inhaling heroin). Paul would often take the night off from working at Heaven so that he could go to Taboo and be with the trendy artist people that he loved.

Paul began frequently fraternising there and made his acquaintance with the likes of Bowery, Boy George, Marilyn and Trojan. It was a cliquey, arty, middle-class set-up where if you were in, anything and everything was accepted. Bowery himself was keen to convey this sense of creative freedom and would say to his favourite regulars, "You've got carte blanche in this club, you can do whatever you like." In Heaven the emphasis was on having sex, but instead Taboo focussed very much on drink, drugs and fashion, and lots of it.

ID and The Face magazine were popular youth culture editions of the time and these magazines promoted an evolving style called 'Heroin Chic' – made famous in particular by a young model called Kate Moss who was a well-known figure on the London fashion scene. She had the look - skinny with a very gaunt face. Paul wanted that look too and he desired the idea of looking like a junkie. Although it sounds strange and somewhat disturbed to think that someone would want to look as though they had a chronic addiction to such a harmful substance, the reality was this was the look many young people strived for.

As long as you were part of the in-crowd at Taboo, you could usually get in, no matter what state you presented in. Paul often turned up 'off his face' on drugs and would be ushered in, past the long line of hopeful punters trying desperately, though often failing, to get inside. As one of the selected people, of which Paul felt very privileged, he also enjoyed the mischievousness of being able to openly take drugs once inside Taboo. These were crazy, fabulous times and Paul craved more and more of this decadence.

When asked about defining tunes of the Taboo era to give the uninformed observer a glimpse of what it may have been like to be part of that time, Paul's response is clear - "I ain't got a fucking clue 'cos everyone was out of their nut. And I can honestly say no-one knew what music was being played. I know I didn't 'cos I was definitely always out of my nut cos that's what Taboo was all about. If you weren't out of your nut, I can't imagine how you would deal with it."

Unfortunately not everyone managed to survive this constant level of drug-taking. One notable victim was Boy George's good friend and the notoriously sharp Taboo doorman, Mark Vaultier, often to be overheard refusing admission with the line "Would you let yourself in?" Vaultier was a casualty of the scene, and died of a methadone and valium overdose at a party in 1986. Ironically, Boy George was due at the same party but never made it as he had been arrested en route on suspicion of carrying drugs.

The Taboo night was extraordinarily trendy and exceptionally difficult to get in to as anyone who was anyone wanted to be seen there. Celebrities from across London would try to gain entry but the rule was if you didn't know someone who was connected, it was extremely hard to find your way in. Famously, Paul remembers some big faces from EastEnders who were turned away as they weren't personally known by anyone in the higher echelons of the Taboo structure. You had to be in the know and have a certain style of dress to get in. If someone turned up, no matter how famous they were, if the look wasn't right or they didn't know the right people, they would surely be turned away. The night was gay and bi-sexual primarily but there were a lot of straight people that went as well, provided they were part of the clique that were involved.

As well as Taboo, Paul would've commonly visited the Mud Club as well as Propaganda and latterly, Pyramid. The big club at the weekend for all the freaks was the Mud Club, held in a venue called Busby's on Charing Cross Road. It was hosted by Philip Salon, a legendary clubland figure who had been part of the original 'Bromley Contingent' that followed the Sex

Pistols as their entourage. Philip was known for his outrageous costumes and cutting wit and would personally scrutinise everyone entering the club. If you didn't meet the grade you wouldn't be let in and would be told why in no uncertain terms. The music policy was anything goes. It was dressed up decadence and trashy disco all the way.

Now a global phenomenon with club nights across the UK, Ireland, Australia and Brazil, and currently operating out of the O2 Academy in Islington, Propaganda started in London as an alternative club night which appealed to Paul as a further venue in which to display his new-found bizarreness.

Held at Heaven, Pyramid was on every Wednesday night and was a mixed night which meant women and straight men were admitted, along with the usual gay clientele. The massive club with its various rooms housed punk and alternative tunes upstairs, while downstairs on the main floor was an endless mix of throbbing electronic music. The sound system in the main room was loud and heavy with bass drums thumping through the assembled throng. The DJ's playing this main room were usually Colin Faver and Mark Moore and Pyramid lay claim to being the first club in England to start playing some of the rare electronic records coming out of Chicago in the 1980's.

With all this clubbing and the related expense, Paul and his friends were often completely penniless during the non-clubbing hours of the day. To make sure they had at least enough sustenance to stay alive, they would often steal bread and cakes from outside cafés and bakers and anywhere else they could make a quick 'grab and run'.

Another way Paul found to make ends meet was through an illicit venture in D'Arblay Street, in the Soho District. Here, Paul and one of his friends from the squat, Andy, ran a male strip show in a shop called Gay Paradise. It worked by customers or 'punters' as they were called, buying a £5 raffle ticket and then going downstairs in the venue where Paul and Andy would be in a dark room on a little stage with coloured lighting and surrounded by plastic seats. The attractive young men would parade around and pretend to be modelling swimwear pants and they would then strip on stage before mingling between the seats hoping to get a few notes put into their hands in exchange for allowing the payer a quick grope. To keep them clear of the law, there was a switch upstairs at foot level and if the police or council officials came around those on the upper level would flick the switch. This would flash the lights downstairs to alert Paul and Andy to quickly put their briefs on and get back on stage. If the authorities did go downstairs they would have just seen two guys modelling underwear on a stage and, as this was allowed, there was never any issue.

Andy, a couple of years Paul's junior, was a big fan of Marc Almond of Soft Cell fame and he and Paul had been to a couple of concerts together. Marc Almond then started to frequent Heaven and Andy, also a regular visitor to the club, began dating the pop star. As a result, Andy would follow Marc Almond on his various gigs around England, and Paul was usually asked to tag along.

They travelled to Sheffield and another couple of venues in the North of England and Marc would put Andy and Paul up in a hotel on the night of the gigs. One night, Paul was in the shower and Marc came in and made a bit of a grab for him behind the shower curtain. Andy was close by as well and although Paul knew it was a bit of a joke, he was also sure had he wanted to take things further, he wouldn't have been met with a rebuttal.

It was during one of these trips that Paul was given his first ever ecstasy tablet from a stash that the band's team had brought back from a recent visit to America. Paul remembers sharing the ecstasy with a barman at the gig who gave him free drinks in return. The bit of the pill he took himself was enough though and as he danced the night away, Paul realised he had just discovered yet another way to lose himself in drugs.

Although Andy and Marc Almond were together a lot of the time, this was an era of many openly gay relationships and it was no secret that Marc was also having a relationship with another man.

It is probable that Marc was having multiple relationships given his new-found celebrity status but the media went overboard with stories of his affairs when they reported that allegedly he was admitted to hospital having swallowed a couple of pints of semen. Although sexual activity was rife that would've clearly been a ridiculous amount of people that would have needed to have ejaculated into his mouth!

Nevertheless, the story made the newspapers. It is only since the advent of widespread information via the internet and other means that stories like this are quickly quashed but back in an age where most people got a piece of information and then followed it up with conversation, conjecture, rumour and gossip, the story was believed by many.

With the progression of time, this particular story has become an established urban myth where the main player changes but the other details remain roughly the same. It invariably follows the same plot where, after collapsing at a post-concert party, a rock star is rushed to hospital, where doctors pump a pint of semen out of his (or her) stomach.

Whilst already debatable, it becomes far less believable when a trawl of the internet today reveals the amount of said rock stars and others that this has been attributed to - Rod Stewart, Elton John, David Bowie, Marc Almond (our protagonist), Mick Jagger, Andy Warhol, Jeff Beck, Jon Bon Jovi, the drummer for Bon Jovi, the lead singer for New Kids on the Block, the Bay City Rollers (presumably all of them?!), Alanis Morrissette, Li'l Kim, Foxy Brown, Britney Spears, and Fiona Apple. In these stories, the amount of ejaculate is often specified and can vary from seven ounces to one gallon and even ten gallons in one instance. In some tellings, animal semen is even said to have been the substance found!

With regard to this particular episode in the life and career of Marc Almond it should be remembered that plausibility has never been a barrier to the spread of popular urban legends and if it had, doubtless no-one would've believed it in the first place. And if by some strange twist of fate it is true, then since the story first broke it has become apparent that he is not the only one to have been caught engaging in such misdemeanours!

Paul's association with the Soft Cell front man was to deepen even further still, when he and another man, Michael, ended up running the official Marc Almond fan club for a short period. This membership club was called Gutter Hearts, ran from 1984 to 1987 and was the first Marc Almond fan club. There was a sleazy connotation to Soft Cell, a dark side, and many of their tracks had a fatalistic, melancholic and depressing side to them. Tracks like Bedsitter, Say Hello, Wave Goodbye and Tainted Love weren't exactly upbeat but they did feed into the emotions that a lot of people who liked their music were feeling at the time.

Marc Almond was constantly evolving and had collaborations such as Marc and the Mambas, a new wave group, which he formed in 1982 as an offshoot project from Soft Cell. The band's line-up changed frequently, and included Matt Johnson from The The and Annie Hogan, with whom Almond worked later in his solo career. But while the line-up changed, the style didn't and the music and Gutter Hearts continued to represent the moody and the misfits who didn't fit into society, those who lived their lives in the dark, the goths and all those who wore big black leather jackets to cover up their emotional frailties.

At the same time he was finding a connection with Marc Almond's music, Paul was also doing a lot of speed, described as the 'cheap man's cocaine'. He experienced regular comedowns where he felt extremely low, dark, moody, destructive and alien. Similar to his emotions as a child, but this time more as a consequence of heavy drug-use, he was sure that no-one understood him.

Marc Almond's music really felt as though it spoke to him though and understood what he was going through and what he was experiencing. Paul felt he fitted in with that level of negative feeling and lots of other fans experienced similar sentiments, that no-one understood them but that Marc Almond's music did.

The question lingered in Paul's mind - did the speed lead to depression or was he using speed to try and overcome his depression? Undoubtedly for anyone who has ever taken drugs, there is a common acceptance that what goes up, must come down. Paul was now relating his excessive use of speed to the rough comedowns that followed, although he reasoned that this wasn't necessarily a contributing factor to his depression then or in the future.

He recalled his visit to the doctor when he was fourteen and living in Dagenham with his mother. Then he was told he was suffering from what the doctor diagnosed as symptoms of depression and prescribed him on a term of anti-depressants. Whether Paul was actually suffering from depression or that this was the right course of action for the doctor to take is uncertain. What is clear is that fourteen is a very young age for anyone to have to consider taking mood-enhancing drugs.

Following this early diagnosis as a teenager, it wasn't long before Paul moved quickly and seamlessly into the domain of alcohol and then on to the drug and club world. As a result, he has always found it hard to distinguish his feelings of depression against the obvious negative emotions associated with come downs from persistent and severe drug use.

As a young man, he had no real understanding of depression as it had never been properly explained to him, nor had he researched his own symptoms. Thus, he found it hard to be subjective when considering his emotional mood set against a backdrop of constant drug-taking and the comedowns that invariably followed.

Paul never really knew what was at the core of his emotional state and he made a conscious decision not to spend too much time analysing it. He simply decided that it would be best to just allow himself to move from one episode to another, without thinking too hard about the feelings that he experienced as a result.

The Gutter Hearts fan club headquarters was located near to what is now the British Telecom Tower, a famous London landmark near Warren Street in the Fitzrovia area. Before it became the BT Tower, it used to have a slow revolving restaurant at the top of the tower and is also famous for a bomb exploding in the men's toilet of the restaurant in 1971, an act that was initially blamed on the Provisional IRA before being claimed by an anarchist collective calling themselves the Angry Brigade.

Here at HQ, Paul and Michael would open up the Marc Almond fan mail. People would also send in money for membership subscriptions or for t-shirts and this would usually be in the form of cash or blank postal orders. Paul and Michael found these hard to resist so they regularly took advantage of the ready money and would take the bank notes or use the postal orders for themselves.

During his time living in the Mornington Crescent squat and through his job at Heaven, Paul became much more sexually active. Whilst mainly explorative, exciting and fun, his promiscuity sometimes resulted in abusive, rather than intimate, sex. There were several older men who seemed to constantly prey on the steady stream of young Heaven staff and club-goers. One was a barman called Scottie who worked in the club. He was an older, stockily-built man and Paul would often go home with him on a Friday or Saturday night after work.

Paul was fond of Scottie as he saw him as a mature father-figure and wanted to share some intimacy with him. But Scottie didn't seem to share Paul's want for affection and gentleness. On two separate occasions, Scottie forced a dildo up Paul's anal passage. The first time Scottie did this it wasn't too threatening and it wasn't a particularly big dildo. The second time, however, was very aggressive. Scottie was extremely forceful and it ended up really hurting Paul as Scottie took him from behind, clearly not caring at all about the pain that he was inflicting.

Sometimes they had moments when they were calm and intimate at Scottie's house, but Paul soon realised this was always a precursor to sex and never just intimacy for intimacy's sake.

Occasionally, Paul wouldn't even get the intimacy or the rough sex as Scottie would take home another bus-boy, Russell, who had similar coloured skin and was the same age as Paul. This would knock Paul back, leaving him devoid of any attention whatsoever and contemplating whether he would have preferred Scottie's rough advances rather than the emotions of rejection and feeling undesired.

Paul was also to become reacquainted with one of his early sexual experiences from Roneo Corner, Hugh. He was very much on the scene in and around Heaven. Hugh was a minicab driver by trade but primarily used this as a cover for hanging around outside clubs with the main intention of preying on young boys that he could later engage in sexual activity either at their house or back at his place.

One of Paul's colleagues was fully aware of the situation and used it for sex in exchange for free cab rides home. Paul was more wary of Hugh but regardless, still saw him a lot. Hugh wasn't hard to miss, sporting his big thick moustache, and appealing to many of his targets with his honest fatherly appearance which always attracted Paul and probably many of the other young men seeking a father-figure in their lives. Hugh would always be standing just outside the door at Heaven, picking on young men to prey on, and Paul did occasionally go to his place and have sex with him.

This took a dark turn though when, one night after work, Paul decided to go back to Hugh's place. As soon as they entered the house, Hugh forced himself on Paul. Whilst the liaisons at the toilets in Roneo Corner and later liaisons at Hugh's house were pleasurable for Paul, this time he was forcibly fucked. Paul initially recalled the experience as being frightening and unpleasant. It was only later in life that he would realise that what had actually occurred was nothing short of rape.

Not long after, Paul was again leaving work and as usual, Hugh was waiting outside. Despite his obvious reservations, Paul was confused enough to think that perhaps he had misinterpreted the previous situation and that maybe Hugh wasn't really like that. Naively, Paul accepted a lift back to Mornington Crescent but as soon as Hugh brought him home, he again forced himself on Paul as soon as they had entered the squat, right there in the hallway. This time was an even more frightening experience for Paul. He was clearly not enjoying it and began struggling and begging Hugh to stop.

On reflection Paul is in no doubt that these episodes, twice with Scottie and twice with Hugh, were clearly rape. Regardless of the situation and the partner, Paul found regular anal intercourse difficult anyway but this was obviously especially problematic when he wasn't relaxed and had someone bigger, stronger and older forcing themselves on him.

These experiences really hurt Paul, physically at the time, and emotionally for a great many years afterwards. Each time, these acts were perpetrated by mature men who misused Paul's trust and his desire for intimacy and turned this into something far more sinister. Paul now sees the similarity in Scottie and Hugh, how they preyed on vulnerable young gay men and how they used the lure of tenderness and intimate moments to garner their own sexual gratification, regardless of what form this took and regardless of how it left young men like Paul feeling afterwards.

He remembers the emotions of the experience, he remembers wiping blood from his backside after each time, but most of all he remembers how confused he felt that men seemed to want to rape him, but not to love him.

Chapter 11 – One Night in Heaven

Paul, just seventeen, had lied to get the job in Heaven. He thought he had convinced them otherwise but the reality is more likely that they knew his real age but liked the fact that they had a fresh, attractive and sharp-witted youth in their ranks who was soon to become an adult anyway.

The bus-boys each had large grey trays and would roam the big nightclub with the two different areas upstairs, each playing their own music, along with the massive main dance floor downstairs. The bus-boys would find empty bottles and glasses on the floor and lying around the venue, collect these and bring them back to the various bars dotted around the club's walls.

Practically all of the staff at this time used stimulants to keep them alert and active and the drug of choice was speed. This became a regular activity for Paul, especially on Friday and Saturday nights when the club was always packed.

On these nights, Heaven would be open to 4am and just before 12am, the main DJ, Ian Levine, would come on. Starting out with Motown and the Northern Soul scene, Ian Levine had transformed the modern DJ arena with endless rare releases that he garnered during family holidays in Miami and other parts of the US.

Once back in England, Levine would spin these previously unheard of gems and soon established himself as one of the UK's most sought after DJ's. He began advising Heaven on its music and then became the club's first resident DJ, remaining there throughout most of the 1980's. Levine was also responsible for founding several bands including Seventh Avenue, and for setting up Record Shack Records. This was a spin-off from the Record Shack record shop which was successfully selling vast amounts of gay disco and other tracks.

Paul would've gone to the Record Shack shop sometimes and usually with friends from the squat. His friend Andy was there a lot. These were the days when record shops were a hive of activity and an all-day experience. Punters would be in there for hours on end, playing different records, requesting new tunes, and hanging out, discussing music like a singular community.

The first record released under Levine's new label was So Many Men, So Little Time by Miquel Brown. One of the big artists of the day, she was a Canadian actress and singer, and as well as being notable within her own right, Miquel was also the mother of Sinitta, famous at the time as being Simon Cowell's best friend. The very first play of this pioneering track was at The Saint, an American gay superclub, located in the East Village neighbourhood of Manhattan, New York. Made as an underground disco record, So Many Men had only been finished in the UK on the Monday and Levine and his team had to get their pressing factory to make white labels so they could be in New York by the Thursday with it.

Robbie Leslie was DJing at The Saint and at three in the morning, at the peak of the night, he stopped the last record dead, plunged the room into blackness, and then dropped So Many Men. By the following Monday it was the talk of New York. It got to number one on the Billboard Dance Chart and would go on to sell two million copies. In addition to So Many Men, Miquel had a few gay anthems out at the time including He's a Saint, He's a Sinner, again produced by Levine.

Sinitta was to follow in her mother's footsteps with a massive club banger of her own called So Macho. Every DJ up and down the land was hammering this track, except perhaps the most noteworthy of them all, Ian Levine himself. Simon Cowell, as Sinitta's friend, possibly lover, but certainly promoter was trying to force Levine to play So Macho during one of his sets at Heaven. Levine despised the track and would later state in an interview, "the record was a piece of shit, cynically designed to get the gay record sales. I banned the record, there was no way I was playing this shit."

Cowell, desperate for the track to be aired at one of the world's biggest gay superclubs, had brought Sinitta and the record to the DJ booth where Levine was playing. Cowell thought that if he brought the artist herself to the decks, Levine would relent and put it on but he refused and was busy cueing up another record to mix. Cowell grabbed the pending tune off the record deck and put So Macho on the deck instead. Enraged, Levine picked the record up and smashed it over Cowell's head. It splintered into several pieces and Cowell, stunned and horrified, grabbed Sinitta and stormed out of the DJ booth.

Despite Levine's extraordinary disdain, So Macho went on to become the number one record on the gay scene and was absolutely huge in Heaven, albeit when Levine wasn't on the decks. It was also massive in other parts of society although those listening and enjoying the tune may not have fully realised the connotations of their new favourite hit!

The iconic tune also provides an essential backdrop to Paul's life story as it is one of the few tracks that he actually remembers from those formative, drug-induced and debauched gay clubbing nights.

Later, Levine would assist in the evolution of Hi-NRG in the UK. This was a genre of uptempo disco and electronic dance music that had originated in the US during the late 1970's and its early beginnings can be found in ground-breaking tracks like Donna Summer's seminal classic, I Feel Love.

The original purveyor of the commonplace 'four-to-the-floor' dance music, Hi-NRG has existed ever since and spawned a huge array of specific labels such as Trax Records and React. It has also had a major impact on the future development of dance music as a whole, giving rise to house, notably Chicago house, and latterly techno, trance, R&B, hip-hop, drum & bass, hardcore and garage, among others.

Paul remembers Ian Levine strolling into Heaven as the big, broad, fat man who was renowned as the go-to DJ for the gay clubbing scene. He used to enter Heaven with one person carrying his box of records and someone else carrying his usual twelve cans of Coke that he would consume throughout the night!

As well as the regular intake of speed, Paul, along with most of the other bus-boys and bar staff, would sometimes take acid, and the main tabs about at the time were ones called Superman, although there were a huge variety of alternatives on offer too. A strong psychedelic and hallucinogen, Superman tabs would start the user off with a bit of a physical tingle, a strong sense of anticipation and some peripheral visuals. This was shortly followed by obvious surges in energy and emotions coupled with a distortion of vision. At its peak, the drug induced clear hallucinations where the most inanimate of objects literally came to life before the user's eyes and this was usually accompanied by heightened and distorted sensations of sound, touch, taste and even smell.

Paul would usually take the acid so it would hit him hard just at peak-time in the club. At this hour, when the club was going off and there was madness abounding, it was really difficult for anyone to spot who was on the dance floor, except by the other staff who either knew what was going on or were, equally, too altered to care. As a result the majority of the bus-boys would be out of it on the dance floor while a small handful of shyer, more reserved bus-boys would do their best to maintain the required level of essential work.

Later in the night, once the bar had closed, which it always did before the music stopped, the bar men would also come down and enter the throng on the dance floor. Into this mix were lots of 'clones' who were prevalent on the gay scene at this time – men wearing leather trousers or leather chaps and braces and showing off big moustaches – and all of them dancing to the booming disco music.

There was also a dark side looming within the scene though. HIV and AIDS were known about but always perceived to be more of an American problem and not something that the London gay scene should be concerned about. As a result, the disease wasn't really understood and the UK as a whole was very late to pick up on it.

Paul was straight in the firing line having, as he was, lots of unprotected sex at the time. In Heaven, men would be having sex in the toilets, in the corners of the dance floor, in the Annex (the smaller club up the stairs), upstairs, downstairs, everywhere, and Paul was never far from the action.

In the toilets it was commonplace to see people openly having sex of all descriptions and in the Annex, the emphasis was devoted to uniform - leather or camouflage or Dr. Martens boots and blue jeans. The Annex was literally anything goes and was rife for sex, often seeing multiple group orgies, and nearly always without any form of protection.

The thought among these promiscuous gay men was that condoms were for straight people to stop them having children and consequently, STI's or more serious illnesses weren't at the forefront of anybody's mind, and certainly not Paul's.

Paul did have little option than to be aware of the dangers though when he contracted non-specific urethritis (NSU), with the only positive being that this was quite a common ailment and was easily treated with antibiotic tablets.

Paul, throughout his older teenage years, had always been good with keeping appointments and would regularly get checked at the local Genitourinary Medicine (GUM) clinic. One visit though would result in severe shock when he went to an appointment at the James Pringle Clinic, near Warren Street. This was an incredibly busy clinic, seeing tens of thousands of patients every year. About half of the patients were men and about half of these were homosexual. This posed a problem for many of the straight, male would-be-visitors who were concerned that the clinic was doubly stigmatised in that not only might others think they had a venereal disease but that they might also think they were gay.

Still, the clinic was ever popular and mopped up much of London's latent sexual conditions. The clinic was where lots of gay men went to get their check-ups for NSU or for wart treatments. And on this particular visit, Paul was horrified to learn that he had contracted anal warts which, although fairly regular among gay men, was still clearly a major inconvenience, source of embarrassment and not the sort of thing that one wants to shout from the rooftops or add to one's CV. But at least it gave him the edge on the 'warts and all' story of his life!

Joking aside though, it would be a fair comment to say that in this era of the rapid expansion of the HIV/AIDS epidemic, that Paul was lucky not to have contracted something far more serious.

Richard Branson owned Heaven during this period and being a proactive and forward-thinking business owner, had brought in a team of people to provide a lecture for the staff at the club. They had to come in to work a bit earlier one night and were given a talk on how to protect themselves and an understanding of how to have safe sex. This level of awareness was quite new to most people and although it was a move to prevent the imminent threat posed by the spread of HIV and AIDS, for many on the gay scene it came too late.

Paul remembers the stark appreciation of that night when he found out that people could have HIV in their system for up to ten years and that it might not always be detectable. When Paul heard this news, he assumed with the amount of promiscuous, unprotected sex he had been having that it was almost inevitable that he would have contracted the disease and describes the following time as "being on death-row" and feeling like "a ticking time-bomb". He felt that whatever had happened to date and whatever he did in the future, he must surely have been exposed to this terrible illness and that he would ultimately die from it. As a result he became extremely stressed out, describing himself as being "completely fucked up" and "going crazy every chance he got".

During this period, when he had some sober moments, he thought that he would be diagnosed at any minute and that each month could well be his last. So Paul being Paul, he found the best way to suppress and bury these emotions was to party hard and try to ignore the fear of his impending death.

Paul recalls many friends and acquaintances that contracted the disease and found themselves largely unaware of how to help counteract the symptoms. Many ended up taking huge quantities of different types of prescribed medication, many with very damaging side effects. The early drugs used to treat the illness were often very detrimental to the host's body and weakened their immune systems, which is precisely what the disease was already doing to their anatomy.

To this day, Paul feels very blessed and extremely lucky that on so many different occasions he could have potentially contracted this awful disease. Looking back, he doesn't really know how he didn't become infected with HIV or AIDS or any other major sexual disease.

But survive he did, and this period of craziness only served to further escalate his already overzealous liking for living life on the very edge of its boundaries.

Chapter 12 – Boy for Rent

With his links to Heaven and central London nightlife, Paul spent a lot of time frequenting the West End nightclub and pub scene. One venue, The Red Lion off Old Compton Street, was one of Paul's favourites. The Red Lion was known locally as a rent-boy pub and Paul had initially gone there a few times out of curiosity and then latterly because he knew some young men that were making money out of offering themselves in the pub for 'rent'.

This was very appealing to Paul as he was desperate to secure an additional source of income. At the pub, Paul would go in and wait around downstairs. There were lots of young boys like Paul and there were also lots of older men, often wearing suits and clearly working professionals. The young men would be dotted around the lower floor trying to attract the attention of someone who would then usually take them upstairs to the main bar.

Although Paul was in it primarily to make money, he would deliberately target the professional men that he actually wanted to have sex with. Partly owing to these experiences, where men of substance would have their needs met by having sex with these young rent-boys, it took Paul many years to understand what intimacy really meant. For a long time, he associated intimacy with sex – that you could only connect with someone on an emotional level if you were actively engaged in the act of sexual gratification. He didn't understand any other levels of intimacy until much later in his life.

Paul would see men on a one-off basis but also began to build up a regular client group. He would know which men would be there on any given Friday or Saturday night and would then use his charm and good looks to secure their custom for the next couple of hours.

In addition to the income to be derived from the pub, there was also work to be had for the active rent-boy at Piccadilly Circus where there were McDonald's, Boots and a variety of other late-night shops and cafés. It was quite easy for prospective rent-boys to walk around the Soho area, moving in the direction of Piccadilly and to eye up any well-dressed business man or shady-looking character. More often than not, these gentlemen of the night would be looking for sex with young men. As the rent-boy and the businessman or other potential 'customer' would pass, either would say "business" so as to be clear as to what was on offer. If interested, the man and the rent-boy would either go to a local bar or jump into a nearby car and go to a car park, situated close by. If the young rent-boy went to a bar with their client, there were usually a few drinks before they retreated back to somewhere more private, usually the man's place.

There were different prices for blow-jobs, being fucked, or staying overnight which was the most expensive of the options available and often involved a lot of money. Paul hardly ever encountered anyone willing to pay huge amounts for an overnight and the exchange was usually arranged by the hour, with one or two hours the norm. The man would usually suggest a price for his chosen service or activity and then the rent-boy would try and increase the payment in any way he could. Through this work, Paul had many random one-off encounters but also had one or two men that he would have seen and serviced regularly.

Paul soon found that there was a local agency involved in offering rent-boys ongoing work with clients in exchange for a cut of their payment. The agency was run by a man Paul knew, called Max, and his flatmate, Gary. Max was well known on the London gay scene and had built up a lot of contacts both with professional men looking for easy and quick gay sex and also with local rent-boys willing to provide such services for money.

Max was a friend-of-a-friend of Paul's and during a night out, Max mentioned that he was looking to take on new boys. The agency was also advertised in gay magazines and other sources but, due to its illegality, the process was very discreet. The concept was incredibly simple. Max and his associate would place ads in local gay magazines and would use their own telephone number in the flat to take bookings and set men up with the rent-boys, often by giving the boys pagers so they could contact them at short notice with the details. The boys would let Max and Gary know they were available for business by keeping their pagers on.

Paul signed up with the agency, and immediately the regularity and the ease of the work increased, but his takings suffered somewhat. In real terms, allowing yourself to be anally fucked would be £80 an hour but later the agency would take their percentage of the payout. The agency did offer the benefit though of regular clients who had their favourite rent-boys, and therefore afforded them an ongoing and steady income.

One man who liked Paul a lot was a short, chubby, Jewish gentleman who always wore suits. He would take Paul to a swanky hotel room and once there, the man would strip off, revealing ladies stockings and would demand to be called 'aunty'. The man preferred to be fucked and enjoyed being passive and being taken as opposed to doing the taking. The Jew always made sure he got his money's worth by pushing it right to the end of his allocated hour and always ejaculated just before his time was up, ensuring it was time well spent.

Another regular through the agency lived in Kent and Paul would go to the local train station near the man's home where he would be waiting to pick Paul up in his small van. Paul would get in and they would drive the short distance to the man's house. As they approached the residence, Paul would have to lie down on the floor so that he couldn't be seen by any neighbours. He soon found out that the main reason the man was so secretive was that he was married, and Paul would only be brought round when the man's wife was away. Paul would only be allowed to surface once the man had safely parked his van inside his garage and closed the door.

Once indoors, the man would always take a bag from the van, which contained whips, chains, nipple-clamps and weights. When they got down to business, the man would attach the weights to leather strings or chains and wrap these around his testicles with a cock ring on his penis. The weight would hang down and pull on his member, in a sadomasochistic style. The man didn't use any of his 'toys' on Paul, preferring instead to have them exclusively for his own pleasure.

Paul remembers one time that the man also wore a mask and on reflection, Paul sees this as the first real 'heavy' experience of his rent-boy life. Not only did he have to hide himself away, ducking down in the van as they approached the man's home, but then later, had to be subjected to the threat of the sadist's environment and the man's twisted sexual pleasures.

Although initially unnerving, Paul didn't see this type of sex as entirely negative and remembers very clearly the buzz that went along with the danger and sadistic nature of the event. This would become more common in the relations that the agency engaged him in. While some of the men were pleasant and even enjoyable to be with, many were not and were simply interested in their own sexual desires and very little else.

Some would be quite specific in their demands and would phone up the agency to find out the size of the available rent-boys penises before placing their order. This would be done discreetly, with the men asking about "shoe-sizes" and requesting a size ten or eleven or larger "shoe" depending on their particular want.

Generally speaking, Paul found a lot of the encounters difficult and he used alcohol to help him deal with the emotions and the situations he found himself in. In addition to his earlier taste for alcohol, these experiences enabled an even greater level of drinking in the young Paul. He would always have a few drinks before these liaisons, to build himself up for the event and to boost his confidence in his role as the sexy, fun rent-boy that he was being paid to be or as Paul describes it "to shut myself down and enable me to do what had to be done". Once with the man in question, they would nearly always have several drinks before and during the sex so it was a common occurrence that with these occasions came lots of alcohol.

Another client had an addiction to cocaine so every time Paul saw him, in addition to the drinking, they would each have a line as soon as he went in. They would start chatting and very soon would be having sex but would still be snorting lines in-between. Paul quite enjoyed these experiences though as he had already developed a clear disposition for alcohol and good-quality drugs and the man in question happened to be quite good-looking so Paul saw it less as work and more as a good time.

While a lot of the work came directly through the agency, sometimes Paul would build up a rapport with certain clients and would arrange to see them privately, therefore forgoing the additional payments due back to Max.

The whole agency operation was founded in illegality. Apart from the obvious laws against prostitution, hiring people out for sex and soliciting money in return for sexual activity, there was the glaring illegal activity of even engaging in homosexual activity with men as young as many of the rent-boys were.

Up until the passing of the second reading of the Criminal Justice and Public Order Act in 1994 the legal age of consent for homosexual acts was twenty-one. Following the amendment in 1994, the age of consent was lowered to eighteen and then, in 1997, the Government introduced the Crime and Disorder Bill, lowering the age of consent for homosexual acts to sixteen, and bringing it in line with the heterosexual age of consent. The reality of the work of the agency was that Paul and practically all of the other rent-boys were under the age of twenty-one, meaning they would have been breaking the law by engaging in any kind of homosexual activity, let alone being prostituted for it.

Setting aside the illegalities of the operation and the liaisons that Paul experienced, there were many other obvious potential risks. Most notably each hour spent with a client increased the risk of contracting a sexual illness or disease or even HIV/AIDS. Further, there was the mental burden that accompanied the activity.

Paul admits that in the early days of being a rent-boy he liked, even loved it, because of the thrill, the secrecy and the mystery of it all. He also really enjoyed a drink so was often happy to go along with the experiences, provided he was alcoholically enhanced for the event. However, after the initial period and the related novelty wore off, things changed and Paul feels that the lifestyle did become detrimental.

This wasn't necessarily due to the fear of HIV/AIDS though because he tended to avoid those customers that demanded anal intercourse so he very rarely got fucked by a client. This was something he nearly always refused to allow to happen, thereby reducing the risk of contracting something during his encounters.

Moreover, what really began to negatively impact Paul was the toll of endless experiences with men who had little interest in him beyond their orgasm. This left Paul feeling increasingly detached and disengaged so it wasn't long before he effectively abandoned his brief flirtation with the world of gay prostitution, returning only occasionally in the future for the odd engagement.

Chapter 13 – Tim & the Brush with Death

During his time working at Heaven, Paul had met a man called Tim. Paul was in full exuberant flow, parading his normal black hair but with three electric blue strands glued to the fluffy bit at the front of his head. When he was in 'normal-mode' these were combed back, but when he was out clubbing he would raise them like antenna. This look attracted lots of attention and one man in particular, Tim, was very interested in the young Paul.

Paul, in turn, was fascinated by this dark handsome stranger, a man Paul describes as, "really attractive, not in a catalogue-kind-of-way but just a really attractive person". Paul was further enchanted by the outrageous group that Tim fraternised with. Tim was part of the trendy, arty crew, many of whom had come through the St Martin's School of Art, between Tottenham Court Road and Leicester Square, a well-known fashion, media and art college and famous among other things for being the first-ever performance venue in 1975 for a, then little known, band called the Sex Pistols.

Somewhat unbelievably, Tim's father was a vicar in Salisbury and his mother, as a result, was a vicar's wife. God alone probably knows what the super-religious couple made of their child sporting Mohicans and doing anything he could for shock value before he had even left the family home. It must have been very disturbing for the whiter-than-white parents to have a son whose main aim in life was to find a variety of creatively esoteric ways to literally tell the world to "fuck off" by portraying endless, obnoxious behaviours, often simply for the shock factor.

Tim had finally found kindred spirits in the eclectic gang that included Leigh Bowery and Boy George and they had been joined in their regular Heaven soirées by a number of other offbeat characters including Princess Julia, Jeffrey Hinton and John Maybury.

Described as 'The Beloved Mother of London's Underground', Princess Julia is a modern day DJ who has been on the scene since she first visited a nightclub in 1976 and who has moved seamlessly through every important era from punk to techno and beyond. Princess Julia was the girl in Visage's Fade to Grey video in 1981, and soon ascended to queen-bee status on the London scene. She began DJing in the early 1980's, originally putting on records at a regular night at the Wag Club in Soho.

In those days it wasn't so much about people mixing records; it was mostly about playing one side of a 12-inch and then flipping it to play the 'B' side. But soon after, bedroom technology came in, and suddenly everything was geared up to beat-matching, with turntables and mixers and their ever-increasing array of knobs and filters.

Princess Julia went and watched a lot of other people DJing and followed this up with endless hours of practice – a method that clearly paid off given her longevity of career in the DJ booth.

As well as Heaven, Princess Julia was often seen at the club nights in Blitz and Taboo, and anywhere else that welcomed the outlandish hedonism that accompanied her and her cohorts. And as a consequence of her increasing DJ bookings, she met many of the regular clubbers, including people like Bowery, Boy George and now, the alluring Tim.

Jeffrey Hinton has spent the past three decades helping to fire the furnace of English club culture. Making a name for himself in the 1980's with Leigh Bowery's notorious Taboo club night, Jeffrey cut his teeth alongside circuit regulars like Rachel Auburn, Mark Lawrence and his close friend, Princess Julia, whom he had met when he was only fifteen.

As a teenager growing up in west London in the 1970's, Jeffrey gravitated towards his elder brother who was heavily into subcultures. His brother encouraged the young Jeffrey to see the world with an open and curious mind and Jeffrey began to learn a certain sort of sexual politics as he and his brother explored the concept of androgyny and how people could play with their own image. This led him to constantly strive to meet new people and encounter new experiences and he found London awash with opportunity at this time.

Jeffrey was soon propelled into the clubbing and later DJ sphere, although he always maintained that despite his obvious love of music, he was a DJ somewhat reluctantly.

In keeping with the mayhem that accompanied everything that went on in Taboo in the 1980's, a recollection of one of his early efforts at DJing there suitably captures the essence of the place. Jeffrey had taken some acid and genuinely thought he was at home in his own bedroom, completely oblivious to the fact that he was actually in the throng of the heaving nightclub. He had been playing just the slip-mat of the deck for about twenty minutes with his headphones plugged into it – all that was audible was an awful grinding noise but nobody batted an eyelid! Everyone just carried on dancing as they were so used to unusual sounds and experiences on those nights, or perhaps it was just that nobody was in any fit state to actually notice. Eventually though, Leigh Bowery told Princess Julia to check on Jeffrey to see if he was alright and if he was intentionally making the horrendous sound. Jeffrey remembers her asking if he was OK to which he replied by asking her to make him a cup of tea. It was some time before he came to his senses and realised that he wasn't in fact at home!

The multifarious crowd of which Paul now found himself acquainted, through his association with Tim, also included John Maybury. He would become a very influential person in Paul and Tim's life and had been another student of St Martin's School of Art before carving out a career as a well known film director. In 2005, Maybury would be listed as one of the most influential gay and lesbian people in Britain and it was he who would enable Paul to join that arty set that he so desperately wanted to gain access to – as a runner on video shoots and then later on as a dancer in pop and music videos.

Tim would come to Heaven and as well as introducing Paul, with his crazy blue antennas and angelic features, to this menagerie of interesting and dynamic people, he would soon also become his partner.

Paul remembers the early days shortly after he first met Tim, when he would see him at Heaven and they would sit and chat. One such time, Paul was working and found Tim sitting in a group with Jeffrey Hinton, another man called Space, who has since passed away, and some other people. They were a collective that lived and breathed the nightlife but they were also renowned for something more sinister. This group were known for their liking of heroin, and Paul was warned by his work colleagues to stay away from them because of this.

Despite the range of illicit drugs that were commonly consumed by many people during the era, heroin remained a dirty word and pastime and it wasn't usually mentioned, far less partaken in.

Not willing to heed any warnings though, Paul began to get very close to Tim, although in truth it was nearly always drug-induced in the early stages.

One of the staff that had concerns for Paul's welfare with regard to potential heroin use, though seemingly not being overly bothered about him taking anything else, was the manager of the Heaven bus-boys, Marcus.

Becoming tired of life in the squat and needing a place to stay, Paul had begun renting a room from Marcus at his flat in Camberwell. But the situation soon became toxic as nearly all of their time in the flat was spent under the influence of some kind of narcotic, though never the aforementioned heroin. One of the drugs that they did often choose was Rohypnol. This was a time when it was quite easy to get access to the depressant, before it became primarily used as a date-rape drug and in today's world where it is highly difficult to get, unless the buyer is prepared to access the dark web or other illegal sources. It was used as a "knocker-outer" and Paul would often combine it with a can of Tennent's Super and go out to concerts or clubs and then try and stay awake, fighting the effects of the drug.

Marcus was a good-looking man, although considerably older than Paul. As Paul's landlord and manager at work, Paul was often in his company and began to find himself attracted to him. This led to them having sex but this was to result in the incident when Paul ended up contracting warts so unsurprisingly, the event only took place once!

Perhaps because it became evident Paul wasn't interested in any further sexual relations or maybe just because it was within his character, Marcus became increasingly manipulative and twisted. This wasn't helped by Paul's relentless drug use, often involving lots of acid, speed and other drugs, which left him very paranoid and insecure, whether on the drugs or coming down off them.

Paul couldn't cope with the paranoia and Marcus' persistent mind games, and the situation was becoming progressively bleak. Paul was worn out from working in Heaven and all that came with the extra-curricular activities linked to the job. The club only shut on a Monday night so he was effectively on the go six nights a week with very little respite in-between.

Paul had decided that he wanted to leave the poisonous situation and go back to the quiet life with horses and the great outdoors. He determined that after so much work exhaustion and the ongoing worry that he was best "doing a runner" and was busy making plans to escape the situation, when another man unexpectedly entered his life.

There was a monthly night in the Annex of Heaven called Skin Two, which also ran an accompanying magazine. This magazine was for those in the rubber, leather and PVC world of S&M. It is still produced to this day and covers all aspects of the worldwide fetish subculture through its highly successful publication, online presence, clothing line and related events. Paul would work on coat check at the Skin Two nights and as the customers would remove their coats, they would reveal that they were usually wearing next-to-nothing, or leather chaps, chains, or dog collars with a lead attached, and being walked along by their master.

It was during one such night, taking coats, handing out tickets, and observing all kinds of the weird and wonderful that Paul met a gorgeously attractive Italian man. As the night wore on, Paul got to know the man a little better and it turned out that he owned a house in Kensington, not far from the famous Harrod's department store.

Paul was invited round the next day. The man, now known to Paul as Michael Lupo, began to see him frequently, once or twice a week. The man was very controlling although Paul found it flattering, got a buzz out of it and thought this must mean that the man really loved him. If the man found someone flirting with Paul at Skin Two, his new friend would say things like, "I'll put a brick in that guy's face!" While the relationship was brief, Paul was very taken with his new partner and was even considering the possibility of moving in with him.

Just as Paul was all set to leave Marcus' flat in Camberwell, he received a phone call from the police requesting that he come down to the station to see them. Paul did as he was asked and found himself being interviewed at Camberwell Police Station in one of the freakiest and most surreal experiences of his young life.

The interviewing police officers informed Paul that they had found his name and number in Michael Lupo's book and that they had just arrested Mr Lupo on suspicion of him being a serial killer, with many victims across London and further afield.

Several times during their brief relationship Michael Lupo had tried to get Paul to take the night off work, and specifically every Thursday. Paul recalled to the police that one time he had done this and had sex with Michael. During the act, Paul was in handcuffs which were locked behind his back and Michael was incessantly forcing him to sniff poppers. Some of the poppers spilt up Paul's nose and he remembers the discomfort of not even being able to wipe them away.

Paul had thought this incident was fairly innocent as Michael had always been very attentive and reasoned this was just a minor accident. But, whilst in the police interview room, he couldn't help thinking maybe it was part of a more deliberate act on the part of the soon-to-be-exposed killer.

Paul told the police about getting regular black cabs from Skin Two at Heaven to Knightsbridge where he'd be in the back of the cab with Michael all over him, groping and openly kissing and fondling him. At the time in London, there was a lot of 'queer-bashing' taking place but Paul remembers never once being told to stop, to get out of the cab or definitely not threatened in any way, despite the blatant homosexuality rife in the back seat of the taxis. It must have been quite a sight for the Cockney cabbie though – with a young mixed race man being ravaged by an older handsome Italian-looking bloke!

The police informed Paul that they firmly believed had he remained in a close relationship with Michael Lupo, that he would have become his next victim. The police felt they had enough evidence to charge Mr Lupo with the murders of four people, and were firm in their assertions that Paul was to be murder victim number five. Luckily for Paul, the police had intervened in time and Michael Lupo was subsequently arrested.

It was only when the case went to trial that Paul realised the full extent of how close he had come to being killed at the hands of this crazed maniac. The arrest, trial and subsequent guilty verdict made big news at the time and the story was featured several times on the front page of many tabloids such as The Sun and News of the World. This ongoing focus on Lupo gave Paul a much greater insight into his background and later crimes.

Growing up in Italy, Lupo went from being a choirboy to serving with an elite military unit in the early 1970's. This army training taught him how to kill barehanded and also enabled him to develop another fondness, that of his homosexual tendencies.

Lupo moved to London is 1975 and began working as a hairdresser, before working his way up to be the owner of a stylish boutique and the lavish home in Roland Gardens, South Kensington.

Not only was he a success in his new career but he was also clearly a success in the bedroom and would boast of having over four thousand gay lovers, the young Paul being one of them. He was also keen on sadomasochism and had built a torture chamber within his new home.

This promiscuity led to his downfall though when in March 1986, Lupo tested positive for AIDS. Immediately following this diagnosis, he ran amok in a violent campaign of revenge against the gay community.

On 15th March 1986, thirty-seven year-old James Burns was prowling London's gay bars in search of a companion for the night, but it would be his last night alive. His body was later found in a London basement, mutilated with a razor, sodomized and smeared with excrement, his tongue bitten off in the frenzied attack that took his life.

Three weeks later, on the afternoon of 5th April, Lupo's second victim, Anthony Connolly, was found by children playing in a rail road shed. In a carbon copy of the first murder, his body had been slashed and smeared with human excrement.

Not content with his deadly deeds thus far, Lupo was leaving a gay bar on the night of 18th April, when he met an elderly, homeless man on Hungerford Bridge. Lupo would later state that something inside of him suddenly "screamed out at the world" and he assaulted the random stranger, kicking him viciously in the groin before strangling him to death and throwing his body over the side of the bridge, into the Thames.

The following day, Lupo met a man called Mark Leyland at Charing Cross and the men made their way to a public toilet for sex. Once there, Leyland changed his mind, whereupon Lupo produced an iron bar and attacked him. Escaping with his life, Leyland reported the incident as a mugging, later telling the truth to the police after Lupo's arrest.

Had Leyland admitted the full extent of what had happened, the police may have taken more of an interest and it might have prevented the final murder of which Lupo would go on to be convicted for. Damien McCluskey was last seen alive in a bar in Kensington on 24th April 1986. It wasn't until some time later that his mutilated body was found in a nearby basement flat. McCluskey had been strangled, raped, and then cut up with a razor.

On the night of 7th May 1986, Lupo picked up another gay man and later attempted to strangle him with a black nylon stocking, but once more his prey escaped. This time though the victim made a full and frank account of what had happened to the police. To track Lupo down, the victim visited all the local gay bars and clubs and finally spotted the murderous culprit on the night of 15th May. The police were called and they immediately arrested Lupo on suspicion of the crimes.

Convicted at his trial in July 1987, Lupo received four life sentences and two terms of seven years each for the two attempted murders, with the judge's assurance that in this case "life meant life". There were also clear suggestions that a series of mutilation murders in Amsterdam, Berlin, Hamburg, Los Angeles and New York may have involved Lupo but, while the crimes were investigated, Lupo was never convicted for these. Any chance of prosecutions being brought for these additional crimes ended when Lupo died in prison on 12th February 1995 of the AIDS-related illness that had sparked his notorious spree.

Paul was struggling to come to terms with the fact that in the weeks and months leading up to these killings, he had frequently been with Lupo and was sure that he could easily have become yet another of his victims. The horror Paul felt was tempered by the sense of relief at having escaped the potential clutches of this most evil of men but this was shattered days after Lupo's arrest when he was once again featured on the front pages of many of Britain's major tabloids – this time when it was reported that he had HIV/AIDS.

For Paul, already struggling with his negative thoughts that kept telling him he had inevitably contracted the illness, the latest news magnified the worry a thousand times. Paul's already inherent paranoia went into overdrive and he was utterly convinced that he too had the disease.

With the Lupo drama and his fragile residential arrangements, Paul literally ran from the hideous environment he had found himself in. He left Camberwell for good and went back to the place where he felt most safe - to the horses at Frencham Farm in Surrey, and back to Roy, his father-figure. Paul was glad to leave it all behind but there was one thing that wouldn't leave him. However relieved he was to be away from London and at escaping his recent situation, he couldn't stop thinking about Tim. Paul soon realised that whatever else had happened in his life and whatever more there was to come, that he loved Tim and he yearned to go back to London to be with him.

Not yet ready to return to the full swing of London life though, Paul had asked Tim to come down to the stables and they went out riding one day. It was a beautiful experience for Paul, doing something he loved with a man he had completely fallen for, and away from the harsh lifestyle he had left behind in London.

Following this meeting in Frencham, Paul said he would get in touch with Tim again. So one night, not long after but long enough that he didn't come across as desperate, Paul rang Tim. They hit it off again and both men began to realise that maybe they were about to embark on something special. They then had a series of phone calls which developed their flourishing relationship.

Tim lived in a flat owned by his friend Ivan, in Cherry Tree Estate, Tulse Hill in Brixton. Ivan was a really attractive, feminine-looking man who would eventually go on to have hormone therapy and begin to grow breasts, before changing his mind and abandoning his new bosom. Ivan was employed looking after the main door of The Fridge nightclub in Brixton, and would be there every Tuesday night at a weekly promotion called The Daisy-Chain, a massive, gay, fashionable and trendy place to go during the week.

After a while, Tim invited Paul to come and stay with him. Paul jumped at the chance and went to stay at Tim's flat for a night, which then turned into several nights. Paul decided that he didn't ever want to be apart from his new love and so he made his final decision to leave horses for good and thus he moved permanently back to London.

Not long after Roy Haggerty came to stay with them in Tulse Hill. It turned out that he was on the run from some dodgy dealings where he was involved in buying and selling various horses. He had ripped off one particularly wealthy client who came after him so he had to make good his escape and used Paul as his hideaway, as Paul had used his several weeks earlier.

But after Roy had spent a couple of weeks at the flat, Ivan had had enough as there wasn't enough space, and so, Ivan moved Roy on. It would be the last time Paul would ever see Roy although he did later hear that the law had caught up with him and he had spent a spell in prison owing to his illegal horse dealings. With Roy's departure went the last contact Paul would have with the equine world.

What now awaited him was a further descent into the relentless spiral of parties, drugs, criminality and sex.

Chapter 14 – Speeding Towards Heroin

Paul had lots of friends from his time working at Heaven, London's biggest gay club, which was full of homosexuals and full of drugs. Pretty much all the staff and customers were using large quantities of speed, Rohypnol and a concoction of other drugs. Paul was no different and was regularly snorting speed, every night he was working in fact. After a while his nose became completely blocked from the incessant drug-taking and he then resorted to 'bombing' the speed (wrapping the drugs in a Rizla paper and swallowing them).

Paul mixed with a wide variety of different people at the club and one of these, a man called Geoff who is now unfortunately dead, invited Paul back to the squat where he lived. Here various people were sitting around, just chilling out and relaxing, before openly injecting speed.

Paul was fascinated by the methodology with which the users got their 'works' out of the cupboard and proceeded with their ritual. Paul was soon joining the group and became equally adept in the art of injecting. It quickly became an obsession for Paul and he craved the buzz using needles and filters, often taken from a cigarette. The filters would be attached to a syringe and used to draw up the speed, which had been dissolved on a spoon with water and citric acid from a lemon to break it down, before the drug was injected into an available vein.

The whole experience, the paraphernalia, the secrecy and the illegality were all components of the massive thrill that Paul sought more and more of.

As Paul quickly learned how to inject speed, he soon found himself with a small group of friends who would enjoy the buzz, and Paul loved having his own little personal kit. Every Friday night the group would meet at someone's house to prepare their kits and inject themselves before heading out for the night. They would always make up extra loaded syringes and while out, they'd quickly pop to the toilets and inject again. This would go on for days on end with the friends continuing to inject as the weekend wore on.

Paul describes the feeling as far more intense than simply snorting a line of speed. Like any drug, it depended on the quality of the speed as well but the product they bought was usually very good. The hit from injecting was instant and produced a real feeling of warmth for a few seconds as the speed entered the bloodstream. The majority of people would never consider injecting but for anyone who is interested in the effects without actually going through with the act, Ed Sheeran's song, Bloodstream, is a good reference point – 'I feel the chemicals burn in my bloodstream'. The way the song describes it is the best descriptor that Paul can relate to nowadays and the lyrics take him back to those weekends of needles and speed and endless nights in Heaven. Although it isn't necessarily true, the accuracy with which Ed Sheeran describes the feelings of injecting and also alcohol use in some of his other songs leads Paul to believe that Ed is probably singing of his own direct experience. Paul can certainly identify with these emotions.

A typical week for Paul involved working week nights in Heaven "out of my nut", and then on Friday night taking a tab of acid so he was still buzzing when the club finally closed and work was finished. Then everyone would go round the corner from Heaven and wait for McDonald's to open. Here, they would each buy a burger and sit there for a couple of hours, talking nonsense.

After this, when the shops opened, they'd all go down Tottenham Court Road, tripping their way down the street, still feeling the full effects of the acid and topped up with a little speed to keep their energy levels up. Back then, embracing the folly of youth, it was easy. Paul would now find it extremely difficult to be in this state in someone else's living room, let alone walking down one of London's busiest shopping areas in broad daylight. But back then it was the norm, and Paul recalls that if there ever was a stage in life when he "didn't give a fuck", then this was it!

Along with the move to Tim's flat in Tulse Hill, came the inevitable progression to the use of heroin, one of the staple favourites of Tim's drug-taking. Paul though is clear that in no way did Tim put it upon Paul or force or encourage him to try smoking heroin. It was in fact Paul who, fascinated by this next stage in his experiences with illicit substances, asked Tim if he would allow him to partake.

In layman's terms, using heroin is mostly associated with the scummy conditions in films like Trainspotting, used only by the bottom-rung-of-society types who have nothing left to live for. But is this a true reflection or is there an alternative side to heroin-users that the authorities and media would rather we did not consider? Paul was soon to find out exactly what it was like to become a heavy heroin-user.

Paul's assorted adventures of heroin use began with him chasing the dragon. This is the method in which heroin is placed on a strip of tinfoil, lit from below and then inhaled directly into the mouth through a pen or other straw-like object. Tim, like Paul, got a buzz out of having an array of drugs – uppers, downers, and in-betweeners. The couple used drugs to 'self-medicate', knowing when they needed to go up or down, or stay the same, and which drugs would be best to achieve the desired effect. To this growing list of mind altering substances, Paul now added heroin.

The couple's chosen recreational habits didn't come cheap. This way of life required substantial financing and to help with this, Tim worked in the iconic West End boutique shop, World, just off Shaftesbury Avenue on a little side street, opposite the Limelight Club.

The first Limelight Club had opened in November 1983 in New York. Described as the 'definition of cool', the Limelight's interior design was handled by fashion maestro Michael Costiff who has had an amazingly varied life and career. Along with his wife Gerlinde, he took London's cultural scene by storm in the 1970's and 1980's, running the impressive World shop, and later starting the infamous drag club, Kinky Gerlinky. On top of this Costiff designed album artwork for Siouxsie and the Banshees as well as being an accomplished photographer, film-maker and designer of his own collections.

Every year the Costiffs would go to the Carnival in Rio, Brazil and they also had loads of contacts in New York and all round the world from where they would gather up items to be sold back home at World in London. Michael would describe it in a later interview, "We were always off somewhere travelling and shopping, and to be honest it just gave us a chance to shop more. We didn't like holidays where you lie on the beach, we preferred to go round the back streets of a market or something and find stuff to send back to London. We had really good staff in the shop, but we all had such a ridiculous attitude as we refused to open until 12pm and closed at 7pm. That was all before coffee shops so it became sort of like a meeting place, a real hub of activity and a great place to come and hang out."

The Costiffs would travel for long periods of the year and then bring back a whole host of trendy, world-wide items, from African bangles to American skull and skeleton and skateboarding t-shirts, big gold hip hop jewellery from New York, like thick chains with the dollar sign, Yankee baseball caps – everything that wasn't otherwise available on the high street in London. In the days before internet shopping, the Costiffs had hit on a brilliant business model of simple, exclusive supply and demand.

In addition to Tim working in the shop, Paul and Tim looked after the Costiffs' house and two cats while they were away. The Costiffs were famed for their feline friends and Paul remembers one freaky cat who had only one tooth in its head. While he was happily stroking it, it would suddenly bite him with its lone tooth. The cats would become legendary for biting and scratching a whole host of famous people from London's hedonistic club and fashion worlds who dared to venture too close.

This house-sitting became a sort of impromptu service for Paul and Tim as they were mixing with lots of wealthy individuals who had nice properties that they needed looking after while they were away. The owners would know their homes were (reasonably) secure and the couple would get to house-sit in some of London's coolest properties. They looked after one opposite The Hippodrome which was the perfect location to get to the club and was also really high up with an amazing view over Leicester Square. They also helped out the highly respected and skilled costume designer, Kim Bowen, when she asked them to look after her flat which was just off Wardour Street, famous for its hotel and jazz club.

Tim worked for the Costiffs in World, and Paul would also get the odd shift there. Most times though Paul wouldn't be found working. Usually he'd be at the back of the shop chasing the dragon. Often Tim would come out and join him and on the odd occasion, they'd lock up the shop and have sex in the back.

At this stage, Paul's heroin use was becoming more and more frequent but even when he wasn't using he never got the chance to go 'cold turkey' as he was always mixing his time with other drugs, mostly speed, marijuana and ecstasy.

For the most part this drug-taking, though clearly excessive and potentially life-threatening on a few occasions, was mostly done through the veil of a 'normal' life. Rarely did Paul get himself into the state that many would expect of a chronic drug-addict, that of a person wiped-out, totally non compos mentis and unable to walk or talk. Paul found a certain state that on reflection was hardly what a person normally seeks from a healthy productive life, but one that nevertheless Paul absolutely loved.

He would take heroin at home or at someone's house and chase the dragon, always to the point of excess. As crazy as it sounds, he would deliberately take so much that he'd make himself sick. Bizarrely, Paul loved getting himself to this state and the reason he enjoyed this particular act so much was that once he had been sick, he felt cleansed and in a state of purity afterwards.

During these phases, Paul would be out of it for an hour or two and then wake up, have another 'burn', light a cigarette and then moments later, suddenly jolt upright as the cigarette had invariably burned all the way down to the end and singed his fingers.

Throughout all of this Paul describes the lovely feeling, the warmth he felt and the absence of the intense worry about HIV and AIDS and bills and money which consumed much of his sober existence. It was pure escapism in a sublime encapsulating numbness which would sound utterly glamorous were it not for the fact that it was achieved via the use of a cripplingly addictive substance renowned for destroying lives, families and communities.

One massive regret from this part of his life though and one which has gnawed away at him is that he did not really acknowledge the passing of one of his earliest influences when his nan died during this hedonistic period in his life.

Due to his relentless drug-taking and heavy clubbing Paul describes himself as being in 'la-la land' at the time his beloved nan passed away. He did attend the funeral in Stratford and he knows that her last act was to be cremated, he remembers that much. He doesn't recollect too much else though owing to the drugs.

It also didn't have much impact on Paul at the time but now, latterly and more maturely, he is disgusted with himself for not being more coherent at the time of her death. Since then, he has had recurring negative thoughts as he was really close to his nan in his early life but doesn't have any later memories or can even fully recall going to the funeral. As a result, he never had a time where he felt he had properly said goodbye to her or thanked her for everything she had done for him while he was growing up.

Often in life we make mistakes or behave in a way that we shouldn't, but we always have the opportunity to make amends. The only time that this isn't possible is when the person or people involved are no longer with us and in these instances, all we are left with are regrets and a deep wish that we had done things differently. These were the overriding emotions for Paul – his cherished nan no longer of this earth, while he stumbled through a haze of heroin-induced absurdity, oblivious to the real emotion of her passing.

Chapter 15 – Being Normal

While Paul undoubtedly enjoyed the nightlife and being at work while high on drugs, it was becoming too much to sustain all the time. He felt the need for a change and decided he wanted to spend more quality time with Tim. He also still wasn't very good with money and was aware that it would cause friction in his relationship with Tim if he didn't contribute more for the essential things like rent, food and, of course, the drugs to while away the social hours.

Paul embraced this desire to change and to make a legitimate income, also reasoning that it might lessen the amount of time that he had available to take his wide variety of drugs. He managed to find work with a market research company, called Market Research Enterprises (MRE), whose main offices were located off Oxford Street.

The work was handy as it was cash-in-hand and Paul made sure to back this up with a fake National Insurance number just in case the authorities ever tried to track him down for tax evasion. Staff were also able to choose their own shifts so it suited Paul down to the ground.

Each employee had a computer running a word-for-word script and a telephone, and as Paul was fortunate to have a pleasant sounding voice, he found it easy to conduct research on behalf of companies such as British Telecom. He would cold-call people before asking them things like, "have you seen the advert with Maureen Lipman and what did you think of it?" There were a wide variety of client companies and Paul could be asking anything from shampoos to shopping trends or eating habits.

In many ways this job was in complete contrast to the rest of his life and could well have been deemed a thoroughly normal existence. Paul though wasn't prepared to fully relinquish all his insaneness and he struggled to maintain his aim of reducing the blurring of his work with his social drug use. Instead, he simply became even more secretive about his relentless drug-taking. His co-workers were none-the-wiser that their colleague would sneak off to the toilet for a 'little boot' before completing his shift and moving out of the telephone pews in Oxford Street and straight out into the debauchery of London's underbelly. He loved the way he could always maintain an air of competency at work and he made sure he never overdid it or ended up leaving himself obviously under the influence – it was always just a little 'bomb' or a snort of speed, enough to make the shift go in a bit quicker and in a bit more of an interesting fashion.

Latterly at MRE, he found himself inputting data on behalf of Jaguar Cars. Paul was tasked with ringing up customers six months after they had bought a Jaguar and asking them about their satisfaction with the car. There is something surreally humorous about the concept of someone having a nice in depth conversation about the qualities of their recently acquired Jaguar XJ6 with its V12 turbo-charged engine and bespoke leather interior without realising that the polite young man on the other end of the phone is well and truly "off his nut"!

For Paul this was all part of the game and he would try and think up new ways of getting mentally altered in his workplace. Towards the end of his brief career in market research, he would bring along a little wooden pipe and frequently pop to the toilets for a quick blast of hash, then come back out and get on the phone again. This was a particular favourite of Paul's if he had previously indulged in some heroin as it helped to straighten him out whilst bringing back a little bit of the intensity of the original hit.

Paul could possibly have been found out for his extra-curricular activities, but he benefited from the fact that the offices were laid out in multiple single cubicles. He could get away with nodding off in a hazy drug-induced mini-coma before quickly straightening himself out before anyone else noticed and thus avoiding being caught by his adjoining co-workers. Most importantly it enabled him to stay out of sight of the floor manager who might otherwise have seen one of his staff members melting off the chair into the cheap office carpet below.

It could also be argued that many of Paul's colleagues were of a similar ilk and wouldn't actually have had any problem whatsoever with his behaviour. Often the staff were a close-knit bunch, of similar ages, with a commonality that they spent much of their leisure time frequenting the same gay pubs and clubs that Paul invariably found himself in. Despite their similarities in other ways though, Paul maintains that it is unlikely any of the other staff were quite as adept at taking mind-altering substances at their workplace as he was, and he secretly enjoyed the fact that he knew he was winning as far as 'the best drug-taker at MRE' was concerned.

Though reflecting on this period and in hindsight with it seeming like a never-ending spiral of addiction, Paul recalls that he didn't ever feel like he was losing control. At the time it was all about getting the required variety of drugs and ensuring access to the range of uppers, downers and in-betweeners he felt he needed to sustain his chosen, self-medicating lifestyle. He knew how to handle it, he knew how to get away with it and he did for a long time, as a self-confessed functioning junkie.

By now, Paul was firmly ensconced in Tulse Hill and was enjoying his fun, albeit chaotic, lifestyle living with Tim and Ivan. Things were soon to change though as, after a short while, Paul and Tim were forced to move out of the flat. Ivan was an argumentative person and Paul was never really meant to be there in the first place. Tim could, at times, be moody and difficult and he and Ivan would regularly clash over the slightest trivial thing. Having Paul there simply exacerbated the situation. Additionally, having Roy to stay for those few weeks hardly helped and the situation was becoming more and more untenable. Eventually as the arguments became more and more extreme, it was clear that something needed to change.

Tim knew a guy who was squatting in a huge disused hospital in Russell Gardens and he managed to get a room for him and Paul. They took it upon themselves to make the place look as presentable as possible and Tim even went as far as sanding down the wooden floorboards in the room and varnishing them. At this stage, Tim and Paul, though they played down the 'fashion statement' personas, were in reality very much like the fashion icons of the day. Though in reality they lived in squats or cramped, shared housing, in their minds and as much as they could, they felt entitled to live as kings among men. However, it didn't turn out well as the man who had offered them the room in the squat took a liking to Tim, and this made things very uncomfortable, so they didn't move in in the end.

Instead, Paul had met a girl at MRE who offered him and Tim a room to rent at the house she lived in, near the marshes at Bodney Road, just round the corner from Hackney Downs Train Station. It was a Housing Association property and all the other rooms were occupied but she had one room available that the couple could rent if they wanted. Although the rent was quite high, it wasn't too much of a problem as Tim was still working at World and Paul was doing the market research job along with the occasional shift with Tim at the shop.

So the couple moved in and for the first time since he was a young child, Paul felt like he was properly settled and that he was getting a grip on his life. He had a steady income, a secure roof over his head and most importantly, was enjoying the intimacy of the close relationship with Tim.

It would have been natural for Paul to start to ease off and embrace the pending conventionality of his existence. But this was the man for whom drama and chaos were always just around the corner. Inevitably the normality was fleeting and merely served as a brief stopover on the next stage of his dysfunctional journey.

Chapter 16 – Nothing Compares 2 U

It was Paul's 20th birthday. He had been working in World with Tim and once their shift had finished, they went round the corner to get a fry-up in a café in Holborn. Paul was wearing Fred Perry bleached jeans and Dr. Martens boots with spurs on the back, like a cowboy would wear. He'd picked these up at World from among the array of weird and wonderful merchandise that adorned the boutique. Paul also had about his person a big bag of branchy weed that he intended to use later on his special day and a penknife which he had for no particular reason.

When they came out of the café, they literally walked into a policeman who didn't know how to figure them out, but was nonetheless concerned enough to tell them to wait while he called for backup. The officer was shortly joined by some colleagues who suggested that they would try to prosecute Paul for being in possession of an offensive weapon as a result of the spurs. He was arrested and taken to the police station where they searched him and found the penknife and bag of weed. The police were obviously clueless in terms of drugs awareness and kept asking Paul if he had been sniffing the weed to get high! Regardless of their inabilities, or perhaps because of them, they just removed the drugs and Paul didn't hear another word about them.

Tim accompanied them to the station but had been told to wait in the reception area. He kept saying that it was Paul's birthday but the police responded sarcastically saying, "don't worry we'll get him the birthday suite!" The police also intimated to Tim that they suspected Paul of supporting the National Front due to his Fred Perry bleached jeans and Dr. Martens boots, perhaps not realising the complete contradiction that he was also clearly a black man!

The police did soon realise Paul wasn't a danger to anyone and released him although first they made him go through the embarrassment of having to throw his little penknife down a drain beside a bus stop full of people who were all watching what was going on, before he was allowed to go. Paul was really annoyed at the potential sabotage of his special day but happy he had escaped and was free to carry on with his birthday.

Following Paul's liberation, the would-be-revellers decided they would visit Kim Bowen's flat near Waldorf Street. Kim was riding high in the fashion industry as an Editor for Blitz Magazine, a major and relevant publication which was rivalling ID Magazine at the top of the fashion mag market. These editions were full of pages of fashionable people like Boy George and Leigh Bowery and often featured Paul's sought after heroin-chic look.

Paul and Tim went round to Kim's a lot in those days and during this particular visit, Paul was to meet Fachtna O'Ceallaigh (or 'Faulkner O'Kelly' to the London contingent), the former head of U2's Mother Records and who, at the time, was most famous for being the Manager of The Boomtown Rats, an Irish rock band headed by vocalist Bob Geldof. Fachtna was Kim Bowen's boyfriend and Tim was friendly with them both, though Paul had never met the affable Irish gent before.

While there, Fachtna began showing them pictures of a young girl, a skinhead wearing Dr. Martens boots and a tutu. These pictures were of a new artist that he had just started managing, called Sinéad O'Connor.

Fachtna then gave Paul a present for his birthday, which he still treasures to this day, a cassette tape of Sinéad's debut album, The Lion and the Cobra. With the title taken from a line from Psalm 91:13, 'you will tread upon the lion and the cobra', O'Connor's first album would go on to sell over two and a half million copies. The second track, Mandinka, is probably the best known of the songs and it would peak at number seventeen in the UK singles chart. The Lion and the Cobra is notable as O'Connor, aged just twenty at the time, recorded it while heavily pregnant with her first child.

In addition to the cassette, Paul and Tim had been given an ecstasy pill to share and later that night the happy couple would round off Paul's birthday by seeing the Kevin Mooney band, Max, perform at Heaven.

Not long after, Paul and Tim were invited by John Maybury to meet him for a drink in a pub called The Old Compton's in Old Compton Street. It was here that they were introduced to Sinéad O'Connor. Interestingly, Paul would actually end up later working at this same pub twice before abruptly getting sacked twice. But during this early visit, they were there very much as customers.

Sinéad, just a year older than Paul, was immediately taken with the cropped hair and clothing style of Paul and Tim. This was similar to how she liked to dress and she loved how the couple looked, and enjoyed being in their company. Spontaneously she said to Tim that if he could find somewhere big enough for him and Paul, in addition to all her requirements, that she would move in with them. She was quite demanding and explained that she wanted enough room for a studio, as well as for her first child, Jake, a room for the nanny, a living room, room for Sinéad's bassist and drummer at the time and a room for Tim and Paul to share.

This was an enticing deal for the young lovers, especially as Sinéad was about to embark on a tour of America so wouldn't even be around that much in the early stages. Sinéad had really taken off in the US long before she made it big in the UK, and this was even before her notorious 1992 event of ripping up the picture of the Pope on the TV show Saturday Night Live which would further propel her into the US public eye.

Her fame wasn't reciprocated initially in the UK where The Lion & The Cobra struggled to be commercially successful. However she did have a track which resonated greatly with Paul, called Just Call Me Joe, written by Kevin Mooney from Max. One of the lines 'I'll meet you on the corner block' showed the true background of the song which was about waiting to meet your dealer to score for heroin.

Paul and Tim ended up finding somewhere to live with the help of John Reynolds, who was Jake's father. It was a beautiful six-bedroom flat in St John's Wood and promptly Paul and Tim moved their belongings in and John moved Sinéad and Jake's things in, as she was by now off touring America.

It felt like Paul had maybe found somewhere that he could finally call home and where he could start to foster the stability that he constantly craved in his life. But as things would unfold, his new-found feelings of security would again prove to be short-lived.

In addition to her undoubted talents, Sinéad also brought with her many issues. She was clearly and openly struggling with her upbringing in Ireland. The third of five children, her parents had separated when she was just eight years old, and Sinéad and her older brother and sister went to live with their mother, where O'Connor claims they were subjected to frequent physical abuse. Her father, Sean, made various efforts to secure custody of his children, but did so in a country which routinely denied custody to fathers and prohibited divorce. This situation ultimately motivated him to later become chairman of the Divorce Action Group, a pressure body advocating for divorce to become allowed under the Irish Constitution.

Aged thirteen, Sinéad eventually went to live with her father and his new wife but struggled with shoplifting and truancy to the extent that at fifteen, she was placed in a Magdalene Asylum for eighteen months. These were horrific institutions, effectively operating as penitentiary work-houses with strict regimes that were often more severe than those found in Irish prisons. As with most inmates, the wretchedness of this period had a profound effect on the young girl. She would later state that "I have never, and probably will never, experience such panic and terror and agony over anything."

Surviving the torment of the Asylum, she was then sent by her father to a school in Waterford with a much more progressive and positive ethos. It was here, with the support of a teacher, that she would record some demo songs. From this breakthrough, Sinéad soon formed a band with a few other members called Ton Ton Macoute. Their early performances received positive reviews and most observers noted O'Connor's talented singing and stage presence. Early in 1985 though, tragedy struck when her mother was killed in a car accident. Despite their difficult relationship, this devastated Sinéad and she left the band and moved to London.

Although she had escaped Ireland, the weight of Sinéad's Catholic upbringing combined with her parental abuse and her litany of other issues meant that she could never escape the inner-demons that permeated her every thought. Sinéad struggled to deal with everything, including the fame in America, and definitely in the period when she became famous back home in London.

Following her return from her time in America, Sinéad moved into the St John's Wood property with Paul and the rest. Fachtna by this stage had split up with Kim Bowen and had started seeing Sinéad.

Things in the flat soon became very fragile. As a result of her life experiences thus far Sinéad was very paranoid and insecure which led to various arguments, both between Sinéad and Fachtna, but also with the other flatmates.

There were many reasons the flat often portrayed an atmosphere of tense conflict and one of the main ones was with regards to the flatmates' choice in garments. Paul's favoured style at this time was wearing bondage trousers and his collection included a corduroy pair, a black cotton pair, and a red tartan pair. They were all in the style promoted by Vivienne Westwood and Malcolm McLaren. To match the trousers, Paul also frequently wore bondage tops. One had two cowboys kissing and another one had a black and white screen print of breasts. Whatever he was wearing at the time always had the same thing in common - the outfits were shockingly brilliant. And whatever Paul wore, Sinéad would say, "oh, let me have it, Paul", and he would say, "no, no, no", and he would think about all the money she had and that she could afford anything she wanted, while he was still doing a research job down the road for a measly salary.

There was also a major issue in the house in that Sinéad and Tim didn't hit it off. It was a clear personality clash. While she was away and the others had moved in, she had a phone line installed just for her, while Paul and Tim were waiting for their own phone line to be put in. One night, the phone was ringing in the flat. Tim answered it, but it was Sinéad on the other end of the line and she was really annoyed that he was answering the phone.

Another time, after she had moved in, she sellotaped a record player of hers down so Paul and Tim couldn't use it. It was petty stuff, but consistently so, and the situation wasn't helped by Sinéad's need and desire to want the clothes that Paul was wearing which he found both weird and irritating.

But despite the difficulties and Paul constantly feeling like his wardrobe was going to be robbed at any given time, often it was a crazy, fun time - living with a soon to be global-superstar in a huge flat in St John's Wood and squabbling over items of obscure clothing.

During his time at the flat, Paul was to meet another star, whose music he adored – the enigmatic Icelander, Bjork, the lead singer of The Sugarcubes at the time. Paul was into her music, style and persona in a big way. He had first come across Bjork's band when he heard their single, Birthday, which was in the charts and had become Melody Maker and NME's single of the week, and had then gone to see her perform at a gig in Kilburn. Paul loved her voice and connected with the abstract lyrics.

One day, he had come home from work, and Sinéad was in the living room talking to Bjork. Paul is not usually starstruck, but he most definitely was on this occasion. He struggled to be his usual chatty self and was barely able to muster a comment. He was saved however by the diminutive star who greeted him and immediately apologised as she had a scab on her lip having been recently attacked by a dog. Paul covered up his unexpected and unusual inability to converse and politely excused himself from the room.

As well as mixing with the stars, Paul and Tim were also keen to develop their own fame. In Paul's own words they "looked the fucking bollocks" both when together and apart. Tim was white, Paul was mixed-race-black, but they wore the same style, usually a perfected look with high-length Dr. Martens boots, bleached Fred Perry jeans and set off with their identical cropped hair.

Paul was regularly approached by photographers and he would be handed various business cards and would usually make a follow-up call. After this he would then either end up in a photo studio on his own or along with Tim and some of their other friends. It was clear from the ceaseless attention Paul and Tim and their wider group got that the image they had acquired, that of the dishevelled heroin look, was very much the in-trend for fashion photographers and editors of the day.

In addition to the various photographs that Paul featured in, he was also beginning to interest those involved in moving media. One of these creative propagators was John Maybury, the film maker, known for his role in many pop music videos but, perhaps most famously, for directing the award-winning video for Sinéad O'Connor's Nothing Compares 2 U.

This production consisted mostly of close ups of Sinéad O'Connor's face with a portrayal of her various emotional states including sadness, melancholy and anger as she sang the now famous lyrics. The rest of the video features the star walking through an area of Paris known as the Parc de Saint-Cloud. Towards the end of the video, two tears roll down Sinéad's face, one on each cheek. She later stated that her tears were real and that while she did not intend to cry, her tears were triggered by thoughts of her mother, and she felt that she should just let them come. It has also been suggested that because Sinéad and Fachtna broke up shortly before the release of Nothing Compares 2 U, the stunning close ups of her crying in the video were attributed to her misery over the split. Regardless of the emotions, the tune would go on to be massive, and the video itself has been described as a genius work of art.

Maybury had asked Paul to be in a pop video featuring Lana Pellay and her track, Pistol in my Pocket. This was shot at Maximus nightclub in Leicester Square where Taboo was held and featured a young Paul as one of the dancers in the club. He loved being in the video as much for the fact he was getting paid to do something he did every week anyway as that he got to hang out with the trendy crew while being given a steady stream of poppers throughout the shoot. It was daytime, but the gathered ensemble partied like it was night time.

Paul would go on to help Maybury with several more videos, either as a performer or a runner. Following the initial Pellay video, Paul would later be employed in one of Wendy James' videos for a track called The Nameless One which again had a club-themed video. As before, Paul found himself intoxicated with drink and drugs while the production was filmed. This video was shot entirely in a club and featured many costume cuts and different actors, including the excited Paul.

Another video that Paul was involved in was for the band, Max. Formed by Kevin Mooney, formerly the bass player for Adam and the Ants, Max was a band that briefly produced a strange mix of drug-induced soft rock.

Kevin Mooney's partner was Leslie Winer, who had featured on the back-up vocals for O'Connor's Just Call me Joe. Winer was also one of the supermodels of the day. She was from Boston in America, tall, slim, very sexy and with an androgynous look. Paul was to meet her several times and always found her sexually appealing - not that he wanted to sleep with her, but in that he appreciated her bisexual attractiveness. Paul also loved the fact that she adored drugs, with heroin and in particular ketamine, the reality distorting anaesthetic, being her chosen dabbles. Mooney and his associate's propensity for drugs often caused problems though and Max found it hard to keep a record label as the band were regularly dropped due to their excessive substance use.

Paul was enlisted for the video for one of Max's tracks, Little Ghost. This featured Kevin Mooney signing with Paul and Tim behind him, sporting their cropped skinheads and naked from the waist up. The black and white models were up a ladder stirring a big tank of water and Paul recalls doing an enormous amount of drugs during the shoot. He remembers having to turn his head away from the camera several times as he was so worried about his obvious gurning due to the narcotic cocktail they had ingested.

Paul was paid about £50 per day for each of his video shoots and although it was early starts and late finishes it was good money for those days, and a lot of fun to boot.

The Little Ghost video was later reviewed on the music and youth culture programme, The Word, by John 'Jellybean' Benitez, an American music producer. Having had early success as a producer and remixer with artists such as Afrika Bambaataa, Jellybean then hit fame with two remixes on the famous Flashdance soundtrack. This caught the attention of Madonna who drafted him to write and produce a track for her 'Madonna' debut album in 1983. Their collaboration of Holiday became her very first hit and they would team up again when they co-wrote Sidewalk Talk, another top twenty hit. Jellybean had commented on The Word that the Little Ghost song was OK but what he really liked were the two guys in the background on the video, Paul and Tim, a commendation that obviously delighted the couple.

Back at St John's Wood, the tension and the issues were piling up and there was always a negative atmosphere in the flat so Paul and Tim were trying to decide if it would be best if they moved out.

Towards the end, Paul and Tim had been living at St John's Wood for over a year and the whole period of living with Sinéad O'Connor is described by Paul as being, for the most part, difficult. Tim had never really connected with Sinéad and she didn't care much for his company. She would have happily gone out of her way to help Paul but the same couldn't be said of her support towards Tim.

One time, Sinéad helped Paul with a hand-written letter so that he could get Housing Benefit. Tim wanted one as well but Sinéad's accountant said that she couldn't do another one for Tim which made it really difficult as Tim had to then pay his own percentage of the rent himself. This was £60 a week that Tim had to find whereas Paul had his covered by the benefits.

Throughout his life, some have doubted Paul's tall tales of having lived with one of the world's most iconic singers but if anyone is in any doubt about the validity of his stories, as evidence he still has the Housing Executive letter and one or two other items including a 21st birthday card that Sinéad gave him.

One major aspect that Tim did contribute, however, was in terms of his musical influence. He used to play lots of records in the house, many of them rare and hard-to-find and one of these was the Prince track, Nothing Compares 2 U. In 1984, Prince formed a band called The Family, essentially a side project as an outlet to release more of his music. They would go on to release only one album, the self-titled The Family. Nothing Compares 2 U appeared on this album and was credited directly to Prince but the tune wasn't released as a single and received little recognition.

Tim loved his music and, being a bit older, had more knowledge and understanding of music than Paul would've done at the time. One of the albums he played a lot was the obscure, The Family. He also loved Prince & The Revolution, Lou Reed & The Velvet Underground and many others but one of his main plays was Prince's version of Nothing Compares 2 U.

Fachtna O'Ceallaigh suggested to Sinéad that she should sing it and Paul genuinely believes that her going on to produce the worldwide massive hit version of the same song was due to Tim's endless plays of Prince's track in their shared house. Although the lyrics were the same, The Family sang the song in a totally different way and version to the way Sinéad O'Connor would later sing it. Paul describes Sinéad as singing her version with depth and passion which made the hairs stand up on the back of his neck, especially when experienced along with the video. In comparison, Paul views The Family version as less impactful and certainly not as enduring as the O'Connor classic.

It's unclear how O'Ceallaigh negotiated the rights to the song but what is clear is that the relationship between Sinéad and Prince was not a friendly one. Later, she would give an interview where she said, "I did meet him a couple of times. We didn't get on at all. In fact, we had a punch-up. He summoned me to his house after Nothing Compares 2 U. I made it without him. I'd never met him. He summoned me to his house - and it's foolish to do this to an Irish woman - he said he didn't like me saying bad words in interviews. So I told him to fuck off. He got quite violent. I had to escape out of his house at five in the morning. He packed a bigger punch than mine."

Unfortunately, Sinéad's early troubles would follow her into adult life and her well-documented issues are often thrust into the public eye. She has constantly suffered from poor mental health and has been diagnosed as being bi-polar in the past as well as recently opening up about having suicidal thoughts. She has also suffered from physical problems including a recent radical hysterectomy with very little hospital aftercare that exacerbated her mental health issues.

Although things didn't go smoothly for her as an adult, Sinéad attributes most of her difficulties from her time as a child. "Every day of our lives, she ran a torture chamber," she says of her mother. "She was a person who would delight and smile in torturing you." These and a multitude of related problems have since impacted on her relationship with others and with herself.

These issues had clearly affected the atmosphere in the flat and undoubtedly had a role to play in Paul and Tim's decision to move out of the St John's Wood residence. Their time here was now at an end and so eventually they parted, Paul amicably and Tim not so amicably. Consequently, years later when Paul would bump into Sinéad, she would have still said hello to Paul but if he were with Tim, she would've usually blanked them, such was her disdain for his partner.

Whatever the background though and however fragile their time living together, Paul has always felt blessed that, in his multi-faceted life, he can count among his experiences a year in the company of one of global music's most endearing figures.

Without a doubt, Paul loves the fact that he has had a closer-than-most link to Sinéad's haunting, penetrating tracks that tend to leave an indelible mark on all who listen to them.

Chapter 17 – No More Tim

During and after their time at Sinéad's, Paul and Tim were heavily into the club scene and frequented one club in particular, Shoom, at Southwark Bridge. The club was run by Jenny and Danny Rampling, the famous DJ and producer. Rampling had been on holiday in August 1987 when he went to Ibiza for Paul Oakenfold's birthday celebrations. While there, they went to Amnesia, an open air club that kicked off at four in the morning, and Danny was struck by the diverse array of clubbers, dancing non-stop to a manifold mix of house, techno, acid, reggae, pop and rock.

He was inspired by what he saw and on his return to London, started Shoom in the Fitness Centre, a gym on Southwark Street. There were several clubs in close proximity, most notably The Wag Club and Le Beat Route but they closed at 3am whereas the gym allowed Shoom to open until 5am.

As it was based in a gym, the walls were covered in mirrors. The club was usually filled with flavoured smoke so many punters often walked into the mirrors head first, mistaking them for an extension of the club itself! The club was decorated with painted banners, smiley faces and slogans. The assembled throng danced all night, many of them began wearing baggy dungarees, t-shirts and trainers – the look that later became the staple of the rave scene as a whole.

The club was a tiny place and the Fitness Centre could only hold about three hundred people so it was very difficult to get in. Jenny would come out and pick people from the long queue to bring inside and every time Paul and Tim were there, they would be selected. They also didn't have to pay and this happened every week that they went.

This was the start of the underground house scene with good, solid music fresh from America, produced by the likes of Frankie Knuckles, widely known as The Godfather of House Music and Ten City, an act who were one of the first exponents of the new deep house genre.

Paul had his 21st birthday at Shoom and he was on ecstasy, as were many of the usual club-goers. Paul remembers being so drug-induced that at one stage, he was dancing with his eyes open but could only see blackness, even though the lights were on. This wasn't a pass out blackness, just complete temporary darkness. The blindness lasted for a few minutes and this night is etched in his memory bank variously for the stunning underground music, the occasion of his 21st birthday, and for the bizarre blackness.

When they parted from Sinéad, Paul managed to get new accommodation through April Housing Association who worked to help gays and lesbians find adequate residences. Paul managed to get a two-bedroom flat above a shop on Kingsland Road, Shoreditch, between Old Street and Dalston Stations. April Housing mainly offered shared accommodation so the aim was to find Paul a suitable flatmate in the near future. Paul quickly moved Tim in and then let April Housing know that his ex-partner was homeless and also needed housing and as they said they were no longer together, Tim got the other room.

Paul was to have a bizarre experience during his time living in Shoreditch. He was on his way back from Stoke Newington, on the top deck of a bus. He looked down at a bus stop and noticed a woman staring directly at him and he stared back, wondering why she was looking at him so intently. Roughly six months later, Paul was in the dance tent at Gay Pride in Kennington Park and there was a friend there who Paul knew from clubland. Standing beside this man was a woman who Paul recognised as the woman he had seen from the bus window. It materialised that the woman was Paul's friend's mum and Paul started chatting to her. During the conversation, she revealed that she lived near to Paul in Shoreditch and the reason she had been staring at him that day six months previously was because she knew someone who was the spitting-image of Paul. They exchanged contact numbers and not long after, the woman arranged for Paul to meet this person at her house.

Paul agreed to go round to the woman's house, but true to form he made sure he had a generous line of speed and a drink or two before he set off. When Paul arrived, he was taken aback as the man he was introduced to did indeed look remarkably like Paul himself and also like his brother John, who is a real likeness of Paul as well. Paul is two years older than John and they look very similar, almost like twins. John, ironically, also grew up to be gay but chose to express this in a very camp way that Paul has never been interested in and as a result, his brother is known locally as 'The Duchess'.

It soon became clear that the mysterious stranger was in fact Paul's half-brother. They talked about it and worked out that they had different fathers but clearly the same mother – this was obvious as their mum had strong genes and they had similar noses, as did all the siblings, even Elaine.

With the excitement of the occasion, combined with the candour brought on by the amphetamines, Paul talked at a million miles an hour and listened little. He did pause long enough to learn that his newly-found half-brother was living in a squat and that he had lost contact with their mother. Paul gave him their mum's number but he was to later find out that he never did make contact. Paul has always held a strong belief in fate and having randomly encountered this woman twice, who it transpired knew his half-brother, he firmly believes it was meant to be.

Paul and Tim were still living together but were beginning to grow apart and their relationship was definitely starting to fizzle out. Tim could be very hard work and Paul had been with him for over five years in this, his first long-term relationship.

Quite quickly, Paul found himself growing up and wanting different things out of life and once this process began, he felt the intimacy with Tim becoming less and less frequent. In addition to Paul's new-found feelings of apathy, Tim suffered from low self-esteem and had childhood trauma which affected him. He was on medication and Paul was finding it increasingly difficult to sustain a positive relationship while Tim tended to be generally so low and moody.

Paul had also been seeing a guy a couple of times so was already on the lookout for something new. Things weren't going smoothly at all for the lovers and although Paul says he still loves Tim to this day, this was the beginning of the end of their relationship as a couple.

After much deliberation and soul-searching, they eventually decided to part, although it was at least an amicable separation.

Paul had already known they were going to finish but what he didn't know was that a chance encounter was just around the corner that would move him straight from Tim into the arms and heart of another.

To help him get over the break up, Paul went to Subterranea, a small, industrial-style club and live performance venue off Ladbroke Grove. He had hoped to see Kevin Mooney and Max perform but ended up waiting for ages with no sign of the performers. Mooney didn't turn up and it would later emerge that he had been arrested on the way to the gig and found to be in possession of heroin.

Disappointed, Paul made his way home via Old Street Tube Station to get a bus back home to Kingsland. Just before the tube station, he went into the London Apprentice, a very well-known gay club.

The LA, as it was known to the regulars, became famous during the 1970's and 1980's when owner, Michael Glover, brought his experiences of gay bars in America back to London. As London began to relax its laws a little, the homosexual community flourished in Shoreditch and the LA became known for its openly gay and transvestite image and its secret parties in the dungeon-like basement, The Tool Box. The club attracted many a gay celebrity and could count on its visitor list such names as Marc Almond, Jean-Paul Gaultier, Lily Savage, Sir Ian McKellen and Freddie Mercury. The importance of the LA as a pillar of the gay community was evidenced when the club hosted the first ever Terence Higgins Trust meeting to spread awareness of HIV.

On entering the LA, Paul realised that he was quite drunk and was suddenly also acutely aware of how deflated he was following his break up with Tim and the no-show at the Max gig.

Feeling rather sorry for himself, he walked towards the bar and waited to be served. As he stood there he turned to see who else might be about and as he did so, he noticed another man who was also waiting. Although he didn't know it at the time, Paul was about to fall head-over-heels in love with this handsome stranger at the bar.

Chapter 18 – Single Ticket to Fame

Paul smiled, maybe outwardly, but definitely inwardly. The man was broad, tall and handsome and soon they began chatting like they had known each other all their lives. The man was charming, and Paul felt himself being pulled towards him like a magnet. Even now Paul can still remember the coat the charismatic stranger was wearing, a large black leather jacket with a fake fur black collar. The size of his frame, his stature and his coat made him look and seem special. He asked Paul if he took ecstasy and cocaine and, never one to look a gift horse in the mouth, Paul answered in the affirmative. The man gave Paul an ecstasy pill and then had one himself.

Within half an hour they left the LA and got into the stranger's red Mercedes. He took Paul to his house in Hackney, just up the road from where Paul was living in Shoreditch. Paul already knew the street distinctly as he had been shown it before as there was a character called Christopher Biggins, the larger-than-life television performer and presenter, who lived two or three doors away from the house he was now about to enter.

It was a lovely property, very expensive with rich carpets throughout and spotlessly clean. Before long, they had drug-induced sex and followed this up with more cocaine and ecstasy pills. The man certainly knew what he was doing both in terms of the right amount of drugs to take, and sexually. Paul was in dreamland, having found a further addition to one of the themes in his life, another sexy father-figure type. The stranger was attractive in a sweet talker way with a cheeky smile and a glint in his eye, combined with the ability to make Paul feel special. They snorted the coke and swallowed the pills and had more passionate sex before they fell asleep.

The next day, the man dropped Paul home. He would see his new lover again a few days later and, as before, they took more ecstasy and cocaine. This became a regular event and Paul found himself being more and more attracted not only to the man himself but to the whole environment surrounding him.

Paul was soon to realise where the man's wealth and much of his charisma stemmed from - he was the managing director of a large record company which was enjoying worldwide success with a raft of diverse artists. The man's name was Nick Lewis and Paul fell for him hook, line and sinker.

Nick made Paul feel wanted and special. This new type of drugs-sex with Nick wasn't something Paul had done much before or has done since with any partner. Paul had had lots of sex while using drugs with Tim but with him, it wasn't as exploratory and there was no anal intercourse. Another aspect of these new experiences that Paul loved and respected was that with Nick, usually he was doing the fucking. Lewis was a big man in stature and in life but he didn't feel the need to act like the big man when he was with Paul.

Paul loved the awareness that Nick was experimenting too and got so turned on when he would say things like, "I've never tried this before". One of the things they tried together was a new experience, certainly for Paul, of him anally fisting Nick. This was something that Paul describes as weird and strange. The feeling and sensation freaked Paul out and he remembers the body temperature of Nick's inner body. He describes it as kneading as you would with dough, except instead of dough it was mincemeat. It was that kind of feeling but with a strong heat to it. This was the only time Paul has performed this act and he wouldn't want to do it again with anybody "for love or money". Before he tried it, he had heard about people being fisted but it wasn't anything he had ever experienced, even during his time as a rent-boy. But it was such an intimate relationship with Nick and because his alluring, older partner knew exactly what to do and what buttons to press to make Paul feel safe, secure and comfortable, he was prepared to go places that he has never been, before or since.

Paul went to lots of concerts with Nick and if there were bands or acts signed to his label, Nick would get tickets for Paul even if he wasn't able to go himself. If there was someone Paul liked who wasn't on his books, Nick would ask his secretary to get tickets and often backstage passes for him. Paul could also get any album or single that he liked, simply by asking Nick who would arrange for a courier to drop it round to Paul's house for him.

For someone so devoted to his music, this was an amazing time for Paul with access to pretty much any record, concert tickets, or backstage passes he desired. He became very accustomed to seeing the name Paul Byfield on various guest lists across London and he felt very honoured and privileged to be with Nick.

Clearly there were fairly significant perks to having a boyfriend like Nick, and it was to get even better. An Italian dance-pop duo had been in contact with Nick to help them break their latest tune into the UK market. They were booked to appear on the popular music and fashion programme, The Word, which was presented by the 'love him or hate him' Terry Christian and Amanda de Cadenet, the young daughter of the famous racing driver, Alain de Cadenet. Being on TV was a big deal at the time as these were still the days when the UK market boasted only 4 channels.

The Italian group comprised only a vocalist and keyboard player and for TV purposes, this wasn't a very interesting visual line-up. Nick asked Paul if he and some of his friends would dance while the band performed the track to make it more visually appealing. Paul, along with his friend, Space, and two others were lined up to be on the show.

Before their big appearance, they were brought to the popular Moschino store, who were using the outfits for advertising purposes, and were allowed to choose from a selection of clothes to wear on the show. Unfortunately for Paul, they weren't allowed to keep them although he does still have a Moschino waistcoat which he managed to hold onto after the shoot. Paul wore the black waistcoat along with black Moschino tape with white lettering which adorned all the outfits. The dancers also all carried home-made fans to add to the effect. The video was filmed at the Limehouse Studios in Wembley 'as live' with only a minute or two delay, so the musicians, along with Paul and his friends, had to get it right.

The track would go on to be a huge success and this resulted in an appearance on Top of the Pops. Paul hoped that he would be reunited with the Italian pop stars for this performance but the band's manager felt the dancers had upstaged the actual artists on The Word, so didn't want them joining them again. Regardless, the fame for Paul was significant and he recalls one of his colleagues at MRE in particular who saw The Word and later said to Paul, "I didn't know you were in a band!"

Paul was still doing the occasional shift at the market research office but as usual was finding it hard to settle down, sit still and engage in a normal office job. He constantly longed to be the class clown and felt the need to be manic, endlessly active and not to sit in the same place for too long. He did though fantasise about calming down and having a conventional lifestyle, where he could enjoy evenings and weekends with less night life, less want to party and more normality through his nine-to-five office work.

These feelings almost certainly stemmed from the notion that, at last, he was cherished and from the intimacy he was being shown. Paul had found someone who was loving and who was good for him. This normalisation process had started somewhat before Nick, as Paul already had the job, and this was the direction that he was naturally trying to head anyway, but undoubtedly the new relationship helped him to see things in a new light. Perhaps this was an inward realisation that however much he enjoyed the hedonistic party life, Paul knew that it was unsustainable at the rate at which he had engaged in it thus far and that unless he slowed down in some capacity, life would otherwise find another way to curtail him.

However the reality was that Paul literally could not sit still and was constantly disruptive and often times, destructive – regardless of his efforts, he was clearly not cut out for a normal nine-to-five lifestyle.

Often in the office, Capital Radio would be on in the background. When there was a music competition on, Paul would invariably know the answer and insist that as many of the other workers as possible kept manically phoning in until someone eventually got through. Paul would then jump on the phone to claim the prize. Through this method, he won tickets to go and see the Senegalese artist, Youssou N'Dour at the Hammersmith Odeon.

N'Dour performed a track with Neneh Cherry, famous for her hit, The Buffalo Stance. Their song was called Seven Seconds and described the first positive seven seconds in a child's life as they are born without knowing about the hardships of the world. This famous track would go on to gain worldwide success and topped the charts in many countries and elevated both artists to global stardom. The night's performance featured a brilliant African musical experience and Paul soaked up the dazzling display and loved every minute of it. And although he could easily have asked Nick to get him tickets, the fact that he had won them all of his own accord added that little bit of excitement to the production.

Back at work, Paul wondered why he wasn't being promoted, although now in hindsight he laughs at how obvious it was that he was a complete distraction to himself and to everyone else who worked there.

Around this time, Paul made friends with a girl called Micky who also worked for the company. He was getting increasingly frustrated with his work so Micky suggested they go for lunch, which they did. They went to The Savoy at Covent Garden as their office was nearby and the pair enjoyed a long lunch and several drinks, with strong cider being Paul's tipple. He went back to work late, wearing red lipstick he had borrowed from Micky. Strolling into the office he told them all in no uncertain terms to "fuck off" and then promptly left.

He didn't actually get sacked but thought better than to come back the next day. Without needing to formalise his departure, he just never returned to the job and there his normal nine-to-five ended.

Paul didn't really care though as he was loving the high life with Nick. In addition to the concerts, backstage passes and endless records, Paul came to know the exclusive and high-end Ivy Restaurant. A short walk from Cambridge Circus, in the heart of the bustling West End and surrounded by several of its theatres, this very British dining institution has become so famous that it has attained almost mythical status and has been charming London's elite since it opened its doors in 1917. The lavish interior boasts a restaurant, central dining bar and private rooms upstairs which are the epitome of real glamour.

In the days when Paul went there, every celebrity who was anyone in London dined there. It was almost a sign that you had achieved stardom if you had a meal there, followed by some photographer taking your picture as you were leaving. The Ivy was famed for its long line of A-listers who frequented its sumptuous interior. Princess Diana ate there, The Beckhams were regular visitors, as were rock legends such as Elton John and Liam Gallagher. Hollywood's finest popped in when in London with Al Pacino and Julia Roberts being just two star names to dine there.

The Ivy was the undisputed celebrity haunt back in the 1990's and now Paul was rubbing shoulders with the rich and famous as Nick had taken him to the iconic restaurant several times. People would normally have to book up months in advance unless they were a certain person or a certain successful star. With Nick's reputation, he would call up on the night or the night before and they nearly always got him a table.

Paul loved the celebrity status and the affluence of these occasions and everywhere he looked there were either famous faces that he recognised or people obviously in very well paid jobs that he didn't recognise. He was always aware though that there was only one reason they could have been in the Ivy and that was that they were either well known people within their own right or, like him, were lucky enough to be familiar with someone who was.

With his widespread links with the music industry, Nick then got invited to a birthday party that Elton John was hosting at the Queen's House in Greenwich. Paul got invited along as well and they turned up wearing hired tuxedos from the London tailors, Moss Bros, that they had been fitted for the day before. They arrived in Nick's red Mercedes and were met by a valet who parked the car as they strode into the lavish Queen's House. The hallway where they entered was adorned with massive ice sculptures of swans, and there was grandeur to behold on a massive scale with tables overflowing with bottles of champagne, and only the best glassware.

All the assembled guests were dressed up in suitable style and fancy. These were the days of Elton John's open drug use and everywhere Paul looked, he could see people brazenly snorting cocaine. Paul lifted a glass and took a sip and no sooner had he done so, than a waiter appeared to top up his glass. Shortly after their arrival, they were summoned into the large banquet area and were treated to a splendid meal of lobster and a variety of the finest meats and hors d'oeuvres.

After the meal everybody moved into the dance hall. Paul put his glass down and then immediately couldn't find it. There were still loads of bottles on the nearby tables so Paul grabbed an open one and started drinking straight from the neck before going out onto the dance floor, still with the bottle in his grasp. There he was in his fancy suit, young and gorgeous, and swigging expensive champagne straight from the neck. Looking around, he realised that Bananarama and Bros were dancing with him and clearly wanting to be part of his exuberant dance. They were the big artists of the day but Paul acted as if he was the star.

Later, and perhaps somewhat predictably, he ended up really drunk. Further into the night, Paul was approached by The Professor of Pop as he was known, Paul Gambaccini. Nick and Gambaccini were old friends and had a game where they would try and get off with each other's partner. Gambaccini said he would show Paul round the house. He took him upstairs and Paul remembers there being a roped-off area and thinking that maybe Gambaccini might try and have a private grope and, although he didn't, Paul was sure he knew what his intentions were, had he been able to find somewhere where they wouldn't be disturbed.

Later, Paul Gambaccini would take Paul to TGI Fridays for his 22nd birthday and then on a tour of Old Compton Street and Soho Village, but Paul got very drunk and became incredibly obnoxious so he ditched Gambaccini. Paul feels he had too much spirit and energy for Gambaccini and was too mad for him so he left him to his own devices as he wandered off in search of more crazed escapades.

By this stage, Nick had decided he wanted to move out of his large house in Hackney. He was starting to view different potential properties and on a handful of occasions, Paul would go with him. Whether by chance or through Paul's influence, on only the second time Paul went with Nick to look at a house, he ended up choosing that one and he still lives there to this day. The property they chose that day is in Clapham South, on the edge of Balham and not far from Clapham Common.

Despite the obvious love they felt for each other, the numerous good times they shared together and the fact that Nick had achieved more for Paul and with Paul than anyone else had managed before, all things in the relationship were however not rosy. There was a feature of Nick's life that was already starting to create tension with Paul and one which would only become more prevalent as time wore on.

Nick was very promiscuous and although his relationship with Paul was reasonably stable, he sought out a greater thrill, usually involving strangers and the great outdoors. During this period, Clapham Common was becoming the new Hampstead Heath, renowned as an area rife in late night gay sex, out in the open. Hampstead Heath has a long history of gay cruising including, famously, George Michael allegedly being caught cruising on the Heath by News of the World photographers.

Clapham Common was now also beginning to develop a reputation as an area where it was customary to have homosexuals moving around in dark spaces and engaging in various sexual acts with random strangers. The norm was for gay men to be looking for sex in the early hours of the morning and there tended to be many an illicit middle-of-the-night liaison taking place in the thickets and clearings around the Common.

So why would a young man choose to be outside in the middle of the night, seeking sexual contact from another man when he could be somewhere far comfier, warmer and safer? Paul suggests that people did it for a range of different reasons – for the discreet side of it, with no-one else knowing or likely to know unless they were unfortunately and unexpectedly discovered 'in the act', or the risk-taking and adventurous aspect of it which provided the added thrill that many of the participating men craved.

There would also sometimes be group sex occurring, hidden away in the Common or the Heath, although not everyone was keen on this with many choosing the safety of one-on-one sex as opposed to the added risk of engaging in sexual activity with a whole group of strangers.

This was also the birth of the modern term of 'dogging' as, in addition to the many men engaged in the physical contact, it was also common to have the voyeurs present - those who enjoyed watching as much as joining in. Nowadays, this form of sexual gratification is played out in car parks and open public spaces up and down the country as couples or groups fondle each other, while on-lookers enjoy watching the show.

Homosexuals, at the height of the activity on Hampstead Heath and Clapham Common, were very promiscuous. At night, the Common was dark but not too dark. Men could easily meet up with a stranger and engage in sexual liaisons with him.

Mainly, the sex was cheap and easy and there wasn't much, if any, talking and certainly no questions asked afterwards. This simple release of sexual tension mostly felt emotionally sterile to the men who viewed it more of a transaction than an intimate act. There was no level of commitment implied to the transactions and men could engage in quick oral sex or mutual masturbation, although penetrative sex wasn't as usual on the Common.

At the time, Clapham Common attracted a wide variety of men, from the openly 'out' gay man to the married man looking to experiment and discover his own sexuality. There were those who were out for the fun of it, men who could find sex in pubs and clubs but enjoyed the buzz of something more risky. Sometimes the men would start talking to a stranger and it would lead to something, other times to nothing.

A great many men loved the thrill of it all, with the anonymous sex on tap. It is an understandable desire for almost any man to be interested in this type of activity and indeed if there was somewhere heterosexual men knew they would be guaranteed quick, no-strings sex, surely many would be frequent visitors too. After all, most men are biologically formed to want to have sex as often as they can.

Generally the participating men didn't think of the danger, even though the Common was also known as easy picking for muggers. The other main danger was of course the fear of getting caught and although the police were usually busy chasing criminals, they did occasionally carry out patrols on the Common.

However the police catching someone in the act didn't always lead to a prosecution. There was the story of the lawyer with the Crown Prosecution Service who was caught by torchlight having oral sex in the bushes. Interviewed later by the police, they accused him of having sex in public. "What was public about it", he asked. "After all, I was in a very private place, a bush, only made public by your torch". He was let go, without charge.

Maybe not on the scale that it occurred when Paul was a young man, but these episodes still go on to this day and it would not be uncommon nowadays to experience the levels of sexual activity on the Common that were so prevalent in Paul's day.

Paul, aged 15, with his class at Erkenwald Comprehensive School in 1982

Paul, aged 17, shows his horsemanship at The Priory Equestrian Centre in 1985

Paul, looking quite the young stately gent, in 1985

The attractive Paul, aged just 19, with his peroxide-bleached blonde hair

Sean McGuigan, the love of Paul's life, aged 26, just after they fell in love in 1993

Paul's beloved mother, Linda, in 1998, aged 66, and as usual, hiding her bandaged hand

Smudge & Ink together
on holiday in Donegal
in 2002

Paul & Sean
in happier
times in
2006

Paul in full party mode
in 2008, the year
before he finally
entered rehab

The final flyer for Trade at Turnmills, one of Paul's favourite haunts

Paul collecting his award for the Adult Learner of the Year for all of London in 2012

← Paul and Horse in 2018, returning to where it all began

This has gradually become more frequent, although the level of sexual activity has only recently begun to return to the promiscuous levels of the past, perhaps experiencing an enforced lull during the dark days of HIV/AIDS and the abundance of other STI's.

Thinking back to those early days, literally being 'out on the Common', Paul feels that there are significant differences to what the young gay men of today experience. Being a homosexual now is largely different to what it was back then. For Paul's early sexual exploits, the legal age of consent was twenty-one. This had come into effect in 1967, the year of Paul's birth, prior to which point sex between men was illegal. The 1967 Sexual Offences Act came into force and made homosexual sex legal for men aged twenty-one or above.

It wouldn't be until 1994 when Paul was twenty-seven that it was legal for him to have sex with an eighteen to twenty-one year old male adult. When he was first on the scene, the situation was that if somebody over twenty-one got caught having sex with someone under twenty-one, the older male was breaking the law and many gay men lived in fear of the potential repercussions of getting caught with a younger man.

Nick himself was to fall foul of this danger when he began to receive phone calls from a young man that he had been sexually involved with for a short while. This younger partner was trying to blackmail Nick, saying that he was going to sell his story to the papers and expose Nick for having sex with an underage man. The young man was no longer with Nick but his new partner heard of his previous relationship and tried to steer his companion into trying to make money from blackmailing Nick. Nothing came of it in the end but Paul remembers Nick being understandably freaked out by the whole situation. This led Nick to become increasingly paranoid and he kept insisting on double-checking Paul's age to make sure he wasn't going to potentially get caught in the same trap again.

This wasn't a major problem as Paul had by now reached the legal age of consent. Paul had been living with Sinéad O'Connor at age twenty-one and then he had met Nick aged twenty-two. The memory of this time is made all the more vivid as he recollects Nick giving him a book about Sinéad O'Connor entitled So Different for his 23rd birthday, which Nick had signed on the inside "Remember the very first night – one of the earliest things I discovered. Happy Birthday. Lots of love, Nick xxx".

Paul fondly recalls this birthday as Nick got him another present which was to go and see Les Miserables at Shaftesbury Avenue, Cambridge Circus, and Paul was allowed to bring a friend with him. Before the big event, Paul and his chosen friend for the evening were in the Old Compton Street bar, drinking lager. With it being Paul's birthday, the drinks were flowing freely and Paul was soon very drunk.

They continued on their way and went to see Les Miserables as planned. Paul remembers that he didn't quite get the storyline although he attributes this to three main reasons. The first of which is that he was so pissed at this stage that he was struggling to concentrate on his surroundings and the lavish performance being played out in front of him. The second is that he kept getting up to go to the toilet so he missed large chunks of the play. The third, and probably most significant, is that he nodded off midway through the show and was only awoken when he heard everyone clapping at the end of the performance. In the true spirit of the drama though, Paul managed to rise to his feet and began clapping too, as if he had enjoyed every second of the excellent production! The humour of the night wasn't lost on Paul, particularly as he was fully aware of the amount of money people would pay to be able to attend what was then the most exclusive production in London's West End, with all its obvious glitz and glamour.

Whilst other areas of his life, particularly his performing talents and his links to the music scene were expanding, the other constant in his young life was beginning to unravel.

It was around this time that Paul and Nick began to drift apart. What drove them away from each other is that Nick slowly but surely began to initiate a third or fourth person into their relationship. They would sometimes go to Clapham Common, near to Nick's new house, and meet other men for outdoor sex in the middle of the night. This whole experience didn't sit too well with Paul, partly the vulnerability of being out in the open and partly the unemotional feeling of having sex with any number of unknown, random strangers.

Paul was easily led into most things so he went along with the idea of group sex with Nick, even though in reality he craved the exclusive closeness of one-on-one contact with his partner. He went and participated in the threesomes and the group sex, though he didn't ever feel completely comfortable with them. Although he was never left out of the acts, Paul just didn't see the need for multiple sex when he felt he had found someone to have a special, unshared, intimate relationship with.

It also irked Paul that one minute he would be feeling really special with all the privileges of concert tickets and aftershow parties and free records, to the next minute having to share Nick and himself with others.

It even went to the point where there was a period of the sexual activity being videoed. It·didn't bother Paul that the footage might be leaked to others, but it did worry him insomuch as it left him feeling detached from the closeness that he had so enjoyed in the early stages of his relationship with Nick.

Paul was feeling as though he had already experienced enough of the open promiscuity of random and group sex and he was still essentially looking for his exclusive love, affection and security.

The way the open group sexual encounters with Nick were developing left Paul feeling increasingly lost and isolated from their once intimate and private partnership. It was no longer just Paul and Nick. Now it was nearly always Paul and Nick and a third party. To add to the confused feelings, it often wasn't the same third person and Paul found himself growing increasingly frustrated with the direction their relationship was heading.

Nick wasn't likely to change anytime soon and Paul realised he needed something to be different so it was inevitable that he found himself and Nick beginning to move further and further apart.

Admittedly, Paul wasn't exactly whiter than white in the relationship as well. Nick knew that Paul had done some agency-escort work and he was fine about it so Paul would've taken on the occasional client, although sporadically. Moreover, it didn't help matters that Paul was also playing the field and was engaged in an occasional fling with a man called Wayne, who lived between Mile End and Bethnal Green, a stone's throw from the place where Paul was born.

Wayne, along with three other black men, were collectively known as the Bliss Brothers and were the main dealers in Heaven. The staff knew this, though it was never talked about. It was never blatant dealing, the drugs were always good quality from a reliable source and besides most of the staff were also customers of the dealers so it was never something that was mentioned publicly. Paul found Wayne attractive, loved the idea of dating a big time dealer and of course also enjoyed the easy accessibility to good quality drugs.

The Bliss Brothers' best product was excellent ecstasy which was a specialised commodity in those days with pills going for as much as £30 for a period, before dropping slightly to a standard price of £25 each. This was pure ecstasy in tablet form which had made its way to Britain where it was embraced by the rave and house music scene that evolved in the mid-1980's. During the late 1980's and 1990's, ecstasy, or the 'original designer drug' as it was often described, expanded beyond the fringes into the mass popular culture and has remained one of the most favoured party drugs since then, becoming one of the most widely used illegal drugs in the world. Ecstasy has long had a close association with the dance music scene mainly because the drug tends to provide a strong sense of euphoria, empathy and a sense of connection and openness with others. The drug also increases sensory perceptions, which is why many people enjoy using it at nightclubs or festivals, with their bright lights and bass-driven music.

The best pills were high in Methylenedioxymethamphetamine (MDMA) content and had names like China White, Playboy Bunnies, White Doves or Mercedes Benz's and there was lots of money to be made if you had access to them. Dealers were rife at raves and nightclubs in the 1990's and early 2000's, where ecstasy, marketed as colourful pressed pills imprinted with logos, was the main drug in supply. Users would be inwardly feeling gorgeous but often outwardly displaying intense jaw clenching, rolling of eyes and profuse sweating. But really, no-one cared. The drugs broke down all the crass social boundaries that permeated almost every other aspect of normal life. Ecstasy brought people together under one heaving roof. For one night at least, the sensations flowing through the gyrating bodies, driven by the ceaseless bass and the throng of smiling, albeit absent faces, meant that all of the usual daily worries were forgotten.

For someone who carried as much emotional baggage as Paul, ecstasy provided him with a simple means of regressing to that balmy state of connection and positive consciousness.

Given the ongoing fragility in his relationship with Nick, now, more than ever, he craved the drugs that would allow him to once again feel in tune with himself and his surroundings, and ecstasy undoubtedly gave him that, at the very least.

Chapter 19 – Dance & Dance

With the feeling that he had invested so much into his time with Nick, Paul now began to evaluate what he wanted and what future direction his life might begin to take.

Assessing his life thus far and exploring the things that made him most happy, Paul decided to throw himself into his artistic, creative side. Through the gay clubbing experience and a stint at Pineapple Dance Studios where he participated in several group choreography dance lessons, Paul had learned how to fan dance. This is a form of dancing utilising two decorative coloured fabric fans which dancers usually make themselves. The performers would typically also spin a square bit of cloth or a t-shirt.

At Heaven there was often a creative vibe, with discerning clubbers trying to outdo each other with more and more extravagant ways of expressing themselves on the dance floor. This often involved going home at the end of a speeded-up night and making these exuberant fans to use the next time they were out. Given his want to dance and to perform, Paul was always keen to watch and learn from others and often, where possible, to surpass their creative exploits.

To this end, he perfected his fan dancing at places like Hippodrome Nightclub in Leicester Square. In modern times, a recent home for burlesque cabaret circus, La Clique, and more latterly an underground casino, in the late 1980's and early 1990's the Hippodrome was a world famous nightclub owned and run by Peter Stringfellow.

On Mondays and most Thursdays at the Hippodrome it was gay night and Paul was on the employee list along with a woman called Frisbee Fox. Usually dressed outrageously and with a shocking mop of pink hair, she was in a long-term relationship with Stringfellow.

For his role, Paul was employed as a fan dancer with the aim of encouraging other customers to get onto the dance floor. He would go to the club early every Monday and be the first on the floor to try and entice the punters to join him. In the early days, he wasn't paid in cash but in drinks vouchers which wasn't an altogether bad thing as the drinks at the Hippodrome tended to be exorbitantly expensive.

The performing also meant Paul could enjoy his fondness for illicit substances, including acid or speed or both, although he had to make sure he was a lot more discreet than he would have been at other venues like Taboo.

At the Hippodrome, Paul would dance on the main floor showing off an impressive array of different moves. With Paul being a Leo and a self-confessed exhibitionist, he loved the dancing, the posing, the demonstration of his art, and of course the attention that he received as a consequence. This was also the first time he had got paid on a weekly basis for doing something that he loved so much and would happily have done for free most nights he was out anyway.

At the time the Hippodrome had a small stage at the centre back of the dance floor that would rise up and out would come whoever was booked to perform and sing that night. Paul remembers some of the acts in particular including Marilyn, who had had his early success when Boy George was making it big in the world of music but hadn't proved anywhere near as successful as the Culture Club phenomenon. Perhaps related to his failings as a global star, there was one poignant night when in a weird moment, Marilyn didn't finish his singing set as he broke down and began crying on stage. Although Paul attributes this to a more probable come down and Marilyn's obvious personal insecurities, perhaps it was the realisation that he was never realistically going to make it in quite the same way that others like Boy George had.

The other act that stood out for Paul was Divine, who was a massive character on the gay scene at the time. A very successful female impersonator, actor, musician and singer, Divine had also performed in many films and had a long association with the independent film maker, John Waters, who gave him the name, Divine, and also the tagline of "the most beautiful woman in the world, almost."

Having made several short and full-length movies, Divine found fame as "the filthiest person alive" in Waters cult classic, Pink Flamingos, a self-confessed "exercise in poor taste", which proved a hit on the US midnight movie screening circuit.

He would also forge a reasonably successful music career with a number of Hi-NRG hits including Walk Like a Man, I'm so Beautiful and You Think You're a Man.

His final role would be in the film, Hairspray, where he starred in drag as the mother of a chubby teenager played by Ricki Lake.

Struggling with obesity throughout his life, Divine died prematurely in 1988 from an enlarged heart, just three weeks after Hairspray was released nationwide.

Despite his untimely death, his life's work certainly didn't go unnoticed and People magazine would later describe him as the "Drag Queen of the Century".

The memorable night where Paul saw Divine was unforgettable with the stage coming up and the artist sitting in the centre on a live, grey baby elephant, singing Walk Like a Man and a collection of his other songs. Given the fact that in addition to being a larger than life character, Divine was also a big, fat man this was no mean feat and Paul was enthralled by the performance, enhanced, as he was, by a concoction of acid and speed. He had heard of this artist called Divine so was already excited to see him perform but the production was made all the more memorable with the addition of an actual wild animal in the act!

Paul would not be the only fan dancer on show and there were regulars from Heaven who performed at the Hippodrome as well. In the beginning, Paul would go every Monday and Thursday, taking over the dance floor, encouraging others and being paid with his free drinks tokens. After a while though, on Thursdays Paul would get the night off work or not bother going in and would instead go to Taboo where he felt more at home, surrounded by the excessive drug-takers and creative madness.

Paul was to follow up his dancing work by landing his next job at a new monthly themed night called Kinky Gerlinky which was started by Mike and Gerlinde Costiff in a club in Leicester Square. The Costiffs had embraced the hedonistic London club scene of the 1980's and had set up Kinky Gerlinky, the most outlandishly glamorous and otherworldly night out in the land. It drew everyone from Boy George to Hamish Bowles, and all manner of drag queens, artists, musicians and anyone else who could get past the formidable bouncers.

Kinky Gerlinky started when a friend of the Costiffs who ran a club called Legends invited Michael and Gerlinde to host a party there. Initially Michael was hesitant, "we'd just come back from the huge carnival in Rio, and everything in London just seemed so dull after all that glitter and feathers. But we thought we'd just do it, and from there it grew like a monster. We told our friends, who told their friends, and we very much encouraged a fun, anything goes atmosphere. Everyone was up for it. I have a great sense of the ridiculous so we didn't take anything seriously at all."

Kinky Gerlinky was housed at a variety of West End venues from the Café de Paris to Shaftesbury's and then the Empire in Leicester Square. A night at the club was definitely one to remember so it was a very popular club to try and gain access to, as Michael describes, "admission into Kinky wasn't necessarily by what you were wearing, it was about your attitude. If you could charm your way past the doormen, you could get in."

Anyone who was anyone frequented the notorious club nights and "it got to the point where we had people flying in from Europe and America every time there was a night on. Everyone in town wanted to know when the next event was, some people planned their elaborate outfits a month in advance." The night was a boisterous jamboree of wigs, slap, DIY fashion and bare flesh, hosted by Winston and Stella Stein, with Roy on the door and regular personalities like Leigh Bowery, Sheila Tequila, Transformer and Amanda Lear on the dance floor.

Once a month at Kinky Gerlinky it would be Brazilian Rio Carnival night. Paul was paid to dance at these events and would be given £30 a night as well as being handed a steady supply of drink tickets. For the night Paul just had to be himself and wear whatever costume his take was on the given theme. He would invariably have taken an ample supply of drugs and, as at his other performance venues, would be dancing to encourage everyone else to join him on the dance floor.

This gave Paul the perfect platform to express his extrovert streak. He was happy to dance and perform and could be creatively dramatic while sober and then the more drunk he got, the more he expressed himself in an ever-increasingly wild way.

Everything was filmed and the organisers released regular videos of the monthly Kinky Gerlinky nights. These videos were on sale in a shop called Boy that had a very high profile at the time. This store was hugely popular among the local club set and was in particular promoted by Boy George, who regularly wore a cap with 'Boy' on it.

Dick Jewell, who is still busy making stylised photos and films to this day, was the main producer and would have usually been present to film the monthly Kinky Gerlinky nights. Having heard about Dick's work capturing the dance moves on the floor at The Jazz Room in Camden on grainy super-8 film, Gerlinde asked him to bring his camera along to the club. He turned up to Kinky Gerlinky armed with some new technology that allowed him to capture longer, more expansive scenes, "This was around the time the first video-8 cameras were available, so I was freed from the limitation of three-minute rolls of film – I suddenly had hour-long tapes that you could let run and ostensibly film in a different way. But then again I soon realised I wasn't actually documenting the club. I was documenting whatever threw itself in front of the camera as soon as the light was turned on - which is a totally different film!"

Dick was himself a precocious club kid, starting out aged fourteen at the Croydon Suite in south London, and had got himself thrown out of the very first Kinky Gerlinky, but for less hedonistic reasons than you might imagine. He'd turned up carrying a baby, his son with resident Kinky DJ Rachel Auburn. "He was one and a half at the time and I had him strapped to my front. But somebody complained. They thought it was inappropriate for a baby to be in a nightclub!"

Capturing Kinky Gerlinky on film was not without its perils – such as the time when the Kinky crew organised a coach trip up the M6 to stage a night at the Haçienda. While filming inside the club, Dick fell off the stage and landed spine first on a metal beam. Luckily the steadicam kit on his shoulder was unharmed and he carried on filming, so the night was saved for posterity. But by the time he shuffled off the coach back in London he could barely walk!

Dick filmed twenty-one nights over the final three years of the club's run and edited the footage into VHS tapes, each with a cover collaged from the flyer for that particular night. Featured on many of these tapes was the outrageous Paul. Dick would always seek him out as Paul would invariably put on a show – he would be wearing outfits like old riding boots with jodhpurs or a dog collar or leather harness and sometimes he would finish it all off by including one of his elaborate homemade fans.

One time in particular Paul had consumed liquid morphine and was dancing manically while drinking loads of water and he remembers projectile vomiting pure water. Paul loved the sensation and so did the cameraman. Dick filmed it, and it was a special moment that Paul will never forget, clearly out of it but managing to hold it together very well and suddenly projecting clear water like a human fountain. Dick loved to stumble across Paul when he was making the videos as Paul confesses that he can do absolutely anything when a camera is pointed at him. Another time there was an androgynous girl with a masculine boy-look who had a massive black dildo down her trousers. Paul took it out on camera before deep-throating the entire phallus!

When the videos were made available and sold to the public, Paul made sure he kept at least six of these much-loved productions for his own enjoyment. However, his fame and the ability to show off his talents and reminisce in later years were unfortunately taken away from him as a future boyfriend lent his videos to someone else without Paul's permission and they were never to be seen again, at least not by Paul. This is part of Paul's life history and he has since made several attempts to get them back, but without success.

But while the films have long since gone, the memories of those endless, crazy nights still ruminate around in the depths of Paul's mind, although these days the madness that accompanied his life back then is now much harder to comprehend in the present cold light of today.

Chapter 20 – From Fulham to New York and Back (via Amsterdam)

During Paul's separation period from Nick, he got together with a young man named Matt who he had known previously from clubland and nights in the Old Compton pub. Paul and Matt went out for a few months while Paul was still living at Nick's and then for a while afterwards when Paul moved into his next place – a flat in Fulham. Matt was different from most of Paul's other partners in that he was Paul's junior by a few years. Paul describes this particular ex-boyfriend as a "liability, but a nice bloke nevertheless!" Owing perhaps to Matt's youthful good looks, Paul was very taken with his new conquest although many of his early feelings would dissipate later on when he learned that Matt had slept with quite a few of Paul's friends while they were going out together. Paul would soon feel his relationship with Matt becoming more and more turbulent and he would quickly catch his young liability out on a whole range of different issues that would lead the brief affair towards its closure.

Paul's move to Fulham had been instigated by a relationship he had developed with a young woman called Deborah whom he had met at Kinky Gerlinky. The two hit it off and while Paul enjoyed her company, she loved the idea of having this crazy young gay man as her new friend and seemed to be almost in awe of Paul's character, charisma and lifestyle. Deborah was clearly impressed by how Paul could get into Kinky Gerlinky's and other clubs for nothing and with all the people he knew on the scene. She loved how he dressed and his wild behaviours and she hooked onto him, her new key to the debauchery of London's clubland.

Deborah especially loved being part of the monthly Kinky Gerlinky nights where she would dress her and Paul up with paint and glitter and gold, sometimes revealing her voluptuous breasts as part of her outfit. Although Deborah was straight, she clearly enjoyed her role of being a 'fag-hag'!

Deborah was a middle-class, arty-type who spent much of her time working on scumble glazing (which involves putting paint and other chemicals onto furniture to make it look old and antique-like) and other aspects of interior design. She had a bit of money, certainly more than Paul, and would often buy quantities of cocaine, which she would use while she was doing her work. Whatever Paul suggested he wanted, Deborah would usually get it for them. It was a mutually agreeable situation for the new housemates – Paul had someone who would take care of him and buy him things that he needed and Deborah had a much sought after prize companion for partying and nights in the city. It wasn't all a free ride for Paul though, and he did pay his way with a manageable rent given to Deborah every month.

By this stage of his life, Paul was twenty-four and Deborah was at least five years older than him. Paul clearly remembers this age as he had always had an ambition to go to New York by the time he was twenty-five and was just about to achieve this lifetime aim.

Paul had gone to Amsterdam for a long weekend by himself essentially to prepare for the big New York trip, where he wanted so desperately to go. As with the planned US trip, he travelled solo. While there, Paul stayed at a youth hostel not far from the main Amsterdam Centraal Station.

On his arrival, he put all his luggage into a lock-up bin and then went out to a café called Prix D'Ami on Haringpakkerssteeg where they sold cannabis. Paul ordered some 'puff' (or hash as it was detailed on the menu).

He was used to the best hash London had to offer at the time, Red Seal and Gold Seal, when it was more common as opposed to today's large scale availability of skunk. Paul sat down with a half pint of Heineken with a nice big frothy head and rolled a joint. He loaded it as he would do back home in London but didn't realise the super-strength of the drugs he had just bought. He had never had hash with this intensity and soon became really stoned and then quickly started feeling very paranoid.

It seemed like he had been in the café for hours and coming as he did from 90-miles-an-hour London, he thought that at any moment the staff were going to ask him to leave. He clearly didn't understand the culture and pace of life in Amsterdam where you are free to sit all day in most cafés, and particularly the ones selling such relaxing narcotics.

On the entrance to the café, there is a corridor and a counter where customers order before moving down to the tables and chairs where Paul was now sitting. Eventually he managed to get to his feet and tried to discreetly leave. He successfully negotiated the way he had come in until he was literally going out the front door onto the street outside when he banged his hip on the doorway like a big, fat, African woman wobbling her way out. He turned in horror to see most of the café staring at him. Hastily, he returned to the sanctuary of his hostel and lay down on his bed, incredibly stoned.

When he finally came round several hours later, he went for a walk and it was only then that he realised it was acceptable to stay in the cafés for several hours and that it wasn't anything like the London attitude that Paul was used to of midday diners being told to "eat up and leave".

Having successfully negotiated the trip to Amsterdam, Paul felt ready to take on the increased challenge of tackling New York. To fund the trip, Paul was in contact with Apollo Couriers which operated by matching people willing to take a package for a reputable company who needed something brought Stateside.

Once at the destination, the item would be dropped off and therefore the individual involved could get a cheaper flight. The packages were usually things like film reels and it was all legal and above board with the only drawback being that the flights were predetermined so it wasn't possible to book your own travel times. This would later prove to be a major inconvenience for Paul when he inadvertently outstayed his welcome but was unable to leave as he had to wait for the prescheduled return flight.

Before he was due to leave for the States, Paul had been working at Kinky Gerlinky's and had heard that one of the DJ's he knew, Tasty Tim, was also going to be in New York during his trip. The friendly DJ had said that Paul was welcome to stay with him, at a friend's place, while there.

Tasty Tim has been on the circuit forever and is still banging out tunes to this day. Back then, he was the original innovative trailblazer, an out-and-out gender-bender, glamorous club doyenne and perennial club tranny. He was also very skilled, as a DJ and producer. Having honed his talents at nights like Cha Cha and the Mud Club, he then took up a long-running residency at Heaven in the 1980's. Through this and a wide variety of other pioneering club nights, he helped shape London's disco and gay scene and has been an integral part of everything flamboyantly fun since then.

When Paul arrived in New York, he got a big air-conditioned taxi and when the driver had brought Paul to the destination Tasty Tim had given him, he charged him the equivalent of seventy English pounds. Paul hadn't worked out the rate with dollars so just paid it, but this already left him somewhat short of funds.

It was to get worse after he arrived when he was told that he couldn't stay there as the owner, Tim's friend, had been injured in a car accident that same day. Tim had found another option for Paul and put him in touch with a different friend called Heaven, a dancer for Erasure who were performing in Manhattan as part of their Phantasmagorical Tour. So Paul stayed on Heaven's floor for a few days while the band were out touring New York.

On the fourth night of his visit, Paul went out clubbing with Tasty Tim and Heaven but Heaven left early as he had a performance the following day. Paul had been drinking large measures and was getting merrily drunk but the staff had a word with Tim and said that Paul wasn't paying tips. A note for anyone who visits the States - the expectation is that you will always tip as, like in this instance, the staff are usually only being paid a minimal amount each night with the rest being made up in tips. This is the main reason American serving staff are always so plastically pleasant and helpful with their endless, "Have a nice day", and, "Is there anything else I can get you?" After this realisation, Paul gave them $2 every time he bought a drink, which was frequently and quickly. After some time, he left the club, alone and very drunk, but feeling relaxed and with the sense that he belonged, being as he did from a big city like London.

As he was walking from Times Square past the meat factories, in a poorer area, he stopped to get a snack. A mixed race man starting chatting to him at the food stand and then brought him up to where he said there was an excellent local club.

As they turned a corner, the man suddenly punched Paul in the face and burst his nose open. The man demanded money from Paul who gave him what he had in his pockets and the man ran off.

During the attack, Paul had noticed someone across the street get out of a car and look over but then quickly hurry off, completely ignoring the assault at the other side of the street. Paul understands this fully though as this was during a period, in early 1990's New York, where gun crime was rife and many parts of the city were incredibly dangerous places to go out in, especially at night.

The only plus side to the ambush was that fortunately Paul had had the composure to earlier stash most of his money in his sock so at least he still had that.

The incident understandably left Paul extremely shaken and vulnerable so he decided to just keep out of the way until his return trip.

Erasure's tour had moved on and Heaven with it, so Paul stayed in a hotel just down the road from Heaven's place. He laid low for the first day after the attack and on the second day, he called Nick Lewis in London to tell him what had happened, that he'd been robbed and had no more money to pay for accommodation. Nick told him to go to see a relative of his in Manhattan to get some cash, and this money secured Paul's room until his departure.

He spent most of his remaining seven days just hiding out in the hotel and waiting for his return to London but when he did venture out, he would often hear people shouting "look, there's Madonna's dancer". Paul had bleached blonde hair and one of Madonna's dancers on her current local tour had the same style of hair. Peroxide blonde wasn't a big thing in New York at the time, so he got mistaken on several occasions!

One of the few times that he did venture out, Paul met a young, funkily-dressed black girl who started chatting to him. The girl, obviously taking pity on the fragile soul, took him to church which was literally a blessed relief for Paul as he was still tremendously scared following his experience earlier in the week.

In the space of just two weeks, his trip had been a real mix of everything that New York had to offer, with the good, the bad and the ugly all thrown in together.

Following his eventful vacation, Paul then returned to the place he knew so well and arrived back to Deborah's flat in Fulham. He had video some of his experiences from New York on a couple of tapes and once home showed them to Deborah and a few other friends. While the tapes captured the visual aspect of life in New York, they didn't however reveal the latest in Paul's emotional life-drama or expose the fact that he never seemed to be able to just have a normal experience, whatever he tried.

Once home, Paul settled back into his life in London. He was fond of this period, recalling the place they shared as a "nice flat" and the phase as a "nice time" in his life, although their relationship would ultimately turn a bit sour towards the end.

Deborah had a good friend called David who lived in a shared house in Acton. By the time Paul had come back from America, Deborah and David seemed to be inseparable. They started going everywhere together as a bit of a package and always went out clubbing as a pair. The friends were very competitive and would constantly try to outdo each other with their extravagant attire on the big nights out.

Now back into the swing of the capital's club scene, Paul found himself in the middle of their company and sometimes felt that he was an addition to the exuberance that accompanied their soirées into the clubbing world, though given the choice, he was increasingly feeling that he would rather be on his own.

David was in awe of Paul's ease of admittance to Kinky Gerlinky's and other venues and loved the opening that this gave him in being able to express himself with his ever-courageous outfits, but Paul began to feel that he was simply a free-pass for them and wondered what he was getting out of the friendships.

Paul began to feel that Deborah was consuming a lot from their relationship and was cramping his style, while he wasn't gaining much from her. Paul felt it had become a one-way street with Deborah being increasingly needy and Paul becoming increasingly tired of her neediness.

On different occasions Paul wanted to go to clubs without her and David, and was often keen to use a variety of drugs, including heroin, which wasn't something that Deborah was into.

The friendship which had started out as an exciting romp through cocaine, fashion and music was by now beginning to reach the end of its course.

Paul still very much loved the flat and having moved about so much wasn't keen to have to relocate again. So, he and Deborah talked it out and decided that they would become less close friends and more conventional housemates.

Paul was happy with this resolution. He had regained his independence that was so important to him whilst maintaining his presence in the nice flat that he enjoyed living in.

He was soon to find a way to spend his new-found freedom by diversifying his income stream in a way that he hadn't previously considered, and as usual, drugs were at the heart of his plans.

Chapter 21 – Sampling & Dealing

Paul had met Damien one night while out clubbing. Damien was a speed-freak who would go clubbing with a group of friends and take speed all night and all the next day. This odd gang all had kits complete with loaded syringes to take on their nights out. They would frequently go to Heaven and other clubs with their secret stash of amphetamine.

By now, Paul was also well used to this way of life and recalls one time in Heaven when he was working as a bus-boy. A bouncer came into the washroom and caught Paul in the middle of 'jacking-up' speed. Given the regularity of such events, the bouncer didn't stop him or even say anything. He simply gave him a look of disapproval, turned and walked out!

Paul estimates that as many as ninety per cent of the Heaven bus-boys were taking speed or acid and, halfway through their shift, most of them would go out to dance. They would always congregate to one side of the huge club where they were covered by a walkway above and where the big speakers helped to hide them from their managers.

Following their first meeting where they got on very well, Paul and Damien, along with another friend, Geoff, would have jacked up all kinds of drugs. They would inject anything they could get their hands on - cocaine, speed, ecstasy, even ketamine. If Paul couldn't find a vein, Geoff was always the one who would step in and find one for him, jack him up and then repeat the 'favour' for Damien.

This behaviour was always obviously a concern and more so due to an urban legend that was circulating at the time of a certain Dr Death, who had killed two people, similarly by injecting them. Usually there would just be the three of them, but sometimes there would be a larger group of people – the 'speed-freaks' as Paul called them.

Paul has always felt like he was different to everyone else and he loved how drink and drugs enabled him to feel like he wasn't the same as those around him. Doubtless, Paul was unorthodox even during his sober times, but the mood and mind altering substances simply served to enhance his desire to be separate from the conventional crowd, especially when he went out on the club scene.

In addition to using large quantities of the drugs, Damien was also dealing and soon offered Paul the opportunity to grab himself some extra cash by helping out. Never one to miss an easy opportunity, Paul gladly took Damien up on the chance and between them, they began to sell at most of London's gay clubs and many of the mixed-straight clubs.

The move from using to dealing drugs was a natural one and Paul took and dealt drugs without perhaps realising the damage he could have caused to someone else, or indeed to himself. Or maybe Paul did realise the dangers but chose to ignore the warnings in his head and around him, deciding instead that this was the way he wanted his life to go and that whatever happened, he was still in control of his own destiny.

He used drink and drugs to fit in with people and to help him get over his inherent, awkward social fears. He felt he needed to be constantly altered and carried with him an impression that this made him more confident. He thought the alcohol and the stimulants made him funny, and it was extremely important to the young Paul to be seen as having a great sense of humour and to consistently be able to make people laugh. Like the small child who walked before him, he felt very needy, constantly craved other people's approval and didn't care what means or methods he needed to administer to gain the wider acceptance of his peers.

The two friends worked together but were also social companions and enjoyed each other's company. In the clubs, they sold mostly hash and some speed, but only on a small scale. They would go to the wide variety of clubs across London and sell their wares to anyone who was interested in buying.

It was always busy. Paul remembers one of the busiest nights being one New Year's Eve when he was jumping in and out of cabs as the clock approached midnight, and trying to get to as many clubs in as short a time as possible to service the needy punters. However, the pair didn't sell for long and they weren't in any way 'big time' dealers.

Paul though was soon to meet a new associate, and would use his earlier experiences to help him evolve into a much bigger and busier dealer. This transition occurred under the wing of his new collaborator, Johnny Fart-Pants, who was soon priming Paul to support his vast and growing drugs distribution network.

Johnny Fart-Pants, also known as Trade John or Trade-Baby John, resided in nearby Peckham and was a major dealer at the time. Johnny Fart-Pants had his finger in many pies and was partly responsible for the overall running of Trade, the famous nightclub, and it's related merchandise. He always wore Trade-Baby t-shirts and Trade-Baby black bomber jackets which were embroidered with the logo of a baby with a dummy in its mouth. Among his current collection of memorabilia of the day, Paul still has a worn out Trade-Baby t-shirt lurking somewhere in the back of his wardrobe.

Interestingly, Paul doesn't know why his recently acquired accomplice was widely known as Johnny Fart-Pants. One would have assumed that this would have been a question that may have been asked early in the relationship? But perhaps it wasn't that important to Paul or maybe Johnny did tell him once but it was promptly forgotten and never asked again?

The club that Johnny helped to run, Trade, had opened its doors in 1990. It was London's first legitimate after hours venue, becoming the first club in the UK to be granted a twenty-four hour licence. As illegal rave culture began to redefine British nightlife, the club thundered out of Turnmills in Clerkenwell from 3am every Sunday and kick-started an intrepid early morning clubbing scene that would last two decades. Masterminded by a man calling himself Laurence Malice, it was billed as a gay club but attracted a diverse crowd and thanks to DJ's like Tony de Vit, it became famous for pushing the new hard house sound.

Trade quickly became a weekly haven for London's late night party boys, many of whom had spent Saturday night in Soho bars and clubs like Heaven and G-A-Y, before ending up at Turnmills on the Sunday morning. Malice promoted it as a safe place for queers to get some safe, after hours 'trade' away from London's parks and other dangerous settings.

At the time, most clubs ended at 2am or 3am and many after hours parties were illicit, even dangerous. The AIDS-epidemic had also erupted and Malice wanted to create a safe environment for gay men alongside a pumping soundtrack. "It was a ridiculously homophobic time," Malice would later state in an interview. "No one knew what AIDS was about so you would have guys leaving clubs at 3am and they wanted to meet, get off with people, whatever, and they were being attacked." It's why Trade's assorted audience was so important. "I wanted straight people to see that gay people are not a problem – that we can mix."

This inclusivity was inspired in part by acid house's togetherness rather than the attitudinal, fashion-focused clubs of the 1980's, "It was a crazy group of characters from different walks of life - rent-boys, trannies, working girls, Muscle Marys, industry people," says regular Trade DJ, Smokin Jo, of the club's clientele. "It was such a mixed bag and that added to the fun. It wasn't a serious night full of musos, it was everyone there with their hands in the air going crazy."

This eclectic flock could often have waited over two hours in the rain to get in, watching the smoke from the main dance room, which was called 'Dante's Inferno', billow under the doorway onto the street. The door policy was simple, "You don't have to be gay or a member to get in, but your attitude and look will count." The 'door-bitch', Tom, was infamous but along with the blokes, bears, lesbians, transsexuals, not-sure-yets and their straight mates, Madonna famously visited, as did Jean Paul Gaultier. Bjork crowd-surfed and even Posh and Becks popped in. Cher was turned away. Her entourage and demands for a VIP area could not be met. There were no VIP's at Trade, Malice told her management, who scuttled back to the waiting limo. Axl Rose got told to fuck off too when he came to the door not long after making some homophobic comments in the press.

Having negotiated the queue and satisfying Tom, the assorted patrons would go through the main door, down an elaborate metal staircase and spill out into the heaving mess below. The path to the dance floor was known as 'Muscle Alley' and would be full to the brim with bare-chested men with their biceps and hard-ons, side-stepping out of time to music that was always too fast for them to dance in time to and still look composed.

Then there was an area where it was easy to get whatever you desired to assist the evening's entertainment. Customers would queue patiently under the arches that surrounded the dance floor in line for dealers serving up cocaine under one, ketamine under the next, and pills in arch three.

When Trade opened its doors, Section 28 was still in force. Introduced by Margaret Thatcher's government, Section 28 of the 1988 Local Government Act stated that councils should not "intentionally promote homosexuality or publish material with the intention of promoting homosexuality". The mainstream media, propelled by righteous moralisers like Mary Whitehouse, saw those participating in nights like Trade as freaks, and they spat disgust at their life choices. Trade was a sanctuary – a paradise of inclusion, unity and belonging. The leather heads and butch dykes from monthly fetish night Fist mixed with Soho's drag queens. Under the Trade lasers the crowd celebrated life away from a judgemental British culture that was yet to accept the weird and wonderful diversity that the gay community brought to London. An article printed in the Gay Times in 1994 perhaps sums up Trade's significance best: "Here there's a real sense of belonging, of community," says its writer, Richard Smith, "Coming here did me at least as much good as coming out."

Trade earned a kind of respect from the mainstream dance music industry that other British gay events had never quite commanded. By the mid-1990's, it had gone international and begun to host events across Europe, notably in Ibiza with Manumission as well as launching in Los Angeles and New York. Carrie and the girls would go on to visit Trade in a 2002 episode of Sex and the City, while the club's equivalent of flyer promoters, The Trade Police, featured in the film Kevin & Perry Go Large.

Ultimately, Trade ran every week at Turnmills for twelve years and Johnny Fart-Pants was integral to its success. Shortly after he began his relationship with Trade, Johnny's partner died of AIDS-related illnesses, and that made Johnny go even more wild than he had been before. His partner had been the main dealer who was responsible for getting all the stock in. When he passed away, Johnny used all the contacts to carry on the empire.

Johnny was obviously well known to all the Trade personnel and punters and was a close ally of Laurence Malice. Paul had met Johnny one night in Trade and quickly became his friend, before progressing to his associate.

The process for supplying Trade would be that Paul and Johnny would get to the club and despite the queues which invariably stretched far around the corner, they would go straight to the front where the door staff would let them in. They would go immediately to the manager's office, sort them out, and then go downstairs to service the punters in the club. All the while, they'd keep themselves topped up with bullet shots of ketamine or speed and sometimes a bit of acid, the odd bit of puff out the back and always loads and loads of ecstasy.

Johnny would always be loading Paul up and they would work together all night, every night. They would start in the gay bars in Old Compton Street, usually with a double vodka and coke to kick the night off. Johnny was flash, and, when he was with him, Paul was flash too and they'd be buying drinks for every "Tom, Dick and Harry" in the place! Paul would copy Johnny and try to be as flash as he was.

While all this was going on though, Paul was still struggling with the same inner demons. He constantly felt like a freak, an alien, and found the best way to alleviate these feelings was to buy people's attention even if this meant destroying himself and them a little bit more as he went along. The drugs, while readily available, resulted in Paul getting more and more paranoid, alienated, miserable and afraid. He would try to convince himself that he loved being out of control, being so different. But the truth was, he didn't. The reality was he would do anything to avoid having to face reality.

There was always lots of cash available too, although Paul wouldn't have described Johnny as rich – it was more just vast amounts of money flowing in and then quickly going out at an alarming rate.

The pair worked together, side-by-side, 24/7 for a long time and with such close proximity, it begs the question - was there ever any sexual contact? The answer to this is that there was one time when they had taken a lot of ketamine in Johnny's flat in Peckham. The episode was really weird as it was a heavily drug-induced state and although Paul was aware of what was going on, he didn't particularly enjoy it, although it wasn't horrible either. Paul wasn't in control, not only of the situation, but of himself and describes it as trying to have sex while on extremely trippy acid. After this bungled attempt, they decided to just keep their relationship purely platonic from that point onwards.

Johnny Fart-Pants was obsessed with Paul and would regularly lay him on with literally thousands of pounds worth of various drugs which Paul would do his best to sell. Paul was dealing in all the West End clubs and, for the most part, the bouncers knew what he and his aliases were doing but didn't care as Paul's outfit were also supplying the club managers, promoters and owners.

As part of the operation, minicab drivers were employed to pick up packages of money, then drop them off and pick up parcels of drugs which usually consisted of ecstasy, ketamine, cocaine, cannabis, speed or acid, before passing these on to Johnny.

Paul would then be given a large quantity of these drugs to go out and sell, but often and not surprisingly given Paul's fondness of the product, he would regularly take large amounts himself or give drugs away to his many hangers-on. But when he would go back to Johnny, and tell him that he was a grand or two down, Johnny would jokingly tell him off and say, "for God's sake, what are you like?!", and then load him up again. And this arrangement continued for some time - Paul being given huge quantities of drugs and then often not quite making the financial return asked of him!

Paul would nearly always be "off his nut" when he was supposed to be dealing so would often drop and lose drugs or give them away to his variety of 'friends' who were regularly in close attendance when they knew he had plenty of narcotics about his person.

Given the combination of circumstances, it wasn't surprising that he'd be down every week. But despite this, Johnny Fart Pants would let him get away with murder. Paul thinks the main reasons for this were because Johnny liked the fact that he could afford it and also some of it was due to the control it gave him over Paul, someone he clearly had a soft spot for.

Whatever the reasons, what was obvious was that allowing someone like Paul to be around such a steady supply of large quantities of drugs would inevitably lead to him taking more and more of the illicit substances and further his voyage into the weird and wonderful world of London's never-ending nightlife.

Chapter 22 – The Love of my Life?

It was late summer in 1992. Near Piccadilly there was a club called Industria and for his 26th birthday, Paul hosted a party there. In typical style he arrived late and all his guests were already there. Paul made his usual dramatic entrance, enhanced by his outrageously loud fashion statement of craziness - a Union Jack t-shirt, fishnet stockings ripped with deliberate holes and cowboy boots. For him, nothing unusual, but for the uninitiated bystander it had all the hallmarks of a really fucked-up outfit! His right arm was covered with cling film as he had just got a tattoo. Throughout the night, quite a few of the guests asked about his arm and he responded be saying that he had a collapsed vein from injecting and passed it off like it was nothing. He loved the drama of seeing the shocked responses of his assembled collective.

As the party got into full swing, Paul went to get more drinks and as he was waiting at the bar, he met the man that he still calls the love of his life, Sean McGuigan. The two men started chatting and before long they realised they had much in common. As a casual introduction they shared some of the drugs they had on them. Sean asked Paul where he lived and Paul told him about Deborah's place in Fulham. It turned out that this was also where Sean's mum lived so he offered to give Paul a lift home. Paul was still in the final throes of his relationship with Matt at the time and so Sean gave them both a ride back to Fulham.

After they got back, Matt went to bed and fell asleep and Paul and Sean stayed up. Paul took some valium and Sean had diazepam eggs and they exchanged these, along with sharing a few joints. Despite the array of consumed mind-blockers, Paul remembers vividly this first meeting and how they got on like a house on fire. After a while Paul went to check on Matt, jumped into bed to give him a cuddle and then ended up falling asleep beside him.

Paul woke up in the morning with a start and immediately felt a sense of blind panic as he remembered having a complete stranger in the house who he had only met briefly and whom he had left all alone when he fell asleep beside Matt. Paul completely freaked out and rushed into the living room, half expecting the TV and other expensive items to be gone.

Thankfully for Paul nothing had been taken and his mysterious stranger had simply vanished, just as quickly as he had appeared.

However much he tried, Paul couldn't get this experience out of his head. Days were spent reminiscing about how much he had enjoyed his chance meeting with the charming Sean and how much he longed to see him again. He found himself looking everywhere for him, in all the usual places, but he could never find him. He remembered the lift home in Sean's very distinctive American Recreational Vehicle (RV) and Paul would look out for the van, especially in Fulham. Then one day he did see it, but Sean was nowhere to be found in the vicinity. Paul fantasised about Sean for the best part of a year, never being able to fully get him out of his mind, and always left wondering what could have been had they had more time together.

Having long since parted with Matt and as it approached almost a year since their chance encounter, Paul began to accept that he probably wouldn't see his fantasy man ever again.

But fate was about to intervene once more. Paul had gone to Turnmill's at Trade, selling drugs for Johnny Fart-Pants. Trade, as usual, was packed out and moving around the club meant walking through groups of heaving sweaty men. Suddenly and without warning, Sean was there in front of Paul. Sean beamed and said, "Hello Paul, bet you don't remember me, do you?" Paul, taken aback and slightly flustered, managed to hold it together and replied, "Yes I do, Sean. Come with me for a minute."

There is a restaurant area in Turnmill's (the term restaurant here could be misleading – it was actually just so the owners could negotiate a licence to serve alcohol!) Sean sat down at one of the tables and Paul said he had to conclude a deal in the toilets but would soon return. This took the best part of twenty minutes and when Paul eventually came back he was somewhat surprised and very pleased to see that Sean was still sitting there waiting for him. From that moment onwards they spent all day, every day, together for the first year of their blossoming relationship.

After the year of waiting, and what Paul describes as something of a romantic fantasy, he and Sean had finally found each other again and they became literally inseparable. Paul found Sean very attractive and loved finding someone who shared his longing for exclusive intimacy. Paul recalls with a sense of pride that, as he had done with Tim before, he spent several weeks sleeping in bed with Sean before they did anything sexual.

This is a common theme with Paul who has experienced so much promiscuous, throwaway sex that when he meets someone he genuinely loves, he deliberately reneges on the physicality until the time is really perfect. It would appear from an outsider that when you have two men who know what they want and are together in a bed, that it's fairly inevitable that they will immediately become intimate, but this isn't necessarily the case.

Aligned to Paul's own sentiments, he also feels that Sean was somewhat mixed up with his sexuality and that may have helped to delay things. Despite Sean being very 'in your face', and a flirtatious show off, underneath it all he was, and is, actually very shy. Sean puts this down to his parentage and his heritage. He was brought up in Belfast in a very old-fashioned, conventional Catholic family. The right thing to do was to meet a nice girl, settle down, get married and then have lots of children. Sean's father passed away shortly after he began seeing Paul and this may have been for the best as the old man would have no doubt had massive issues with one of his offspring being declared as an out-and-out homosexual.

Sean describes this time as him "testing the waters" and that he was essentially straight before he met Paul. He had had numerous girlfriends and the odd liaison with a couple of men but never before had he felt that he was fully gay. It was Paul and the feelings that this stirred up in him that moved him from testing, to swimming, in the waters.

Another mitigating factor in their early lack of sexual intimacy was that Sean wasn't as attracted to Paul at the start as Paul was to him and in Sean's own words, "he grew to love" Paul as time went on, in what was Sean's first serious gay relationship.

There was also a key aspect to Paul's early relationship with Sean which meant that sex wasn't always high on his agenda. Unknown to Sean, Paul was struggling with an intense and deep-rooted dependency. What Paul was endeavouring to keep from his new love was that he was in the grip of what he describes of his first major heroin addiction.

This spiral into the lure of the White Lady happened just after he started his relationship with Sean and was still living with Deborah in the flat. True to Paul's form when finding real and true love, the couple weren't having sex but they were sharing a bed together and in Deborah's place, this was just a single bed. Paul was engaged in 'poly-drug use' and was using anything he could get his hands on – uppers, downers, and everything in between, as well as the heroin – to get through it all.

One of the major symptoms of this cocktail of drug ingestion was severe sweats which he passed off as having flu. He needed to invent something as it was impossible to deny that there was an issue when the small bed was invariably soaked come morning time. Sean didn't have a clue – he was to find out later on – and Paul did everything he could to hide it from him. During this period, on top of the heroin use itself, Paul would experience many bouts of 'cold turkey' in the initial stages and would use a variety of different drugs to try and control it.

What was different to his previous heroin use with Tim and others was that this time round Paul found his usage was at the stage where it was almost a daily occurrence. He would do things like go missing for two or three days in a row, often waiting for an argument with Sean as an excuse to "fuck off to Clapham" to visit his friend, Waqar, an Asian girl who worked in the clothing design industry.

Waqar was in a relationship with a man called Ian, who worked in an arty, avant-garde boutique, design studio and shop that sold designer shoes and clothing. In their experimental and creative world, they loved having Paul around as it gave them another avenue into the outlandish domain that he inhabited so frequently.

Paul would disappear to their flat for a couple of days, buy heroin and take it there, chasing the dragon while Waqar and Ian injected. Paul also injected sometimes but usually it was just chasing – it was his secret heroin getaway and enabled him to shut himself off from every other aspect of his life, without judgement or disturbance.

Due partly to the amount of drugs they were taking as part of their normal routines, Sean didn't really notice Paul's occasional absences. Sean had his own interests outside of Paul, and when Paul went away, Sean had the opportunity to do his own things without worrying about his boyfriend.

Sean knew of Waqar but had no idea Paul was there so Paul was free to do what he wanted. As the disappearances usually followed an argument, it was probably to everyone's benefit that there was a bit of a break.

No-one else in Paul's circle of friends seemed to be too bothered where he was, and this was still a time of relatively limited technology so he was hard to trace. In today's invasive world of global location devices, mobile phones and social media platforms, it would be much harder to disappear in this way. Looking back, Paul really enjoyed the whole secrecy of the trips - that only he knew where he was and what was going on. It was obviously what Paul felt he wanted and needed and he would frequently and deliberately negotiate arguments so he could make another getaway.

For the average person and even for the occasional recreational drug-user, using heroin is still a million miles away from what they have experienced. So what is a heroin addiction like? Do you wake up in the morning and crave a fix? Do you have constant internal devils telling you that you need to take heroin? It is not uncommon to hear stories in the media where addicts are lambasted for begging and stealing hundreds of pounds every single day to feed their habit.

None of these standard trends however seemed to apply to Paul, despite his obvious and self-confessed addiction at the time. He was dabbling nearly every day yet had convinced himself that he had it under wraps and it was fine as he wasn't hooked. For Paul it wasn't just the lure of the drugs themselves, it was also a lifestyle choice - he wanted that chic-heroin appearance and craved both the look and feeling of misery. Linked to the self-harm process, for Paul a large appeal was also the secrecy and ultimately what he craved was the feeling of the heroin numbing him, warming him, and making him not have to think of anything.

As with his previous heavy heroin use with Tim, Paul loved the physical feeling of vomiting. He would regularly take enough heroin to make himself throw up and afterwards, he would feel a lot better, more content, warmer, balanced, cleansed and in control. It was a process Paul followed to get him to the place he wanted to be. Most users try to take drugs without being sick or take too much and end up unwell and don't enjoy it but Paul did precisely the opposite and loved every minute of the twisted process.

This addicted phase lasted for months but Paul still maintains he was in control as it was on and off drug-use, and although close to it, he wasn't using every single day. Paul knew he would need to back off for a few days when his 'clucking' (cramps, shaking legs, restlessness, cold sweats and pain throughout his body) became more intensified and he knew he would have to let himself 'come down'. His body would crave the heroin when it wasn't there but Paul liked to know that he was always in charge of the drug and wouldn't let himself give in to every single craving, preferring instead to force himself to have a few days off to prove he was still in control of himself and his body. However, he would always inevitably slip back into that familiar warm and secret state.

There are usually two main ways in which users handle heroin addiction – they either take increasing amounts of heroin and end up in a really expensive, damaging habit or they use other drugs and self-medicate the addiction. The latter is what Paul chose to do. As he had access to multiple different types of drugs he had the opportunity to substitute and passed off any of his comedown clucking symptoms as flu and sickness or a bit of a cold.

Prior to his relationship with Sean, Paul enjoyed regular social heroin use. But with Sean, he suddenly realised he had to stop. This was when he had his first proper bout of cold turkey and he came down with severe sweats, diarrhoea, and vomiting while noticing how adversely affected his psychological functioning had become.

After a few weeks of this traumatic experience, Paul decided he would prefer to 'dabble' with some amount of heroin rather than go through the horrors of trying to stop completely. As a result, he would either go off to Clapham for a few days or make a quick visit and bring some heroin back with him. He would do a little bit here and there with no-one knowing and that was all part of the buzz. Sean didn't know Paul was involved in heroin so it was a big secret, and Paul loved the thrill of using whilst trying not to get found out.

Around the corner from where his mum lived in Fulham, Sean was friendly with a woman called Sue Bennett and he spent most of his time there. Sue loved her drugs as much as Paul and Sean and when she found out that Paul had access to hundreds and hundreds of acid tabs, she couldn't have done more to accommodate him and quickly asked him to move in so Paul soon moved out of Deborah's and into Sue's house.

There was another reason that Sue loved having them there as she was, and still is to this day, besotted with Sean. Sue had had a one-night stand with Sean's older brother, who is unfortunately now deceased, and was always keen to try the younger version too. Sue could get quite twisted and would sometimes invent stories to try to move Sean away from Paul but it never worked, due in no small part to the fact that Sean was clearly more gay than bi-sexual.

This is something that most people are surprised to hear though as Sean is an interesting, multi-dimensional character and if you met him you would be hard pushed to believe that he is gay, as he very much portrays the manly Cockney geezer who would be far happier knocking a bloke out than letting him touch his nether regions!

Before the start of their relationship, the 'geezer' Sean had purchased a new RV – a glorified van with room for swivel seats and tables in the back. Sean used the vehicle as a commercial business, and would most famously soon be driving the Dreamboys male strippers and their manager, Bari Bacco, round in it.

The Dreamboys had an office in Russell Gardens and Sean used to park the RV near there. He had just come off the back of a week-long club bender when he went back to collect his van and was approached by a couple of men - Bari Bacco and Jimmy, the dance choreographer. They walked up to Sean and asked him if he would hire the van out and drive the group round Europe. Sean accepted the offer and would go on to drive them around the continent on and off for the next three and a half years.

Bari's real name was Barry Solomon and he was a Cockney Jew who was at the forefront of the male stripping scene in the late 1980's and early 1990's. He founded the Dreamboys after watching the now-infamous 1985 Levi's advert that saw Nick Kamen stripping off in a launderette.

This led to him founding the male stripping troupe and they kicked off with a small show in a club on Wardour Street in 1987. The show went down an absolute storm and Bari suddenly realised he had a new and highly sought after product on his hands. Since time began, women had been taking their clothes of for the pleasure of men. Now, all of a sudden, Bari realised that scantily-clad men could be seen as sex symbols and that women were every bit as eager as their male counterparts to get a close up look at the opposite sex wearing little to no clothing.

The Dreamboys would go on to achieve global fame, even meeting famous faces including Princess Diana in 1991. As she moved along the queue of handsome young men, she was heard to remark to one of them, "You aren't wearing very much today!" It would later transpire that one of the Dreamboys, Jason Steele, actually worked as Princess Diana's personal trainer although the royal had no idea about his double life.

Following the Dreamboys' initial success, it wasn't long before they were travelling all around Europe and in between performing, they made it their mission to sleep with as many women as possible, often boasting to each other of their multiple conquests on a daily basis. Sean's job was to drive them to and from their various shows and they did two-week tours of Germany, Denmark, Belgium and Holland.

The irony of Sean's business was that as much as he was an accomplished driver, he didn't actually hold a driving licence having never got round to doing his test, nor did he have any legitimate insurance cover. Ironically in many of the countries they visited, they were given police escorts to and from gigs but he was never asked by those helping him to prove that he was even allowed to be on the road in the first place.

While the Dreamboys were performing, Sean initially watched from a safe distance but after a couple of shows, he noticed an area for improvement. Generally the strippers would remove everything save for a skimpy pair of underwear so after the show, the stage was strewn with items of clothing. The Dreamboys would gather up all the clothes but Sean thought this looked unprofessional so suggested that immediately following the performance, they would leave the stage and he would go round and pick up all the clothes. Thus the Belfast Cockney van driver was promoted to 'Road Manager'.

In addition to his driving duties with The Dreamboys, Sean also diversified his transport of people willing to remove their clothes for a living. He offered his services to The Blobbendales, a novelty version of The Chippendales, who were headed up by the voluptuous Flabio and who only admitted performers who were pushing the wrong side of twenty stone. Sean would only do two trips with this group owing to the fact that, as he put it, "they were fucking my suspension up!"

He also did a few trips for The Dreamgirls, the female counterparts of their more illustrious male group but again this only happened on two occasions as Sean found himself at the shows surrounded by huge Welshmen who wanted to touch the girls. Not fancying being responsible for stopping the inevitable gropefest, Sean instead concentrated his efforts on just driving The Dreamboys to their shows.

When Sean wasn't working, he, Paul and Sue, the curious threesome, would hang out at Sue's house together and take copious amounts of green and yellow temazepam eggs. These used to come in the jelly-egg form but this had to be stopped as many hardened drug-users were extracting the jelly and injecting it.

The intravenous misuse of temazepam was first reported in Scotland in 1987 where users would heat up the capsules and then draw the contents up into a syringe to use in combination with heroin. These capsules which were obtained from doctors and on the street were injected to enhance the experience of heroin intoxication, to offset effects of psychostimulants such as cocaine or methamphetamine, to deal with stress or psychological distress or to enable the users to sleep. They injected because the effect was quicker and more intoxicating and despite clear awareness of the harm associated with temazepam injection, these people were prepared to sacrifice their health for the pleasures they perceived to be afforded by injecting the gel capsules.

Despite the obvious risks linked with the practice, users continued to inject the capsules, and the results were often severe. Most suffered some complications including abscesses, cellulitis, skin ulcers, nerve damage or distal limb amputation. A number reported using deep veins in the groin and neck because they could no longer access peripheral veins.

As a result of the problems, temazepam was then sold only in pill form. It mattered little to Paul though as he had never slipped to injecting the eggs and was happy to take the drug in whatever form it came, along with his additional chosen array of other substances.

Although the lovers' relationship was generally positive at the start, Paul recognises that he was extremely insecure and jealous. He feels that he is still like that today but back then he was far worse. To compound things, Sean was very outgoing and flirtatious which fed Paul's paranoia and often led to arguments. In the beginning, their disputes were usually brief and easily resolved. They were clearly in love with each other and there were plenty of positives to make sure that they always quickly got things back on an even keel. But as time wore on, the arguments became more frequent and more vicious. Their ability to resolve their differences seemed to be getting worse and the situation was nearly always worsened by the impact of drugs or alcohol or come downs.

Paul clearly remembers one Boxing Day when they were in a pub, not far from Sean's mum's house in Dawes Road, Fulham. They had smuggled in a bottle of vodka and while managing to drink it very discreetly, they undid all their excellent incognito work by then having a full on brawl in the bar. Following their altercation Paul walked out of the pub, got into Sean's RV and attempted to drive off. Sean came out and stopped him getting away by hitting him over the head with a crowbar which he had procured from the back of the van. Paul then hit him back, again over the head, and this time with a bottle which he still had from the bar.

After the melee, they stumbled in opposite directions with the intention of getting to their nearest emergency department. Purely by chance, Sean went to Charing Cross Hospital and Paul ended up at Chelsea and Westminster Hospital, the two being less than two miles apart from each other. Paul was relieved and hoped they didn't end up in the same hospital, spending most of the time freaking out that at any minute, Sean might appear in the next cubicle.

The net result was however a pleasing one for Paul as he ended up with four stitches whereas Sean needed five stitches, something that Paul saw as a minor victory and made all the more memorable by the fact that it took place on Boxing Day!

Whilst in retrospect a funny story, there is the obvious concern of tangible domestic violence that permeated the relationship, and it raises an interesting point on homosexual abuse. Different from heterosexual relationships, both partners tend to be physically stronger, and there is perhaps less of a perpetrator-survivor scenario where it might be more common to have two strong males who could both be deemed the perpetrator in their own right.

Paul feels that homosexual domestic abuse has only really begun to be addressed in the last few years. He has noticed more public exposure of domestic violence being between men, although it remains a difficult subject in which to shift society's perceptions and consciousness. While domestic abuse is still mostly carried out by male perpetrators on female survivors, there is ever increasing evidence of males being the abused, whether in homosexual or heterosexual relationships.

Yet male survivors of domestic violence are largely invisible, as indeed female survivors were until the feminist movement forced society to take notice. Men who experience domestic violence, whether in heterosexual or gay relationships, have until relatively recently been largely ignored. Work on improving society's response to domestic violence against women has not been matched by responses to male survivors.

One of the factors leading to this is that not only do the professionals tasked with supporting male survivors of domestic abuse not always respond appropriately, but further the men themselves don't always recognise the abuse for what it really is. Male survivors often reveal recurrent disbelief and dismissive responses to their disclosures of the abuse they have been subjected to and there are chilling accounts of the joking response given by some GP's and other professionals. To compound all this are the views of the male survivors themselves. In a recent study of men attending UK primary care health clinics, only a third of the men who had experienced domestic abuse thought they had been in an abusive relationship.

But perhaps things are slowly changing. Although homosexual domestic abuse has obviously gone on for generations, Paul feels it's only now that it is recognised as a serious thing, "years ago if you'd gone to the police station and said your boyfriend hit you, they would've laughed at you."

One of the most serious incidents was when Paul stabbed Sean after a fight. Paul was at home with his friend Fiona and a male acquaintance who he knew from the local housing estate. They had all been out drinking at the Richmond Pub and the man had come back to Paul's as he was interested in Fiona. At 1am, Sean got a female friend of his to drive him over and he came round to the house. Paul was by now very drunk and had had some cocaine with the couple. Sean, as was the norm for him at that time of the night, was also intoxicated.

When Sean came in and saw who was there, he and Paul went to talk in the kitchen and Sean flatly accused the man of being there as he was with Paul. An argument quickly ensued and before Paul knew what was happening, Sean had pinned him to the ground with a broom handle across his throat. Panicking and in self-defence, Paul grabbed for anything he could use to defend himself and set his hand on a small paring knife. He stabbed it into Sean's left leg, just above the ankle. The blade entered about an inch into Sean's body and then Paul pulled the knife out. It was enough to have the desired effect and Sean got off Paul and immediately left the house. Paul followed Sean out as he got back into his friend's car and they sped off with Paul trying in vain to chase after them. When he went back inside, there was blood on the floor and up the walls and door of the kitchen. Much of this was Sean's but Paul realised he was also bleeding heavily from his nose.

Reflecting on it, Paul was not proud that he had stabbed his boyfriend but reasoned that it was 'needs-must' as he genuinely feared for his safety at the time of the assault.

Another night, round at a friend's house in Bolingbroke Road, West Kensington, Paul and Sean were still awake after a long night's drinking. What had started off innocuously enough as a bit of drunken banter soon escalated into a serious fight, as was the pattern of the majority of their arguments – it was almost as if they would squabble and fight for show and because it was expected of them but it could very quickly turn into something much more aggressive.

In this instance, punches were thrown and there were genuine threats of televisions and computers being thrown out of windows. Eventually the situation settled down and whilst seemingly normal enough for the couple, it was quite a scary experience for the handful of friends who sat watching proceedings and wondering where the violence would end.

Paul and Sean also had occasional trips to visit friends in Ireland. One of these friends recalls picking the couple up from Derry airport where they had been drinking heavily on their flight from London. When they were collected, they were already mid-fight and this continued in the car on the way to the friend's home. It got fairly heavy, and Sean, who was sitting in the front seat, turned and threw a big punch at Paul's head with such force that the car seemed to lurch backwards though they were travelling forwards at sixty miles per hour!

Paul though didn't recognise that much of what was happening with his partner was essentially a series of volatile domestic abuse incidents and saw it more as the norm of their relationship.

There was also an ongoing element of denial which Paul found difficult as Sean always maintained a persona of the masculine man and would've refuted his homosexuality to most people, including his mother and close family members. This was a common theme in arguments between the couple where Sean would always act like the hard man and try to demean Paul as being the "poof" and the "gay" in their relationship.

The turbulent juxtaposition of love and violence which percolated through their time together soon began to define their relationship. It was a constant flux of the best and worst parts of having an intimate partner and Paul describes their time together as, "when it was volatile, it was horribly volatile, but when it was good, it was definitely good."

Unfortunately for the couple, despite their obvious love for each other, the sinister nastiness that constantly murmured under the surface was always there as a negative force in their time together and would ultimately prove to be their undoing.

Chapter 23 – Cleaning Cars and Sean's Incarceration

It wasn't all drug or alcohol-fuelled nights out mixed with arguments and fights though. Sean was also in the process of setting up a new business, a car valeting venture called Starcraft, located in Putney, South London. Sean always seemed to have some scheme or idea on the go, with this being the latest one, and Paul was happy to help him get the project off the ground.

Sean had been helped to set up Starcraft with the Prince's Youth Business Trust. He had attended a twelve-week course and then presented his business plan to a board of business people including CEO's from companies like Woolworths and Boots and the famous entrepreneur, Peter Jones. He presented his case for a car wash and the assessment panel liked it as they especially wanted to give disadvantaged people a start in life. They gave him a start-up grant and a business mentor who was a commercial banker, but Sean only saw him once as he probably scared him off with his exuberance and unstable mannerisms!

Paul and Sean were trying to get ready for an opening in the New Year and they were busy mixing cement to make steps on Boxing Day, a year to the day after their very public brawl. Sean was committed to making the business a success and did courses on car valeting, upholstery and bodywork. Paul remembers being enrolled on a three-day course in Kent but never quite making it for a reason that he has long since forgotten.

Sean had the 'gift of the gab', perhaps partly due to his Irish roots. Sean's mother was from Belfast, and Sean would have spent much of his younger days in the Emerald Isle, before his family moved to London. You would never know it from being around him most times, but anyone who had ever heard him on the phone to his mother would immediately make the connection as he would always break into a pure Belfast lilt!

As a result of his undoubted charm, Sean was able to attract lots of people to his new venture and once opened, the business brought in a wide variety of cars that tended to be a mix of the regular punter along with more high-end vehicles and commercial business contracts. The idea with Starcraft was that it was much more than today's throwaway £5 car washes that adorn every side street in every town and city. Sean wanted Starcraft to be an experience, and Paul wanted to help him achieve his vision.

They soon had the business up and running and things were starting to go well. But there was a problem. Sean's love of the high life, combined with his negligent approach to the law and authority meant that he would soon be compromising the future of the business. Soon after opening, Sean started stealing cars out of the car wash.

One of these times was when a customer asked him if he could leave his Porsche at Starcraft for four days. Sean's eyes lit up and he told the man that he could leave the car there for as long as he wanted!

Sean took the car out that night along with a special guest – he had chinchillas in the garage and he took one along with him! First they went to the pub next door, the Rose & Crown in Parson's Green, and Sean swears that the animal was smoking cigarettes, among other things. The odd couple then moved on to the West End together, with the animal jumping all over the dashboard. As with most other parts of Sean's life, it was all about how much fun he could cram into one night.

But it wouldn't last as Sean was to be arrested later that night. This wasn't the first time he had endured this fate and in the short time since the business launched, this was the third time he had been arrested for stealing vehicles out of the car wash. The previous times he had just been given a caution as the police were perhaps lenient when it came across that Sean was a bad boy made good who was trying his best to turn his life around with the new business.

The theft of the Porsche however was the final straw. Sean ended up in Old Compton Street where he burnt the clutch out of the car doing doughnuts. There was so much of a smell that those passing by must have thought the Council were out tarmacking the roads!

Before long the police appeared and when they opened the driver's door of the Porsche, Sean literally fell out onto the street. One of the police officers picked Sean up and said, "Is this your car, sir?" to which Sean responded, "What car?" It was fairly evident that Sean was already in a lot of trouble, but this was compounded when the police tried to take the keys out of the ignition and he attacked them.

He was taken immediately to the nearest station and found himself in court the next day. In total he was facing thirty-seven charges and the judge took just twenty minutes to sentence him to four months in Brixton jail. He would end up serving two months in prison for this series of car thefts and the other charges.

When Sean was sent to prison, Paul was left with the responsibility of Starcraft which he absolutely didn't want but equally, he didn't want it to close while Sean was away. To help him through the stress of carrying his partner's business and missing him terribly at the same time, Paul turned to his tried and tested means of escape and again began using heroin on a regular basis.

The local addicts used to regularly pop in to Starcraft and offer to sell a bike or whatever they had stolen to feed their habit and would often sell a £10 bag of heroin to Paul while they were there so the temptation was nearly always a daily occurrence. He was also able to fund his habit by doing a bit of work for Johnny Fart-Pants, using the Starcraft takings, the benefits he was able to claim and whatever other bits of wheeling and dealing he could engage in.

As before, Paul convinced himself that he was in control. He would never buy anything more than a £20 bag, not enough for a "big hit", just enough to purge, then a bit more, but assuring himself that he was never falling into a major addiction in terms of taking huge amounts.

An incident was soon to occur though that would put a serious dent in Paul's ability to generate additional income and push the ever-patient Johnny Fart-Pants' good nature to the limit. While in prison, Sean had become friendly with a fellow inmate and taking him for a solid acquaintance, had opened up about Paul's access to large quantities of drugs. The inmate, released before Sean, had visited Paul at Starcraft shortly after he had regained his freedom, and asked him to set up a major drug deal.

Paul made the necessary arrangements and organised for Johnny Fart-Pants to come to KFC in Marble Arch. The plan was for Sean's co-convict, along with his associate, to meet Paul and Johnny who brought with him the requested purchase – nine thousand pounds worth of ecstasy tablets.

Once at the rendezvous point, Paul waited at a table as the other three men went to the toilet to conclude the deal. All of a sudden, the two men came running out of the toilet, quickly pursued by Johnny Fart-Pants. Without really understanding what was happening, Paul started running after them as well, and shortly overtook Johnny in the bizarre race. The men turned a corner and jumped into their waiting car. Paul managed to keep pace with them and climbed into the back of the car just as they sped off.

The men drove to Lewisham where they exited the car and entered a house. Paul went in with them and it soon materialised that Sean's new friend was simply a con man who had pumped Sean for information. The men had grabbed the drugs in the KFC toilets and literally ran for it, without the intention of ever paying for their hoard. During the earlier proceedings, Paul had been told he would get a cut from the deal so was lingering impatiently for his cash, but the men refused to give him any money. After two days of waiting and receiving nothing but takeaway food, it dawned on Paul that he was never going to be paid for his part of the scheme, so he finally gave up and left.

Although Paul knew that Johnny would've known he wasn't part of the scam, Paul felt it best to avoid him anyway. Paul wasn't out on the club scene any more and the chances of running into his old associate were slim, so he just rode it out and eventually it all blew over.

It also helped Paul's cause that he was even harder to trace than before, having moved out of Sue's place. He was now living in a small, rented studio flat between Baronscourt and West Kensington, just behind Queen's Tennis Club. The new pad became somewhere that Paul was out of more than he was in and when he was there it was invariably just to sleep off his latest binge.

Again, Paul didn't want Sean to know he was using heroin but he was about to be found out as Paul's friend Damien had been using heroin at the flat. Paul had a problem with the sink and asked the letting agent, Julie, who was also a friend of both Paul and Sean's to get it fixed. Julie got her partner, Dave, to fix the problem but it materialised that this had been caused by syringes stuck in the u-bend which Paul is convinced Damien had left there. Dave told Julie what had happened, and she told Sean during a visit to him in prison.

After Sean was released, Paul came clean and told him about his heroin use. Sean said although he had never tried heroin in prison, he did try Subutex, the heroin substitute, but only did it once and didn't like it. He had put it under his tongue and let it dissolve as you're supposed to but then wrote a far-too-honest three-page letter to a female acquaintance who was an ex-girlfriend from many years ago, and posted it. However, as soon as he came down he realised what he had done. He described sending the letter as, "like releasing a Cruise missile", so he then desperately, but unsuccessfully, tried to retrieve it. Not surprisingly, he has never spoken to the woman again!

Fairly obviously, with such a volatile ownership, things didn't always go according to the business plan at Starcraft. One time, a customer had brought his white MG to be cleaned and wanting a full valet, had left it overnight with Paul. Another customer returning from a foreign trip that day had given Paul a bottle of brandy.

The combination would ultimately be a tempting and dangerous coincidence. Paul drank the brandy with the customer and then they went to the Rose & Crown up the road and took a couple of ecstasy pills together. Paul went to make a call to Sean from the Starcraft payphone and he said he was at Sue's house. It's a ten minute walk from the garage to Sue's but Paul thought he would instead take the MG for a spin.

It was beginning to get dark. Paul got as far as Sue's road and heard a click and thought it was the wing mirror clipping a parked car. Then it happened again, followed by a scrape, and Paul realised that it wasn't the mirror but the actual wing of the MG that had hit several parked cars. Paul stopped and got out to have a look. The whole of the MG's wing was severely dented as were the line of parked cars, although luckily none of the owners of these were in the vicinity to see what had happened.

Paul decided to do what he tended to do in these situations - he rang Nick Lewis. Round the corner from where the accidents had occurred was 'Roy's Garage'. Roy was a good friend of Nick's and was able to get the MG repaired. The bill came to £500 which Nick gave to Paul to settle the account.

The next day when the owner came to collect his car, Paul told him that some kids had jumped over the wall and done some damage but that he had sorted it. The man with the MG later sold that car and bought a red Corvette, and Paul would often see him drive past Starcraft but strangely enough, he never brought his new car in!

The business model was actually a very good one and Starcraft could have gone on to much bigger and better things but for one other major flaw – the owners weren't overly concerned with ploughing any profits back into the business. The more money they made, the more money Paul and Sean spent, usually on 'essential' items like drink and drugs.

There was also an issue with the location of the car valeting business, under the arches, near Putney Station, in that the next two businesses on the street were the pub next door, The Rose & Crown, and a wine bar further up the road. The norm was to collect the daily takings, then go next door and spend most of the profits in the pub.

The wine bar was called The Pen and this was where they spent a lot of time as well, although it was much more upmarket than the pub. Sean claims to have met Jeremy Clarkson here one night. Sean was partaking in some nice cocaine and kept making a point of telling Clarkson that it was "top gear" that he had consumed!

The Pen was a fancy wine bar with a restaurant upstairs. At the end of the first full year of Starcraft, Sean decided to throw an end-of-year staff Christmas party. As the 'staff' were just Paul and Sean, along with a couple of students, Brendan and Danny, who they had roped in when they weren't able (or more often couldn't be bothered) to be there, Sean also invited Danny's girlfriend, Siobhan, and a selection of his friends and extended family members along too.

It was an extravagant affair and started off in fine style with an opening starter dish of muscles but before the main arrived, the night disintegrated into a free-for-all riot with Sean's family suddenly having an explosive falling out with a full scale fight ensuing. While this startled many of the guests, Paul was completely unperturbed, stating that this was the usual outcome any time Sean's family were together.

As the night wore on Paul became aware that he hadn't seen Sean for a while. The manager of The Pen had approached Paul and was asking where Sean was as he wanted him to settle the bill. Paul managed to get hold of Sean by phone, who by this time was at his mum's house. Sean had realised at some stage that he wouldn't be able to pay for the night out or perhaps the plan had always been to do a runner, but either way the outstanding bill remained unpaid.

Paul left shortly afterwards and met up later with Sean. Having no money to pay the bill, Sean called round the next day to The Pen and settled up with a few hundred acid tabs that he happened to have stashed away so it all worked out well!

Despite the initial success of Starcraft, trouble was never far away, especially financially. Paul and Sean would come round, pay the boys and then take all the earnings. This meant there was never any money for anything else.

To try and get things in order, Sean visited Starcraft to assess the state of the business and found a pile of unpaid bills for things like business tax and utilities. The signwriters from whom he rented the space for the valeting hadn't been paid for months and were putting the pressure on. There were no materials left to speak of and almost all the Autoglym cleaning products were empty. Sean took the money that was left and told Brendan and Danny that the business would close that day, once all the cars were gone.

The students quickly set about getting the remaining cars finished. They got most of them done and were down to the last few cars when the air began to get cooler. It was winter and it was close to freezing so they doubled their efforts and had every car ready for collection, bar one, a nearly new VW estate.

The boys set to work on the final one, hoovered and cleaned the interior, washed the exterior and then applied polish to the paintwork. They then began to clean the windows as the air started to freeze. The boys just had to complete the removal of the polish and to buff the car up before it was finished.

They removed the polish from one side of the car but as the air was by now so cold, the polish on the other side of the car had frozen and was impossible to get off. As the customer was shortly arriving for collection, the students turned the car around so that the polished side was visible in the street light that shone into the yard. The customer arrived, paid the boys, thanked them and then drove off.

Immediately, the students took the last of the money, quickly closed up the gates and posted the keys back through the letterbox. No doubt the owner of the last car to ever be cleaned at Starcraft came back the next day to complain but would've been shocked to find that not only was nobody there, but that the business had closed for good with no sign of any of the staff or the owners. It was 1995. Paul was twenty-eight. Starcraft, and with it the latest of Sean's dreams, had come to an end.

To make up for the closure of the business, Paul soon got a job working at Substation as front of house staff. Substation was a basement gay club with an industrial corrugated look about it in Falkenburg Court, just opposite Centre Point on Tottenham Court Road. He had got the role through an acquaintance called Martin Confusion who used to work at World doing the shifts that Tim didn't do, and through a friendship developed at Shoom with Wayne Shires, who owned and ran Substation.

Shires was a local club promoter who had originally been influenced by clubs like Shoom and Kinky Gerlinky and was now beginning a long-term role at the forefront of London's underground queer culture by opening his own venue. Substation was extremely popular among London's gay community and in addition, featured in several pop videos, including the huge Stretch & Vern hit, I'm Alive. Paul had met Shires at Shoom and these social liaisons, along with the connection to Martin, helped Paul get the job.

Shires also set up and ran Substation South in Brixton and was soon to move the main Substation venue to Dean Street, although this venture proved something of a headache for the promoter and his team. The police would often turn up at the club where there would always be a throng of young men with their shirts off. The police would say to Shires, "your licence says people need to be properly attired, tell them to put their shirts back on" and Shires would stand at the door arguing with the police saying, "you go and tell them to put their shirts back on!"

This happened on several occasions and eventually, Shires was taken to court owing to one Friday night when the club was visited by the

Vice Squad. All of a sudden, five officers arrived in trench coats and asked, "can we have a walk around?" Shires took them through the back entrance to the club and literally as they walked onto the dance floor, one of the clubbers dropped to his knees and started giving another man a blow-job! Shires immediately whacked him round the back of the head and said, "Security! Throw them out! And if they have memberships, take it off them!" It wasn't enough though and when Shires and the officers finished walking round the club, the police turned and said "Mr Shires, you are not obliged to say anything…….."

Subsequently, Shires was prosecuted for running a 'disorderly house' and ended up at the Magistrate's Court. However, his business partner at the time had been getting grief from the police for years. He wasn't having any of it so he got the best barristers and eventually the case was thrown out.

In the present day, Shires now runs clubs for 'bears and cubs'. In the homosexual world, bears are big and hairy (in layman's terms - fat blokes) and cubs are essentially young bears who are less fat and less hairy. There are literally hundreds of terms that have been invented to describe gay men and it is usually gays themselves who coin the descriptions. Clones is another commonly used one, with a clone being a gay man with an exaggerated macho behaviour and appearance. Among the vast list of other homosexual slang words are popular terms including chicken (a young man), gym bunny/Muscle Mary (a man who works out purely for the aesthetic look), wolf (someone who falls between a chicken and a bear), twink (a young, small man with no body hair), bear chasers (men who desire bears), bottom (the receptive gay man who takes it rather than giving it), top (the gay man who gives it), otter (a thin, hairy gay man), poz (a HIV positive man) and daddy (an older, financially established gay man) – the latter being one of Paul's personal favourites throughout his life.

Sean would be a frequent visitor to Substation though this began to irk Paul greatly as the barmen would give Sean free drinks as he was Paul's boyfriend. This was probably intended as a friendly gesture but Paul became increasingly jealous and annoyed about it. He was the one that was at work and felt that Sean was just riding on his wave and getting all the benefits without actually doing anything.

Paul's insecurities were heightened with Sean being very attractive, and gaining a lot of attention. Paul felt Sean was overly-friendly with a lot of people that Paul knew and the green-eyed demon was out in full force when Sean got very friendly with one barman in particular. This annoyed Paul immensely, having to watch his boyfriend having more fun than he was and enjoying endless flirting with his friends while he was at work!

There was a fun aspect to the work though in that Sean would drive Paul to Substation early each night and for the first hour, before anyone came in, Paul would go and play tunes in the DJ booth. He loved spinning tracks in the empty club and hammered favourites such as Electribe 101's, Talking With Myself, the S'Express banger, Theme from S'Express and a variety of other house tunes that he loved.

True to form though, along with the flirting and the partying, Sean was also always on the periphery of violence and danger. One night, he had gone to the toilets in Substation and at the urinals a man kept trying to grab his penis. Sean kept telling him to "fuck off", but the man persisted. After several attempts, Sean gave the man a backhand punch to the face, splitting his nose and knocking him to the floor. As the man lay bleeding and clutching his nose, Sean stepped over him and said, "oh, I'm sorry", and walked out of the toilets!

At Substation, Paul's job was on the door. Customers would have to get past the outside door staff, including, as Paul recalls, a gorgeous guy called Rob. Punters would then either pay to get in or be down to get in free on the guest list. Each member of the bar staff had two names they were allowed to put on the list but if the staff were nice to Paul, they would get more. The bouncers would click the customers in and the paying ones would then give Paul their money and he'd put it into a tray under a shelf at the door.

Paul also used the job for one of his life-long habits – the ability to wangle more than he was actually meant to get. At the weekend, on Friday and Saturday nights when it was really busy, Paul would often secretly help himself to a handful of money, often hundreds of pounds.

After Paul had finished doing the door at Substation, he would also top up his earnings by doing a bit of club promotion for various other clubs around London. Paul would go to venues and hand out fliers to the next club. This was a great time to be out if you wanted a night that just kept on going with free buses that would take punters to all parts of London and onwards to another late-night club.

Paul had quite a degree of control over who could get in at Substation and certainly who had to pay for the privilege. The club was nearly exclusively male and while there were the odd one or two lesbians, generally it was all men.

One night however he made a serious error of judgement when three foreign, clearly heterosexual couples, all wearing dressy clothes and announcing that they had just been to the theatre, arrived at the door of the club. They were met by Paul, sitting there chewing gum and ungraciously looking them up and down. As was his prerogative, Paul gave them a bit of verbal abuse and refused to let them in. He told them in some colourful language that the club was for gays only and that the policy was to not let heterosexual people in.

The group looked like they were lost and had stumbled upon this large industrial gay nightclub so Paul thought he was doing them a favour by turning them away. But, unknown to Paul, the visitors were good friends of Shires who had insisted they come and see the club during their trip to London! Owing to the way he had treated them, Paul got the sack and thus his time at Substation came to an abrupt end.

The footnote here is simply another case of Paul starting something but never quite being able to make a prolonged go of it, as is his blueprint.

Chapter 24 – Guilty, Your Honour

Sean's situation would become very complicated when alongside several new driving offences and non-payment of fines, he was prosecuted for a serious assault where he violently attacked a man with a Gucci shoe that he had been wearing. This very serious offence took place in Victoria and was later deemed in court to be an offence worse than Grievous Bodily Harm, and only prevented from being a manslaughter charge because fortunately the man didn't die.

It was now four years after Sean's previous stay at Her Majesty's pleasure and Sean was working as a ticket seller for the Original London Sight-Seeing Tour Company who ran tour buses all across London. He was working at Grosvenor Gardens in Victoria and after work, he went to an old Irish gay bar called The Stag. Sean started chatting to an attractive man in the bar but shortly afterwards, news began to filter through about a bomb going off at the Admiral Duncan.

The Admiral Duncan was a bar in Old Compton Street in Soho and that evening, on the 30th April 1999, a neo-Nazi called David Copeland carried out a nail bomb attack that would kill three people and injure seventy more, many of them seriously. Copeland, intending to stir up racist and homophobic tensions, had already carried out two hate-crime bomb attacks that month in Brixton and in Whitechapel.

For his final attack, he left a bag containing the bomb in the Admiral Duncan. Some of the patrons had noticed it and the bar manager was in the process of investigating it when it exploded just after 6.30pm. The front of the bar was literally blown into the street in the blast, and glass and debris filled the air as the burnt, injured and maimed victims stumbled out of the now destroyed bar into the road outside.

Once the news of the bomb reached The Stag, the man that had been chatting to Sean made up his mind that it must have been a terrorist attack carried out by the IRA. Earlier in their exchanges, Sean had mentioned to him that he was originally from Belfast. Now with the news of the Admiral Duncan attack filtering through, the man began personally singling Sean out and saying, "it's one of your mob, you Irish cunt."

Soon after though, the emotions settled down and Sean left the bar with the man with the intention of going back to his place. But on the way the man would not relent and kept picking at Sean, blaming him in an ill-founded and misguided association for the Admiral Duncan bombing.

Eventually Sean became so annoyed at the man's persistent accusations and, with his blood boiling inside of him, elbowed him full in the face, knocking the man to the ground. Sean is neither an aggressive nor a violent man but when he fights, he fights hard. With his full force, Sean then stamped on the man's face, so hard that he left a Gucci stamp just above the man's eyebrow. It was this imprint that would later condemn him when the police caught up with him and found him to be in possession of the offending footwear.

In court for the Victoria 'Gucci' assault, Sean initially pleaded not guilty as the man had provoked him, but he would later change his plea. Following the trial, he got sentenced to three and a half years in prison.

Of these, Sean would serve eighteen months with a further four months on licence, where he had to wear an ankle tag. This was on a twelve-hour timer and he had to be home every day from 7pm to 7am otherwise he would've breached his conditions of release.

Sean though was no stranger to prison. He had served his first term in 1985 when he was given a three-week sentence for wearing a t-shirt with indecent drawings and inciting words on it. He would then go on to spend the next twenty years in and out of prison, although nearly always his offences were as a result of being intoxicated.

Sean describes prison as very violent, unforgiving places. The safest ones are actually the highest category ones, called 'A Cats or Cat A's', like Belmarsh in south-east London and Frankland in Durham. This is due to the fact that they house many of the country's most violent and dangerous criminals and therefore, there are more officers per prisoner, intensive searches are commonplace and there is less opportunity for violence within the prison.

The more dangerous institutions are Cat B's, Cat C's and Cat D's. Throughout Sean's time in prison, he has done the tour and has been in Belmarsh on four separate occasions, Wormwood Scrubs in inner west

London (a Cat B prison that was built in the Victorian era) eight times, and Wandsworth in south-west London (Cat B, and one of the largest prisons in Western Europe) four times.

In Wandsworth, famous for being the prison that Ronnie Biggs, the Great Train Robber, escaped from in 1965, Sean was 'tea-boy' for the 'screws' for a period of eighteen months. This meant looking after the staff while they were working, which in turn led to massive privileges for Sean.

It is a surprise that Paul has been involved in many criminal activities and has often been before the law but yet he has never received a custodial sentence. Ironic too that he would have a partner that spent a lot of time in prison, before and during their relationship.

Sean thinks this may have something to do with Paul's uncanny luck as much as anything. Prisons are aligned to serve the courts in the area in which they operate and prisons will accept all suitable prisoners from the courts in their catchment zone. For example, Wandsworth Prison will serve Westminster Magistrates, Southwark Crown Court and Isleworth Crown Court, while Belmarsh serves the Old Bailey. What seemed to always go in Paul's favour was the factor of where he was arrested, which then had a direct correlation to the court he was committed to attend. These courts were often more lenient since they were located in areas where the prisons were at maximum capacity, thus meaning lesser charges weren't deemed worthy of a custodial sentence.

While good fortune was undoubtedly on his side, Paul, despite not being squeaky clean, didn't carry with him quite the level of baggage that Sean brought to every court hearing. Throughout his criminal career he has amassed almost fifty previous convictions and somewhere in the region of eighty charges have been brought against him. This means that every time he is brought before a magistrate or judge, they look at his 'previous' and this will certainly work against any individual as the charge sheet racks up.

Like many criminals who haven't committed any terrible crimes, Sean started off in courts by being fined. As he puts it, "If Satan had a business, it would be courts", and he is convinced that POLICE stands for "Paid Officers Lying In Court Evidence!"

Then, the transgressor usually moves on to Community Service although Sean maintains that he'd rather go to prison than carry out eighty hours of unpaid work in a week. Sean found this type of sentence especially difficult when he had spent a Saturday night out raving and then had to report the following morning to "paint a shitty fence out of my nut!"

Out of all the time he has spent in jail, Sean certainly doesn't see it as all bad. He has had some of his favourite times inside and definitely some of the funniest situations and best laughs. He describes Belmarsh as a "top nick" and has always remembered meeting different people as he has invariably been sober. On the outside, he has had many experiences but they are usually clouded by drink and drugs so the memories are hazy. But he recalls vividly most of his time spent in prison.

Many people make criminal associations in prison and instead of being the intended setting for constructive rehabilitation, it can often become a breeding ground for developing relationships between convicts that they then use on the outside to further their illegal pursuits. And Sean was no different, forming many friendships that continued to serve him long after he had left the respective jails.

Sean also ensured he trod a careful line of staying friendly with most of his fellow inmates. In Wormwood Scrubs there were a lot of prisoners from the Irish Traveller community on 'A wing', along with the native English gangs. Fighting was frequent and it wouldn't be uncommon for one or other side to go to a rival cell and issue a severe beating before retreating to the sanctuary of their own. Due mainly to the name he carried, he was accepted by the Irish contingent and because of his accent, character and humour, he remained on good terms with the English too. If push came to shove, he was loyal and stuck with the Irish but he was also mindful that, when the pushing and the shoving became overtly violent, he was aware enough to maintain a respectful distance from both factions.

Prison isn't a nice place - it's a dangerous environment where people constantly hide behind a mask and where you have to watch your back all the time. It can be hard to accurately gauge a man's genuine personality. Sean has often met people inside who he really liked and felt were nice, decent characters. But when he met them again on the outside, he realised how nasty and violent many of them were.

In prison, Sean wasn't seen as high-risk so always shared a cell and in the main, kept himself clean and stayed out of trouble. For Sean, half the battle was getting a good cellmate and this, he feels, can make all the difference between a positive or negative spell in prison.

After two years, Sean was released, on licence, for the Gucci shoe attack. When he got out, he moved in with Paul and managed to borrow £30,000 from a long-standing family friend called Pat. Sean needed the money for his latest idea – to start a limousine company – and he used the cash to buy a black American Lincoln Town Executive Series limo which was thirty-two feet long.

Through the limo business he met many interesting people, including some of the Gumball 3000 organising team, who he drove around for the duration of that year's race calendar.

It wouldn't last long though as, true to form, he destroyed the car later on that same year. This occurred when he was driving the limousine for a booking which involved taking three generations of the same family out – the grandparents, parents and children – for the child's birthday party.

Sean drove the family to Planet Hollywood on Coventry Street and once there, the clients went inside the restaurant. Sean decided he would use his spare time while he waited to go and have a drink, which inevitably turned into several drinks.

By the time Sean returned to his car, he was staggering slightly and inadvertently got into an argument with a man who happened to be standing outside Planet Hollywood.

Unknown to Sean, there were several police officers in the vicinity who had observed the incident. When Sean's clients came out, he helped them into the limo and then went to drive off. As he did so, a police officer jumped in front of the car but instead of stopping, Sean instead floored the accelerator, and the officer had to jump out of the way. Sean would later note that, "the cunt scratched my wing mirror with the buttons on his jacket."

Sean sped off down Coventry Street, flew into Wardour Street where it connects with Whitcomb Street and then threw a hard right into Panton Street. As he approached Haymarket, there was another policeman in the road waving his arms but Sean just floored it again and the policeman jumped out of the way.

Sean screeched into Haymarket and got the limousine up to about 80mph but when he looked in his wing mirrors, he saw that the street was awash with blue lights and the sound of sirens.

He careered on down Haymarket past Her Majesty's Theatre and took the bend towards Trafalgar Square but as he did so, he clipped the kerb and was forced to pull over.

Sean was promptly arrested by the pursuing police and charged with dangerous driving. His passengers, who had spent the hair-raising, short trip laughing in the back of the limo, instead had to find themselves a couple of cabs to get home.

Ironically, the date of the court hearing featured Sean involved in another case of speeding, though it was to materialise that this particular 'need for speed' was ultimately in vain.

Sean had driven to the Haçienda in Manchester in his limousine which he had just got back from the repair shop, along with Paul, Johnny Fart-Pants, Felix (the digital music artist and DJ) and Natalie (Adamski's "ugly bird", as Sean describes her). They all got absolutely hammered and Sean remembers literally rolling around on the floor of the club.

The following morning, Sean awoke and found himself lying on the floor of the hotel lobby they were staying in. As he slowly opened his eyes, something awful dawned on him and he suddenly jumped up and shouted, "fuck, I've got court today."

Sean drove back to London doing 90mph down the hard shoulder in rush hour traffic. But when he arrived at the court, "sweating like a rapist", they told him he was a day early! He couldn't believe it.

Ironically, when he turned up the next day, which was the correct date, he actually appeared a bit late for his hearing! They tried to throw the book at him but Sean pleaded that the day before he had been there early. The judge eventually relented and fortunately for Sean, he was released on bail.

It wasn't to last though as, while on bail, Sean was arrested again, this time for falling asleep at the wheel while paralytically drunk.

He was driving near Hyde Park and had been partying for the best part of four days when he dozed off, claiming that it was because he had no-one to talk to in the car to keep him awake. Although, in reality, it was perhaps more honestly that he hadn't slept in days and had been drinking solidly for most of that time.

As he was falling asleep, his foot slipped onto the accelerator and the car quickly sped forwards.

Suddenly, Sean was awoken by a loud explosion and as he stumbled out of the car and noted the damage, he was alarmed to see that he had essentially turned his limousine into a saloon car, although he was struggling to see what he had actually connected with. Before he knew it, a man appeared shouting, "you cunt, you've hit my motor." Sean realised that the point of impact had been him destroying this man's car so he decided to make a run for it. He got about ten feet away, before collapsing into a nearby bush!

The police promptly arrived, arrested him and removed him to Paddington Green police station. On account of the serious breach of his bail conditions, he was taken straight to Belmarsh Prison for yet another stint.

He had finally managed to get a legitimate driving licence earlier that year and had business insurance so he told the insurance company that he had been driving some clients who had got him drunk and he then crashed the limo.

Amazingly, the insurance paid out as the incident was seen as being covered under the business policy and therefore the liability was not attributable solely to Sean as the driver. It worked against him personally however as he was prosecuted for driving a public service vehicle, as opposed to a private car, and this was one of the reasons that he went straight to prison for the crime.

Aside from the car valeting business, Sean's other main responsibility that was impacted by his regular visits to prison was his dog, a Dalmatian called Pepper. Paul didn't have room to keep the dog in his small flat, and Pepper had already been passed around a bit as Sean had originally bought the dog and given it to Sue but then Sue gave it back after a while.

When Sean went to prison, the only option was for Pepper to stay at Sean's mum's house. To help out, Paul used to go down there every day to walk Pepper and clear up the dog mess in the back garden and this led to Paul getting to know more and more of Sean's mum.

As with most Irish households, the kitchen was the hub of the home and they would sit for hours, playing cards or the game, Frustration, often with Sean's sisters Maria and Liz. Ironically when Sean was on the outside and on the rare occasions they would visit, they never played cards or Frustration but for Paul, without his partner, this became something of a daily custom.

When he wasn't in prison, Sean mainly stayed with Paul and kept his family at arm's length so Paul had only known Sean's mother vaguely. Up to this point, Sean's mum and sisters thought that Paul was simply a mate of Sean's.

Every time Paul went to visit Sean in prison, he would always go round to Sean's mother's house straight afterwards to let her know how her son was getting on. Often Paul would be very emotional after seeing Sean and it was becoming increasingly difficult for him to hide his feelings from Sean's mum. Eventually after one such prison visit, Paul told Sean's mum that Sean was gay and that they were partners. Although Paul maintains that up to this point she didn't know, he feels that to a certain extent mums always know so she must have had some idea.

The conversation just carried on after the disclosure, a kind of 'nothing has happened' scenario, although Paul puts this more down to her need to fully digest the information or her contemplating her response as a holy Catholic Irish mother before she revealed her true reaction.

It had been so difficult for Paul to contain himself in the weeks leading up to his confession, but afterwards he felt relieved that he had done what he had. Paul still of course had to tell Sean what he had said, which he did the next time he visited him.

In response, Sean wrote a letter and asked Paul to bring it to his mum. On arriving at the family home, Sean's mum couldn't bring herself to read it, instead giving the letter to Maria. Maria read it aloud and the letter confirmed that Sean and Paul were together and that he was indeed gay.

Following this, Paul was relieved to be embraced by the family, by everyone except Sean's mum's sister. Sean's aunt effectively accused Paul of making Sean gay. If Paul went to the house and asked if everyone wanted tea, the aunt would blank Paul completely and he didn't know why but was later told it was for his horrendous crime of turning the young nephew into a homosexual! Sean though maintains that his family always knew about his homosexuality and that they knew from 1994. As Sean puts it, "I didn't actually come out, I just appeared!"

In the end, all the family accepted Sean for what he was. He reveals that he didn't actually say, "I'm gay", because he maintains that he isn't gay – he says he is "an iron", from the Cockney rhyming slang 'iron hoof' or 'poof'. Sean declares that the difference is that he doesn't register on the 'gaydar' and that he sends out straight signals. He is sure that he scares the gays off and that it is women, and not men, who are generally attracted to him, describing it as having "all these birds" on his case.

Sean does feel an attraction back towards some girls but as he puts it, "I like the little pink bit in the middle, but it's the rest of it around it I can't handle!"

So is he a 'straight-gay' then, as it were? "I'm just me", he asserts, and that is probably the best way to sum up, or not sum up, the undoubted love of Paul's life.

Chapter 25 – Moving Around & Seeking Traction, Mr Jarvis?

Paul had decided that the studio flat in West Kensington was too small and that he wanted to move. In order to do this, he would need an eviction letter from the local Council. To help with this process, he stated to the Council that he was getting intimidated by kids on the steps near the flat who were annoying the dogs and that along with his depression, he was finding it hard to cope. It was mostly true but as everyone who wants to be rehoused in London does, Paul played up on the issues.

Eventually, the Council gave in and moved him temporarily to a tiny B&B in Russell Road. It was so small that although it was classed as a double-bed property, it was actually just two single beds laid widthways. Paul wasn't happy and phoned the Council every day to get moved. Fortunately he would only stay in the property for one month before he was moved to Hesketh Place which was described as a hostel but was really a studio flat. Paul would spend the next nine months of his life here while he waited to be properly rehoused.

Finally, after the months of waiting, Paul was relocated to somewhere he actually wanted to live and was given a larger flat in Oxford Gardens, near Portobello Market.

After so long, Paul was beginning to feel settled and for the first time in many years, he felt he was building up a secure level of traction.

To accelerate this process he managed to secure employment, as a postman with the Royal Mail.

In the beginning the job really suited Paul. He would start work at 6am and be finished his round and back on the nice balcony of his flat in Oxford Gardens by 11am each morning. He would have his breakfast, and then enjoy the rest of the day which would invariably involve drinking, sometimes in the flat but often going to the pub with some of his postal colleagues. The others would usually leave at some stage but Paul would often stay until closing time, crawl home to bed and then get up and go to work the next day.

Occasionally he would just keep drinking through the night and turn up for work completely inebriated. However, the managers at the delivery depot didn't care what state their postmen were in as long as they could still do the job. If a postman was unfit for work for any reason, the managers would have had to deliver the mail themselves, a task that they generally felt was beneath them, so they didn't care as long as the mail kept getting delivered.

The pay was good and the hours were good. It was a great job to have back then, perhaps not so good now, but in Paul's day it was a nice position to be in.

To build on his sense of stability, Paul made a conscious decision to do something that would make him less likely to go out all the time - he got a little dog and named her Smudge. Paul got Smudge mainly as he knew it would force him to take on more responsibility and to keep him out of the pubs and clubs, and it worked. At this stage of his life, he literally couldn't sit in his own company. If he was out of his nut, he had to go out and he couldn't sit around sober at home for too long either.

Smudge was a Parsons Jack Russell. This type of dog is a terrier which is bred more for showing than working. It is taller than a standard Jack Russell, with a longer head and larger chest. Paul saw her in the paper and although it went against everything he knew he shouldn't do, he couldn't help himself.

He phoned the number in the ad and arranged to meet the person, a Traveller woman, at a nearby train station. Paul went as arranged, and there they had the dog for sale. He never saw the puppy with its mother as you're supposed to, but he couldn't resist her once he had set his eyes on the tiny animal. Smudge was definitely the runt of the litter and this was something that resonated with Paul as he has always called himself the runt of his own litter.

Paul then headed away for another trip to Ireland and brought Smudge with him. On this occasion, they went with his friend Micky and her friend from Kenya, who has since sadly passed away.

Micky's family had an old thatched cottage that had been left in a state of disrepair and this is where they resided. After a couple of weeks, Micky and her friend went back home but Paul stayed behind for a while to paint the cottage. He loved the freedom of living in the wilds of Donegal with its simple pleasures and laid-back approach, far from the craziness of London. The sense of calm Paul felt during these extra few days in Ireland were to stay with him and leave him often yearning to come back to this way of living.

When Paul flew back to England, Sean met him at the airport and as a surprise, had brought him another little puppy, completely white save for a black dot on his back. The dog would be called Ink and was to become the latest addition to the Byfield family.

Smudge however wasn't that old and the two dogs didn't like each other at all. They were always growling at each other, especially as Ink was a short Jack Russell. Paul didn't think too much of it though and as it was a present from Sean, he felt obliged to keep him, which he did for two more years.

During this time, the dogs constantly battled for supremacy. Paul had again returned to Ireland and this time he brought both dogs with him. He was in a car with Micky with the two dogs on his lap when unexpectedly, they started viciously fighting over a bag of crisps. Micky had to stop the car and Paul literally threw the dogs out to let them finish their battle at the roadside.

Back in London, Paul went to the vet who said that he would have to get rid of one of the dogs or one of them would literally kill the other. So Paul took Ink to Battersea Dog's Home to say goodbye and experienced one of the saddest, though most humane, things he has ever had to do. Although he knew it was for the best, Paul was inconsolable for several days afterwards and missed the little rascal that he had grown to love as one of his own.

Although Ink was now gone, Paul had enjoyed having two dogs around him, when they got on at least. So he then decided to deliberately get Smudge pregnant.

There was a girl who lived round the corner from him in Oxford Gardens and she had a tan and white, male Parsons Jack Russell. They let the dogs mate in a little park just off Portobello Road and soon after, Smudge gave birth to four pups.

Paul kept the first born and christened him Bruise, a pup who was the same tan and white colour as his father. The litter also included Charlie, who lived for a while with Paul's mum, although he turned out to be a "right nutter" and was ultimately rehomed to Sean's brother, Joe, a recovering alcoholic. Paul's old friend, Waqar, took another one - a female pup called Sally who ended up getting run over near Clapham Common. And the other one was given away to a friend of Paul's.

Paul's second attempt at managing two dogs together started out much like the previous effort. Smudge couldn't stand Bruise as the new pup got lots of attention where before she was the only dog in the household. Smudge worked out the best way to definitely stay top dog was to let Bruise think that he was the master but just once in a blue moon, she'd pin him down with her paw to remind him who was really in charge.

Paul observed all this behaviour and loved seeing the dynamics of the wonderful canines. He understood the attitude of the young pup who "took the piss left, right and centre". And he admired the calmness of the long-suffering mother and marvelled at her occasional, though very forceful, reminder to her son that whatever happened, she was still the one in control.

Sadly though, Paul wouldn't have long to enjoy the two rivals finding their way in life together. Unexpectedly, Smudge began suffering from liver shunts when she was eight years old. This is a condition that affects dogs when the main vein that processes blood though the liver is not properly connected and therefore blood normally detoxified by the liver will bypass it and go directly into circulation throughout the animal's body.

This is usually a very serious issue and, as would happen to poor Smudge, can often prove fatal. Paul had taken her to the vets on numerous occasions where he was given lots of medicine and he had to give her mouth syringes every three hours for a period. But, it was ultimately in vain, and soon after, she had to be put down.

Having been around dogs all his life, Paul knew that eight was a very young age for a dog to die and he felt robbed of his precious mother-pet. Paul had lost his nan before, but the way he grieved for Smudge was the most he had ever suffered in terms of the impact a loved one's death had on him. And Paul's sadness at losing Smudge only heightened his great affinity with the dogs that he cared for.

What was far less tangible in his life was the link he felt to the name that he carried. Increasingly, he was building up feelings of resentment that he should be walking around carrying the surname, Byfield. Paul was very aware of how his step-sibling's father, Mr Byfield, had domestically assaulted Paul's mother, forcing her into leaving several of her own children with him. For years Paul carried Mr Byfield's name, but this was a man that he had no affinity with, had never met and whose first name he didn't even know.

He came to the conclusion that he didn't want to carry the surname of someone that was so alien to him, that he'd never seen and who had been abusive to his beloved mum.

Paul's alleged biological father, Mr Brown, had always denied that Paul was his so he didn't want that name either.

He decided instead to take his mother's maiden name which was Jarvis. Paul went to see a solicitor near where he lived, a very feminine, almost transgender, Asian man. Paul brought along his passport, filled out a form and paid his money, just £50. As it is so simple, with this easy process anyone can just pick a name that they want, anything from Mickey Mouse to his chosen new name of Paul Henry Jarvis.

Paul has always felt a lot more Jarvis than Byfield. At the time of his change his brother, Johnny, carried the name Brown and his other siblings were, and still are, Byfield. Later, Paul would speak to Johnny and find out that he had gone from Brown to Byfield, thinking it was his mum's maiden name. Johnny and his dad, Johnny Brown, didn't work out as Johnny the boy was always being looked after by whoever his father was seeing at the time so he ended up resenting the dad who had taken him in, but not really followed through on his paternal duties.

As well as denying Paul, Johnny Senior had also always denied that Elaine was his. But with Elaine in her early twenties and her father getting older, he realised that he would have no daughters so he then suddenly tried to claim her, showering her with gifts such as a Mini and a Triumph car. This really annoyed Paul as Elaine welcomed her father with open arms after so many years of him denying them. Paul's pain was made all the more graphic by their father finally claiming her, but still not him, let alone buying her the cars.

In total, Paul would spend six years at Oxford Gardens. But towards the end, he felt like he had outgrown the place. Paul craved more space than he currently had and was getting increasingly frustrated with the amount of young people constantly hanging around at the end of the stairwell by his flat, smoking and annoying his dogs.

Paul had moved so much as a child and throughout his adult life and really didn't like staying anywhere for too long. In hindsight, he feels that his family should really have been Travellers, such was their liking for continually being on the move!

He felt that his time at Oxford Gardens was done and that again, it was time to move.

Chapter 26 – A Broken Hand to Steal the Post

By now it was 2003. Paul was gearing up for his next move, this time to Carlton House on the Henry Dickens Estate on St Anns Road in Notting Hill, where he would reside for only a short period of four and a half months. It was a one-bedroom property but was quite roomy and was on the ground floor so was handy for the dogs to access the outside.

Paul was involved in the Council house bidding process where points are allocated to prospective tenants for a variety of reasons. The more points an individual has, the more choice they get in finding their next property. Paul was informed that he was behind someone in the bidding phase but they decided against taking the Carlton House tenancy, so it was offered to Paul.

He was just beginning to get settled in when, not long after, there was a major incident which affected Paul greatly. Around Carlton House, there was a large group of teenagers who were born and bred on the estate – this was their manor, they were known to everyone and they didn't answer to anybody. Suddenly Paul had moved in, a strange combination of mixed-race, gay and a postman. Then there was Sean, who was driving around in the big, flash, black stretch Lincoln limousine. It was difficult for the local cartel to work Paul and Sean out.

One time, shortly after he had moved in, a drunken Paul came back from the pub and as he made his way home, the group of young people shouted something at him. Paul sneered at them and went into the flat to get Bruise to take him to the front of the flat where there was a small green.

Paul took the dog out briefly but when he went to go back inside, the teenagers started throwing rocks at him, before attacking him. There was a cleaning truck nearby with wooden brooms in it that they used to hit him with. There were about twelve in the gang and although Paul put up a good fight, he ended up taking a beating. He was left with several superficial wounds and, worst of all, ended up with a fractured wrist that he was later told couldn't even be wired back together. His hand still hurts to this day and he can't play guitar, something he used to enjoy before, although he could only ever play a few chords.

The police had been after these boys for a long time, for property thefts and stealing bikes, among other crimes. The police wanted the perpetrators prosecuted and issued requests for information pertaining to the serious homophobic attack. Some neighbours, who Paul is still friendly with, helped to identify the culprits and while this process was going on, the Council rehoused Paul just around the corner in Holland Road.

This new residence was a lovely flat with a huge, hundred-foot garden. Paul was really happy with the new property but the close proximity to the Henry Dickens Estate posed a major problem - there was no way he was going to court to convict the teenagers, having just been rehoused in a nice flat where the young people and their associates would know exactly where he lived. When Paul told the police this, they said they would put Paul up in a safe house but he was aware this might mean being placed in the middle of nowhere, somewhere like Leeds as he was led to believe, where he would probably again be persecuted for not being local to the area.

So he made a difficult decision and dropped the charges. The police were fuming as they wanted to convict the young troublemakers but Paul knew it would've ended up making his life hell if he went through with the prosecutions.

As a teenager, Paul would've gone to the occasional West Ham football match and would steal Stanley blades to cut up people's jackets from behind. The victim wouldn't even know it had happened. Looking back, Paul knows it was just stupid, but the kind of stupid thing that teenage boys get enjoyment out of, so he had some sympathy for the youths that had attacked him.

He also knew that if he moved around the corner, he wouldn't know whose brother or father or friend he might bump into in the very close-knit community and therefore would always be living in fear.

Paul now knows and talks to some of the perpetrators who are now adults, and they respect him for not hanging them when he could have and also for the fact that at the time of the incident he did his best to hold his own, despite the obvious odds stacked against him.

Although the situation had clearly shaken Paul and wasn't the sort of thing anyone wants to happen to them, it did have the plus side of moving him to his new flat in Holland Road, which he really loved. It was a basement flat, with one bedroom, a very long hallway with a kitchen at the end, a left turn that led to the garden and a right turn to the living room. It was a great property and the best feature was undoubtedly the large garden which was perfect for Bruise.

Recovering from his attack, things seemed to be on the up for Paul. But, as was a characteristic of his tumultuous life, he was about to become embroiled in yet another escalating issue during this time.

Paul was still working for the Royal Mail, although he was also continuing to enjoy quite a bit of partying. To fund his social activities, he had got into a dangerous habit of taking credit cards out of the post, waiting for the accompanying PIN's and then taking out as much cash as he could, either doing it himself or getting other people to do it for him.

It was hard managing the nightlife and then having to get up and 'do the rounds' but Paul realised that he needed the job to give him access to the cash that enabled his ceaseless want to party. Through his postal thefts, Paul found he had plenty of disposable income to supplement his chosen lifestyle and between his decent wages and the credit card income, he was fairly flush.

But the more he had, the more he spent on drink and drugs and on any of the weird and wonderful variety of stolen goods that would turn up in the pub on any given day.

Brendan and Edel, a couple from Ireland who had known Paul and Sean for years, had come over to visit them. When they arrived in London, the couple arranged to meet Paul in a local pub. They got there, rang Paul and awaited his entrance. When he finally entered the pub, he was clearly already very drunk despite it being just after lunchtime. He had his postman bag with him, still full of post.

The couple realised how drunk Paul was when he came in as he stopped to talk to two random girls, which he did for about an hour. Brendan and Edel were sat at the bar watching and shouting over that they had come all the way from Ireland to see him and here he was stuck on these two strangers! The couple didn't take any offence though, knowing Paul as well as they did.

This was a trait of Paul's, his combination of being the evergreen socialite along with something of a nervousness where he built up to a big occasion but then almost overwhelmed himself and tried to create a diversion, rather than deal with the event in hand.

Eventually though, Paul did come over, and after a few more drinks they all went back to Sean's place to continue the partying. In the morning, the bag of post was still there, full and lying in the hallway. Brendan asked Paul if he was meant to deliver the contents but Paul said he would always get round to delivering the post but sometimes, this wouldn't be until the next day.

Non-delivery of items was serious enough but what was more amazing was that it took so long for Paul to get caught with the credit card thefts. This had started when Paul was doing some additional night shifts and sorting as opposed to delivering. By being in control of arranging the post, he thought he could put away the required letters and not be singled out as the culprit.

However, the Royal Mail have their own internal police who had cottoned on to the thefts and they were about to set him up. One night, during a shift at Wood Lane Sorting Office, Paul found three of the credit card letters and surreptitiously put them to one side. But the internal police were watching from an upstairs window and as soon as he went to put the letters inside his jacket, they pounced.

The Royal Mail police took Paul to his flat, and Sean was there. As they walked in, they observed a couple of lines of cocaine with a blade on the coffee table, but they weren't interested in that.

Instead they searched the flat, looking for evidence to back up their investigation. In a cupboard, Paul had left four hundred pizza delivery leaflets that are worth an extra 1p each to the postal worker when they are delivered. They would later try to prosecute Paul for four hundred items of non-delivery which Paul would successfully argue was ridiculous as most of the postmen would've binned these extra deliveries anyway.

Fortunately there was no other mail in the house but he was ultimately prosecuted for the credit card fraud and they attempted to add the individual cases of non-delivered pizza flyer items as well.

The case was heard before Croydon Crown Court, a massive intimidating place. It was an incredibly serious matter as stealing from the Royal Mail is, in effect, stealing from the Queen.

Paul had heard stories from other people, a girl who was a friend-of-a-friend who was a Royal Mail employee and had stolen a VHS tape from her deliveries. She had ended up "getting bird...getting time" for it.

In an attempt to find mitigating circumstances to help Paul's situation, his solicitor pleaded that owing to Paul's use of drugs and alcohol, he wasn't fully responsible for his actions. His solicitor claimed that Paul's severe addiction issues had led him to think that stealing money was the only viable option open to him to continue to fund his habits. The solicitor also played up on the intimidating work environment that Paul suffered in, and that due to his sexuality, he was victimised and harassed by his colleagues.

The reality was that Paul actually managed to hold his own in the male-dominated workforce and saw much of the 'harassment' as just jovial banter which Paul was always quick to join in with. In truth, he became renowned as a 'top bloke' for his quick-witted banter and he was well able to verbally slaughter anyone who attempted to have a go at his sexuality. Where he would frequently be told to "shut up, you poof", Paul would come back with a retort like, "shut up, you love shit-shagging your wife so what are you talking about?"

But while in reality Paul held his own, when it came to him being prosecuted it was a case of him gaining any advantage to try and avoid a custodial sentence. Thus, it was described in detail by his defence solicitor how he was constantly being picked on at work and how he used alcohol and drugs as a coping mechanism.

Paul gave evidence himself and was very convincing, but despite his outstanding performance in the dock he was still extremely close to being sentenced to prison. What ultimately saved him was his, and his solicitor's, ability to milk the extenuating circumstances and to effectively play up on any opportunity to evidence how difficult Paul's work and personal life was to bear.

What made Paul's performance following his arrest and throughout his trial even more remarkable was that he was faced with going to court with an already extensive criminal charge sheet and record to his name. He carried with him the caution for shoplifting when he was a teenager along with the caution for carrying the air rifle. And he also had the adult caution for getting arrested with the spurs and the bag of grass on his 20th birthday.

Fortunately for Paul, the court felt prison would not be best served to rehabilitate him in this instance, instead issuing him with a DRR, a Drug Rehabilitation Requirement. This order stopped short of stating that he had to go on a course of residential rehabilitation but it did mean he had to attend an addiction centre and was assigned a key worker to support him with his problems. In addition to the DRR, Paul also had to attend regular probation sessions and was handed a two-year suspended sentence.

As a result of the DRR, Paul ended up working with Tommy, who was his assigned key worker. Tommy was an excellent ally, not only in helping Paul, albeit fleetingly, to come to terms with the negativity surrounding his drug and alcohol use, but also in supporting him with the past and recent life events that had so adversely impacted and scarred him.

Paul had barely survived the thing that has always remained the most fearful eventuality throughout his life, being sent to prison. He had come through the recent trauma of being attacked by the teenagers. He was still coming to terms with the loss of his recent bereavements. And at any rate, he had experienced well over a decade of extremely hard and heavy drug and alcohol abuse. Now, he was being offered the opportunity to finally address many of his long-standing addiction and other issues.

Paul looked out at Bruise happily playing in the nice big garden at the back of his new flat in Holland Road. He was relieved that by good fortune he still had his freedom and his health. Paul determined then that he would never again put himself in a situation that might compromise his greatest desire, to be allowed to live his life as he wanted, without the constant worry of the law lurking over him.

But as he had done many times in his life before, this was just a temporary sense of being. The real question was whether Paul had the capacity and the will to avoid making the same mistakes again?

Only time would tell.

Chapter 27 – The Royal Blackmail Plot

In 1997, Sean had met a man who, from here on, will be known as 'Witness D'. Witness D worked as a royal aide and right hand man to some very prominent royals and was introduced to Sean as a friend of Bari Bacco, the Dreamboys manager. The reason he must be known as Witness D is because he was to become the main player in a major court case, involving Sean, which became known as the '2007 Royal Blackmail Plot'. To this day, there is a 'gagging order' on revealing Witness D's actual name and he will be joined later in the story by other anonymous 'Witnesses'.

After their first meeting, Sean became friends with Witness D and they regularly went out for dinner together. Usually, Witness D would call one of the waiters over and tell him that he could turn him into a Dreamboy. The waiter would invariably be flattered and later, would often go back to Witness D's house where Sean would then be required to supply them with a variety of chosen drugs.

One time, Sean was called round to Witness D's house. Sean was brought into the living room and gave Witness D some cocaine. Witness D then immediately disappeared off to the bedroom and left Sean there for a while.

Sean soon wanted another line so he went to the bedroom where he came across Witness D who was out of his head and having a "three-course meal" with a waiter that he had picked up earlier that day (a three-course meal in this instance meaning licking, sucking and biting the waiter from his anus to his mouth and then to his penis).

Consensually, this may have been fine but Sean noted that the waiter was unconscious and told Witness D that what he was doing was totally out of order. Sean proceeded to remove the rest of the drugs and had a few lines while finishing a bottle of vodka that was in the living room, deliberately prolonging his exit so he could keep an eye on the would-be-rapist, before he eventually left.

Sean wouldn't see Witness D again until ten years later, in 2007. Sean was on his way to see his friend, Ian Strachan, who would later become Sean's co-defendant in the case, when he happened to walk past an upmarket, bespoke furniture shop on Pimlico Road in Victoria which was owned by a nephew of the Queen. He looked in and saw Witness D and thought it was an illusion. The man waved at him, came out of the shop and they exchanged a few words. It was the first time they had been together for a decade, but despite the niceties, there was still the palpable taste in the air that revealed that Witness D remembered what he had done and that Sean knew exactly what had taken place that night all those years before.

Sean went on his way and later told Ian what had happened. Ian wanted to go back to the shop to see it all for himself so Sean took him there. Ian got on famously with Witness D and ended up spending lots of time with him thereafter.

A short period later though, Ian confessed to Sean that Witness D had raped him and all the memories of what Sean had seen that night, ten years previously, came flooding back to him.

Sean decided that they should record Witness D and get enough evidence to get him sacked. So the pair began to do just that and for the following five months, they spent as much time as they could with Witness D while gathering the maximum amount of covert evidence possible.

During this time, Witness D made several disparaging remarks about his employers, the Royal Family, and Sean and Ian ended up with eight hours of video and ten hours of audio recordings.

Initially, Witness D came out with several interesting but not terribly exciting bits of information. He started volunteering details on the Royal Family, what they were like in private and secret peculiarities of what they got up to out of the public eye. For example, Sean and Ian would later allege that Witness D revealed that Fergie had bought the Queen a Puffin Billy set of bellows for Christmas. According to Witness D, this was one of their quirks - that they bought each other silly presents, and the sillier the better, and they would then jibe each other about their choice of gifts.

But then, as part of the ongoing sting, Sean and Ian unexpectedly recorded Witness D insinuating that Witness A, a prominent member of the Royal Family, used cocaine. Sean and Ian claimed to have filmed Witness D taking some cocaine out of an envelope that carried the royal insignia in red wax on it. Witness D then used a Harrod's store card to chop up several lines before verbally disrespecting the Royal Family and disclosing lots of juicy and potentially explosive information. He revealed something very startling which was that the member of the Royal Family, in addition to the cocaine use, had allegedly given him a blow-job. Sean had known Witness D for a long time and knew him as someone who, although he was a gossip, didn't tell lies so he and Ian soon realised that they might be in possession of something very valuable if they could find someone willing to pay for what they had uncovered.

Sean took it upon himself to see if he could get someone to buy the story and started contacting the press to see if anyone would respond to the evidence that he now claimed to have in his possession. As part of his plan, Sean approached James Weatherup, the newspaper journalist from News of the World. Weatherup invited Sean and Ian to a building in Clerkenwell which the paper used for keeping a variety of covert recording equipment and told them that they could use anything they wanted in order to garner more substantive evidence. However, Sean left unimpressed and told the journalist that he would keep using his own equipment.

The press then told Sean that they wouldn't run with the story as it was a legal minefield. They couldn't print the rumours as what was revealed was essentially 'pillow talk' without any real foundation, and they would have left themselves wide open to legal challenges if they published the information, which ultimately boiled down to the royal aide's word as evidence.

Realising that they weren't getting anywhere with the sale of the story to the press, Sean then changed tack again and decided that he would phone the royals up directly and revert to the original aim of getting Witness D sacked.

Later, the Telegraph would report "The first alleged contact with the royal was made by telephone. The caller, who identified himself only by his first name, claimed that he knew that a member of the royal's staff had an envelope containing drugs bearing his insignia. He then allegedly told him about an alleged sex video tape. There were several more calls which was when a detective from Scotland Yard's kidnap and blackmail unit was seconded to the royal's office."

In Sean's own words, he claims that he rang the Chairman of Christie's auction house and spoke to 'Witness B', who was Witness D's Secretary, and told him what he knew about the cocaine and the blow-job.

He asked for the royal to call him back but the next day, Sean went to Springfield Mental Health Centre in Tooting for a pre-arranged rehabilitation spell due to his alcoholism.

At the rehab centre, Sean was parking the car he was now driving, a Bentley T2, in the doctor's car parking space when he got a phone call from an unknown French man. Sean said he was busy and would ring him back when he got out after two weeks.

It later materialised that the caller was 'Witness C', who is a famous French divorce lawyer. Unknown to Sean at the time, the French police were also listening in to the call. The lawyer was calling from Marseille and was acting on behalf of the royals, having been appointed to try to get to the bottom of the ensuing scandal. Witness A has family connections in France which is why the French contingent had become involved

Shortly after he had finished his two-week stint in rehab, Sean was driving down Imperial Road in the Bentley with Ian Strachan in the passenger seat. All of a sudden, the police were at the side of the road, waving at them to stop. Sean was on a driving ban at the time so when he pulled over the police initially arrested him and confiscated his keys. But then shortly afterwards, they handed him the keys back and let him go on his way. Sean was baffled and it was only much later that he would realise that it was because MI5 had them under surveillance and wanted to monitor their normal, ongoing activities.

Shortly after this confusing incident, Sean contacted the lawyer who told him to give his details, and they would book him flight tickets to come to France to discuss the situation there. So Sean gave the lawyer his and Ian's name and their dates of birth. Sean maintains there was no blackmail plot and that they simply wanted to make sure that Witness D would be sacked for the rape of Ian and his other previous misdemeanours.

As planned, Sean was ready to go to France, but at the last minute they aborted the plans as Sean had a bad feeling that they were maybe being set up and had become annoyed at what he perceived as a lack of genuine interest in what they were trying to achieve.

Sean was with Ian and asked him to ring the French lawyer on their behalf and Ian left the room to make the call. Later, Sean ascertained that this was when Ian asked for money, hence changing the scenario into one that could be perceived as blackmail. Ian came back into the room and said to Sean, "they've offered us fifty grand."

Sean went along with it. They arranged to meet a representative of the royals at Room 713, on the 7th floor of the Hilton Hotel in Park Lane. Sean thought he was going to exchange the video and audio recordings on his laptop and mobile phone for the £50,000. He believed that (as far as he was aware) as they had not asked for money but had been offered the £50,000, they weren't in danger of being prosecuted for blackmail.

So, Sean and Ian brought everything they had to the Hilton Hotel. What they didn't know was that in the hotel room next door, there were thirty SO15 police officers (specialist operations anti-terrorist officers from the Met Police) led by Detective Inspector Paul Harty of the SO15 anti-terror unit along with Royal Protection Squad officers, MI5, MI6, and Special Branch personnel.

Sean and Ian went to the room where they had arranged to meet. They knocked on the door where they were met by a man known as 'Paul Butler', who was, unknown to them, actually an MI5 agent. Not sensing the imminent danger they were in, Sean was more interested in the man's height and was immediately amused by how small the agent was, standing before him at barely more than five feet.

The trio would end up spending the next hour and a half in the room. At one point, Sean opened the fridge but there were no drinks in there which he thought was a bit strange. The reason the event took so long was because Sean and Ian were showing the man what they had, while the agent was trying to get them to verbally ask for the money. Although the agent had the money to show them, Sean maintains he never saw it as they categorically did not ask for it.

Sean was becoming increasingly bored so wandered off to examine a bunch of flowers that were on a small bedside cabinet beside the bed. He sniffed them and as he did so, some pollen from the flowers fell onto his jacket. As he looked down to brush the pollen off, he noticed a series of small red dots on his hands and upper body. Looking up, he realised there were suddenly ten officers pointing guns at him. They had come into the room silently and were now training their weapons on Sean and Ian.

The Telegraph report would later state, "They met in a suite but the meeting was filmed secretly by officers in an adjacent room. Part of the video with the royal aide making his sex and drugs claim was allegedly being shown when the police burst in and seized the two men. The arrests took place on the 11th September 2007, five weeks after the first approach was made."

After they were arrested, it was revealed that they had been followed and filmed by MI5 for the previous two days. Apart from themselves and the arresting team, no-one else knew that they had been arrested. It was only when Sean rang Paul, who asked where he was, did it become apparent. "I'm in Wandsworth", was the response. He then went on to explain that they had been arrested for blackmailing the royals.

Thus, Ian Strachan, listed in court as aged thirty and a property developer, and Sean McGuigan, given as aged forty, appeared at the City of Westminster Magistrates' Court on the 13th September, each charged with one count of blackmail.

It wasn't until the 29th October 2007 that the story broke in the national newspapers. The Telegraph reported that "Two men in custody for allegedly attempting to ensnare a member of the Royal Family in a £50,000 gay sex and drugs blackmail plot have been named. Ian Strachan and Sean McGuigan, both from London, will appear at the Old Bailey in December accused of demanding money after threatening to release a video which they allegedly claimed showed the royal engaged in a sexual act with a male aide. They also allegedly claimed that they had evidence that he supplied the assistant with an envelope, apparently bearing a royal insignia, which contained cocaine. A second video allegedly exists showing the aide taking the drug."

The following day, the same newspaper ran a story which claimed that the royal at the heart of the scandal had been named. They said "The royal who has been targeted in an alleged £50,000 gay sex and drugs blackmail plot has been allegedly named for the first time on American television and in an Australian newspaper. Buckingham Palace is now braced for other foreign media outlets to name the alleged victim as they are not covered by the British reporting restrictions. A relation of the Queen was first named in the United States on Fox News by a British author, Nick Davies. He was then allegedly identified in a newspaper report in Adelaide, Australia. There has also been speculation on internet chat rooms. Ian Strachan, 30, of Chelsea, west London, and Sean McGuigan, 40, of Battersea, south London, have been charged with attempting to blackmail the royal. The pressure on the royal intensified when lawyers for Strachan said that he would plead not guilty to the charge. A full trial would almost certainly require the royal to go into the witness box to give evidence which would test the anonymity rule to its limits and would raise the prospect of a member of the Royal Family being called into the witness box for the first time in a blackmail case. While in line to the throne, the royal in question is not a senior member of the family and does not carry out official engagements. He is deeply upset by the impact the publicity over the alleged £50,000 plot is having on his own family and the House of Windsor. The Queen has privately indicated her support for her relation who has been through a 'fraught' few days since the revelation that two men had been charged in the first alleged royal blackmail case for more than 100 years."

The report went on to state, "Immediate doubt was thrown on the claims when the lawyer representing the 30-year-old suspect said: 'I wish to state that there is no tape of a sex act in existence. What there is in existence are tapes, both audio and visual, of an assistant to a member of the Royal Family boasting of how he received a sex act from this [member of the] Royal Family — whether that act took place I do not know.' The video footage of the royal aide was allegedly shot in a flat close to Buckingham Palace in an upmarket residential area. It allegedly shows cocaine being cut up on a coffee table with a Harrod's charge card before being sniffed by the aide who made claims of a sex act that took place between the two before asking for 'more cocaine'. The hearing before magistrates was held 'in camera'. Reporting restrictions have been imposed which prevent the publication of anything that would lead to the identification of the victims or witnesses."

In the intervening time between Paul finding out what had happened and the press releasing the story, he had seized the opportunity to make a quick bit of cash, with Sean's blessing. Although Sean had been arrested and the story was about to go live to the public, none of the papers had a photograph of him. So Paul decided he should sell a picture of his partner to the press before someone else did.

Paul telephoned the Mirror and arranged to meet a reporter at Wetherspoons in Shepherds Bush. Paul brought four different photos of Sean with him and managed to sell two to the reporter who gave him a cheque for two hundred pounds in return. During the transaction, Paul had given the reporter a fake name of "Darren" so he could remain anonymous. In the middle of the deal while Paul was sitting in the bar, a friend of his came by and said, "oh, hi Paul", which left the reporter looking somewhat bemused!

Sean had been able to secure the services of a top lawyer, Barrister Ronald Thwaites QC, along with Mike Mansfield QC (who shortly before had been involved in the case of the shooting of Jean Charles de Menezes, the innocent man shot at Stockwell underground station when he was suspected of being a terrorist).

Sean's defence team had told him that there was no real evidence and he was informed that he wouldn't be convicted on evidence as poor as the prosecution team had. In court, Sean's lawyers claimed that what the prosecution had was unsubstantial, incomplete and unjustified but still when the case was heard, Sean and Ian were tried for blackmail.

Sean had also been able to get support from Henry Milner, a top lawyer who doesn't usually look at a case for less than £100,000. The reason he was able to secure such high profile support was because these lawyers wanted the case as a badge of honour and it was to become a battle of the giants, both on the defence and prosecution side. This was the first blackmail case for one hundred years and the previous one hadn't even made it to court so there was a lot of interest in the case from the higher echelons of the legal world.

Ian Strachan had hired Giovanni di Stefano, who is known as 'The

Devil's Advocate' for taking on a series of unwinnable cases and whose previous infamous clients include Saddam Hussein, Slobodan Milosevic, Harold Shipman, Tariq Aziz and Gary Glitter. At the time, Sean was confused as to why his co-defendant had hired a lawyer whose previous clients were all either dead or in prison! Ian had an additional lawyer on his side called Jerome Lynch QC, another famous legal expert, with a special interest in Human Rights issues.

Ian and Sean also had a role with the jury - Sean said he didn't want anyone who was related to a police officer, a royalist, anyone who worked for the royals or was a friend with the royals. Out of one hundred and eighty jurors who came into the court, they ended up helping to select the final fifteen.

Further to his struggles to ensure a fair trial with the correct jury, Sean had also tried and failed to get the hearing moved to the European Court in The Hague as he felt the procedure would otherwise be biased. Certainly he had a point as at the end of every court session, the Clerk of Court would stand up and say, "God Save the Queen", whereupon everyone would bow so it was fair to say that the hearing may already have been swayed in favour of the prosecution.

In the end, it was the weight of the Royal Family against two men who were made out to be low lifes, with Sean in particular being painted as an alcoholic, violent criminal.

Despite this, Sean entered the court case sure that he wouldn't end up being sent to prison for what had happened. In hindsight though he admits he had tunnel vision and didn't really consider all the options. In truth, he hadn't really paid much attention to the detail and was actually more concerned with enjoying the excitement he got out of feeling like the main protagonist in a star-studded courtroom drama. Later, when one of the probation team asked him what the hearing felt like and Sean told them it was a buzz, they labelled him a 'thrill-seeker'.

The MI5 agent that the accused men had met in the Hilton Hotel room was in court for some of the hearing but was always hidden behind a curtain – Sean and Ian could see him, but no-one else could. During the trial, Sean's barrister asked the agent some difficult questions and kept pressing him with enquiries such as, "what is your position?" and "what is your job?"

The agent was clearly uncomfortable and didn't want to or couldn't answer. Several times the agent appealed, "my Lord, I'm asking for your help". Sean was desperate to shout out that he was an MI5 agent but managed to refrain. The barrister persisted with, "don't ask my Lord. Answer my questions."

Eventually the judge became so annoyed with the exchange that he dismissed the MI5 agent, leaving Thwaites to proclaim that the proceedings were a farce and saying, "he's meant to be the main prosecution witness in this case and you're giving him grace not to answer any questions". The judge knew this but had been put in an extremely difficult position. And this wasn't any old judge either - in the Old Bailey there is only ever a sword above the top judge and this famous sword hung during this whole trial. During these particular exchanges, the judge had to ensure that whatever happened, he didn't compromise the MI5 agent's position.

The longer the trial went on, the more Sean became convinced that he was going to be found guilty. And sure enough this is what happened. Before the sentence came down, he and Ian were told that they were potentially facing between eight and twelve years in prison.

When it actually arrived, it wasn't as bad as that but nevertheless, both men were sentenced to five years imprisonment. By this stage though, it didn't really bother Sean. He had long since accepted his fate and had spent most of the sentencing process so bored that he actually dozed off and when he was eventually sent down, he simply laughed.

The Crown Prosecution Service later issued a press release that reiterated the need for confidentiality in all aspects of the case and in the defendants' subsequent prosecutions. When Sean and Ian went to prison, nobody, even the screws, believed that they were inside for blackmailing the Royal Family, such was the cloak of secrecy that had accompanied the case.

Shortly after the sentencing was handed down, the Telegraph reported on the trial, stating, "Two men have been jailed for five years after being found guilty of a £50,000 gay sex blackmail plot against an unnamed, married member of the Royal family. Ian Strachan, a 'Walter Mitty' character with a cocaine addiction and his friend Sean McGuigan, a recovering alcoholic, demanded cash for a set of recordings featuring 'scandalous' remarks by a royal employee. The tapes claimed that the married member of the royal family, witness A, performed a sex act on the male aide at a party and took cocaine with him. The senior aide involved was described in court as a 'predatory homosexual', a 'mincing and boastful braggart', and was compared with the camp actor John Inman in Are You Being Served?"

The article proceeded to criticise the time and expense committed to the trial process, "It was the first case of royal blackmail for more than a century, but the expensive trial was described as an 'overreaction'. Large numbers of anti-terrorist officers were diverted from their duty to investigate the blackmail because the Royal protection squad do not have an investigative arm. Huge resources were devoted to the case because of the identity of the alleged victim, it was claimed. Liberal Democrat MP Norman Baker said: 'We are all equal before the law and members of the Royal Family like everybody else are entitled to the protection of the law - but also they are entitled to excesses not available to other people. It seems something of an overreaction to involve anti-terror officers in what is essentially a blackmail case'."

In addition to the trial itself, the cost of the operation to ensnare Sean and Ian was also brought into question during the court hearings and the Telegraph reported that, "In court police refused to say how many rooms they had hired for the operation, citing operational secrecy. Stays at the hotel range between £179 and £913 per room per night. Together with the costs of the three-week trial, including solicitors and two top barristers for each defendant and the prosecution, the total cost was estimated by a legal source as at least £1 million. The secrecy surrounding the trial was described as a 'charade' by Jerome Lynch QC, defending Strachan - since the name of the royal involved could easily be discovered."

Following his conviction, Sean would spend the next part of his life on a tour of prisons across England. He recalls many of the journeys between the prisons and one in particular when he was so bored that he masturbated in the back of a 'sweat-box' (prison van)! Although he was initially sentenced for five years, because of the Bentley being pulled over, he was given an additional four months for driving while disqualified.

Generally speaking, an inmate can hope to carry out about half of their sentence if they commit to an unblemished record of good behaviour while incarcerated.

But in the end, although neither of the defendants served their full sentence, Sean still felt aggrieved, as Ian did a total of thirteen months while Sean was inside for thirty-two months. What made this all the more galling for Sean was that, throughout the saga, he maintained that it was all Ian's fault for getting them into the situation they found themselves in, by asking for the money during their botched plan.

In a strange twist to the tale, on Christmas Eve, 2016, Sean was cycling round to Paul's house at about 8pm when he was hit by a car. He managed to get up, dazed and confused, and stumbled to Paul's house where he looked in the mirror and realised he was covered in blood. An ambulance was called and Sean went off to hospital where he would stay for eight hours. He should have stayed longer but pulled all the wires off himself and staggered out, citing the fact that he was freezing and hadn't even been offered a cup of tea as just cause for vacating the hospital!

Months later, Sean read in the papers that the other royal blackmailer, Ian Strachan, had died from a drug prescription and milk overdose (the milk helping to retain the drugs in the system for longer) on Christmas Eve, 2016, at 6pm. Up to this point, Sean didn't know anything about Ian's passing and it was only several days later that it hit him that it could've easily been that both men might have died within hours of each other, in completely unrelated incidents.

Sean now feels though that this was the ultimate redemption as he always felt that Ian had stitched him up and got him sentenced to five years in jail.

This recent period was also significant for Sean as he feels it was the beginning of the end of his long relationship with Paul.

Sean though maintains that Paul was "always a cunt" and that every summer, Paul would throw him out of whatever place they were living in. There was a pattern, Sean muses, and he began to see that Paul wouldn't throw him out in the winter as it was cold but he would invariably get his marching orders in the summer when Paul knew his boyfriend, or perhaps soon to be ex-boyfriend, would more easily find somewhere else to live.

Whether this is true is open to interpretation but what is clear is that Sean and Paul both have the same understanding of what their time together was really like. Sean describes the relationship using the exact same word as Paul does - "volatile".

Sean though, like Paul, knows that it wasn't all bad. Sean has a different reason however for suggesting why their relationship lasted as long as it did – the fact that he spent six years of their time together in jail. As Sean puts it, "thank God for prison!" He feels that the prison breaks always helped their relationship by giving them an enforced separation that ultimately strengthened their bond. Paul always waited for Sean which was a positive although Sean notes that he was always accused of having affairs in jail.

A further issue that Sean cites as an ongoing reason for their eventual break up was that he always felt that Paul's dogs came before him, which made him feel jealous, in a strange way.

Regardless of the other relationship issues, Sean's involvement in The Royal Blackmail Plot certainly had a major impact on both his and Paul's life. What had started out as a vague idea and a plan to perhaps do the right thing by exposing Witness D's misdemeanours had eventually turned into one of the biggest legal cases involving the Royal Family that has ever been experienced.

And although it was Sean who paid the highest price for the situation, it has at least given him yet another story to add to his vast and bizarre collection.

Chapter 28 – Denise & More Chaos

Just around the corner from where Paul lived in Holland Road, there was a pub called The Duke of Edinburgh, locally known as 'The Dip' as it was located down a slope, lower than street level. The pub has long since closed down but at the time that Paul was settling into Holland Road, it was very much open. Open, but horrendous in every sense of the word. The bar resembled something out of Trainspotting – the toilets looked like they had never been cleaned, and the same could have been said for the majority of the customers who resembled a cast of poorly-paid extras from a low budget horror movie.

Paul however enjoyed his visits to The Dip, perhaps secretly appreciating the satisfaction that came with knowing that whenever he went in there, it would invariably be safe to say he wasn't the punter with the most negative issues at any given time.

It was during one of these visits that he first became acquainted with Denise. She was there with her partner at the time, Ray, and his niece, Tanya. Tanya would invariably be with them and literally stuck in the middle, sitting between the couple. Paul, true to form, was loud and confident and jovial. Denise was the same. Paul would always play his favourite songs from the juke box and would see Denise frequently.

In the same local area, there was a wide variety of other pubs and bars including Wetherspoons and The Stewart's, and invariably Denise would be in one of these whenever Paul went in, so he would keep bumping into her.

From there the friendship grew, they exchanged phone numbers and often arranged to meet at the pub. They hit it off immediately. Paul would soon discover that in addition to enjoying her alcohol, Denise also enjoyed another pastime and was something of a kleptomaniac.

It was almost a part-time job and the pair would go stealing a lot from local shops, illegally procuring goods worth anything from £2 to £200. Paul always ensured he was self-medicated and would have a drink in advance so that if he was caught, which he was on a few occasions, he could plead that his addiction had caused him to steal and therefore he was far more likely to avoid a prosecution or certainly a custodial sentence.

One time while out shoplifting, Paul did get caught but as the cells were busy and there was a changeover of staff, they let him off with an £80 fine.

Also, the 'All Shoplifters will be Prosecuted' statement that many retailers are so keen to propagate isn't necessarily the case. Sometimes they can't be bothered with the hassle, perhaps being aware of the complexities and cost of bringing an attempted prosecution against an apparent drug or alcohol-fuelled addict. Or sometimes, it depends on the specific store. Some simply see the inevitable, occasional theft as a poor debt that they then write off.

Paul would often exploit this with visits to Asda, Tesco, Morrisons or Sainsbury's where he would pile a trolley up with expensive legs of lamb, large bits of steak, packs of salmon and other luxury items before brazenly wheeling the trolley out of the store and off up the road. He did get caught twice from Morrisons and once from Asda while trying this though.

The punishment at Morrisons was simply to be banned from the store on both occasions. At Asda, they took his photo and banned him from there. But each time, that was the end of the matter, and clearly a relief to Paul as another appearance in front of the courts would've almost certainly landed him in jail.

It was a major contradiction for Paul to be dealing with as, on one hand he had the two-year suspended sentence and massive fear of prison hanging over him, and yet on the other hand, he kept on stealing. He was shit-scared that he might get caught but equally sure that he had an air of invincibility and a literal 'get out of jail free' card due to his addiction issues.

On reflection, Paul describes this time as him being like a headless chicken and when thrown into the mix the behaviours of his new accomplice, Denise, it was an even more dangerous concoction.

Something would have to give. Paul was all too aware that he would either get caught and finally sent to prison or that his relentless use of drugs and alcohol would become too much and that this would cause some serious complications for him.

But despite his inherent fears, Paul was on a merry-go-round of self-destruction and was finding it very hard to get off.

On one occasion, Paul and Denise went to Homebase. Denise got a large trolley and went into the store while Paul waited outside. Denise put two Henry Hoovers and two large chandeliers, all still in their boxes, into the trolley. After a few minutes, Paul rang Denise to give her a signal and as he walked in and opened the security barriers at the entrance, she wheeled the trolley straight out into the car park.

They managed to get away with it and on reflection it was due to the confidence they both had, being completely brazen and never a thought that they wouldn't be able to just stroll out with a trolley laden with stolen goods. Looking shifty would've merely made them look suspicious and could've led to them getting caught.

There was always some fear for Paul but as there tended to be long periods of time between getting caught and very little in the way of recriminations, the worry always subsided and the confidence grew again.

As his constant back up, Paul always made sure he had drugs in his system although, not unsurprisingly, he found the most difficult times to be when he was stoned. He would turn up for one of their free-sprees and Denise would be mightily annoyed at the state he was in. A large part of the scheme relied on them being able to not look obvious and when Paul would appear with red, bloodshot eyes, Denise wouldn't speak to him in disgust!

Often they would keep their acquired produce for themselves, but sometimes they would try and sell it on. Back then, it was easy to steal to order and go round the pubs selling whatever had been asked for. Nowadays, it's more difficult although you can still expect the occasional junkie outside various pubs, trying to sell their latest acquisition.

Another aspect of their relationship which was both a positive and a negative was Denise's regular and exuberant trips abroad, often several times a year and to places like Goa in India. These were beneficial for Paul in that the odd time, he was able to tag along, but also they carried a disagreeable side as when he didn't go, he would invariably be left responsible for Denise's dad who would often have a turn for the worse and end up needing constant care. Paul would then ring Denise and she would always ask if she should come home. But the reality is she had no intention of returning early and would instead expect Paul to once again take care of her father for her.

However, despite their undoubted problems, Paul and Denise found something of a kindred-spirit in each other. As much as their relationship was difficult at times, it was also a very important and positive one for Paul for a long period of his life and he would certainly turn to Denise in times of need.

One example of this was when Paul needed Denise to make sure he kept his composure and was able to get home safe following a random night out in Sheffield.

Paul had been to see Bjork in Hammersmith and, Paul being Paul, had managed to blag his way into the aftershow party. Once accepted into the pop icon's secret inner sanctum, Paul got chatting to a man, one of her back room staff. The man arranged for Paul to come to Bjork's next gig, which was a few weeks later, in Sheffield. The plan was for Paul to go to the concert, then go out later with the entourage, and to bring with him a healthy supply of drugs for those that wished to partake. Paul would then be invited to sleep on the man's hotel room floor later that night.

Paul had obtained the required amount of ecstasy tablets and temazepam eggs and all was going according to plan as Paul sat on the National Express bus, three quarters of the way from London to Sheffield.

But then Paul's phone rang. It was his back room staff friend who told him that the gig had been cancelled as Bjork was having relationship issues and couldn't face having to perform. As a result, her team hadn't gone to Sheffield, instead moving on to the next tour venue.

When Paul arrived in Sheffield, he got into a waiting taxi and told the driver that he needed to collect his sister who was in a gay club in the city, thus ensuring he got to a friendly destination, but hopefully not arousing the suspicion of the taxi driver, who may or may not have cared!

Paul was delivered to said club and once inside, he followed his usual behaviour in these circumstances and proceeded to go mad on the dance floor. Awash with the excess drugs, he began handing out ecstasy pills "like it was Christmas". Unsurprisingly, Paul soon began finding himself slightly the worse for wear but just about held it together well enough to strike up a disjointed, but otherwise friendly, conversation with the gorgeous coat-check girl who worked there. Paul managed to dial Denise's number before spilling the phone into the girl's hand. Denise, being Paul's close aide, was able to immediately understand the situation and asked the girl to make sure she looked after Paul, being, as he was, all alone and lost up North!

The girl duly obliged and stayed with Paul until the club closed, before making sure he got a taxi back to the bus station in order to complete his journey home to London.

While Denise's ability to help Paul when he needed a friend or ally wasn't in doubt, what was less obvious was the answer to the question of how someone on benefits, with a drink problem, could afford to go abroad so often? The answer was that Denise was also a prescription drug dealer. One of her favourite destinations was India, where she had been going, on and off, for the past twelve years of her life. These holidays were always a minimum of three weeks duration.

At the time in India, anyone could walk into a chemist and ask for pretty much anything they wanted and the chemist would give it to them. Denise would buy literally thousands of valium tablets and bring them home in her luggage, in addition to posting batches of five-hundred tablets to Paul and her other associate's addresses.

The purchase price in India would be £70 for five-hundred valium and once back in London, these would sell for £1 a piece so the mark-up was massive and was funding Denise's lifestyle and holidays, even allowing for the odd package that wouldn't make it to its final destination.

Another quick seller was Viagra which she would again buy cheap and sell on for a large profit.

The entire process was also supported by the fact that, as Paul noted, Denise could sell sand to the desert as she is such an accomplished salesperson.

However, the authorities soon cottoned on to the fact that many Brits were involved in similar schemes and they quickly put a stop to it. It became much more difficult to purchase valium in such large quantities and the new batches tended to not work as effectively as in the past. To circumnavigate this problem, Denise diversified and instead bought and sold large quantities of zopiclone, which is a stronger type of anti-depressant. It's not as straight forward to shift though, as not as many people like it, so the operation wasn't on the same scale as it was in the early days.

There was also another problem in their relationship. While Paul was clearly a heavy drinker during this time, Denise took it to another level and would be drunk most days. The excessive drinking became difficult to sustain, even by Paul's addictive standards. Seeing Denise meant drinking heavily and Paul didn't always want to do this, so it began to put a strain on their relationship.

Paul started to stay in more, and then a chance encounter led to him taking on a lodger, essentially as a handy means of getting some extra cash, which was vital as Paul was by now unemployed and usually strapped for money.

Paul had met Eddie, a Lithuanian man, who needed somewhere to stay while he worked in London. Paul began renting his bedroom to Eddie while he stayed mainly in the living room. Paul didn't know much about his new flatmate so had given him a set of house rules to follow, the top one being that he categorically told Eddie he didn't want any drugs in the flat that could lead to him being lured into taking any.

Through his ongoing drug therapy work with the DRR, Paul was becoming more aware of his addictive triggers and was trying to learn processes that would limit his exposure and subsequent temptation to take excessive amounts of substances.

Along with the house rules, Paul especially stressed that, on no account, should heroin be brought into the house in case he got tempted and it activated a relapse to the dark old days. Paul was as clear as he could be and thought that would be the end of it.

But then, still weak from his recent issues and still feeling vulnerable and emotional from the grief of losing Smudge and his nan, Paul was tidying the kitchen one day when he found some tell-tale burnt tin-foil.

He held the silver paper in his hands and knew immediately what is was. Suddenly, the urges and the excitement bubbled up inside of him. He sniffed the tin-foil and instantly felt a spark lighting the internal fuse that would propel his descent into his second major heroin-addiction.

Despite his professional help, Paul was feeling extremely low and hurt and when he saw the tinfoil he wasn't annoyed at Eddie, he just craved some of what it had contained as he knew what it could do. He allowed himself to think that this was exactly what he needed at the time.

So, Paul went back to that place he had been to so many times before. He bought some heroin and went through the familiar ritual of burning it on the tinfoil before inhaling the smoke through a straw. Initially, the drug had the impact he desired – he felt numb and forgot, albeit temporarily, about all the things that were troubling him.

He enjoyed the state immensely, as much for the immediate sensations as for the place it brought him back to - earlier in his life when everything had seemed so much more simple and fun.

But, as before, Paul struggled to contain his usage. He found himself waking up every day and thinking solely about how he could score. He was eternally restless and could only find sanctuary when he eventually managed to get the drugs in his hands.

Having been in this exact same place before, Paul knew he had to do something constructive or else he feared he may go under and never come back. So, he bit the bullet and confessed his latest addiction to Tommy during his next appointment.

When Paul opened up to Tommy to get help, he told his worker he was taking a bit more heroin than he actually was, so Tommy prescribed him with a new, expensive, heroin-replacement medication called Subutex. Paul knew about this drug as he had bought it once or twice in the past. He knew that if a user ground the Subutex down and snorted it that it gave the same effects as heroin.

Paul had become aware that the usual procedure for prescribing medication like Subutex to addicts was that the staff would prescribe the user more than they would usually take if they were using the illegal version of the drug and then try to reduce the amounts over a set period of time. So Paul told Tommy he was taking more heroin than he actually was. This meant he was able to sell the excess Subutex and ensure that he wasn't taking it all himself, therefore avoiding getting hooked on the substitute-drug as many users did.

Initially, to access the Subutex, Paul would be supervised and have to go to Boots pharmacy where the staff would give it to him and watch while he dissolved it under his tongue. This would happen daily, every week day. Then on Friday the staff would give Paul what was required for the weekend.

This was just in the early stages but then, as the staff trusted Paul and he didn't fit the 'normal' profile of a junkie, with his relaxed character and personality, they gave him the full amount for the whole week. This meant Paul was able to take what he wanted and then sell the rest. Paul, like most addicts, was also still using a bit of heroin in addition to the prescribed substitute.

After a while, the rehabilitation staff asked Paul if he wanted to reduce the Subutex with a view to eventually coming off it or if he wanted to 'sustain and manage'. He remembers at the time thinking how he thought it was outrageous that a treatment process could be for an addict to be encouraged to come off heroin while continuing to maintain the constant use of a heroin-like substitute instead.

The staff also offered Paul methadone but he knew this was more addictive than heroin itself and that it's renowned for being nastier so he didn't want to get hooked on that. Paul was aware that heroin itself won't kill you, and it is actually what it's mixed with that can kill, but that methadone will destroy your bones and your body and certainly can kill you, so this was a road he definitely didn't want to go down.

With the endless spiral of Subutex and occasional heroin use, Paul knew he was going nowhere fast. He was running out of options so went and had a frank conversation with Tommy. Paul described what his life had become like and Tommy agreed that it was unsustainable and that something had to give.

They explored the options together and after a short while, Paul made a monumental decision to completely stop taking drugs and alcohol for a prolonged period.

With a fear in his eyes but a determination in his heart, Paul shook Tommy's hand and signed off on a residential rehabilitation programme.

Chapter 29 – Rehab

At the time, Paul didn't know what rehab was. But an accumulation of his history of depression from the age of fourteen, his related life behaviours, later addiction problems and run-ins with the law, had led Paul to a situation of chronic chaos which necessitated a serious and prolonged intervention.

Following the Royal Mail prosecution, he had been attending probation meetings which were initially weekly, then fortnightly, and then monthly for a year. During these meetings, rehab was often discussed as an option although Paul never thought he was quite at that stage yet.

It was really the ongoing attendance during the DRR and through his work with Tommy that he began to genuinely assess the possibility of rehab as a means to finally find resolution to his litany of life issues.

During the early discussions, Paul remembers being somewhat reluctant and he used excuses like not being able to get funding as a reason not to realistically consider it is a feasible option. There were also practical considerations like the issue of needing his dog looked after but eventually the practicalities, the funding, and then latterly the realisation that this was something that simply had to be done all clicked into place and Paul finally agreed to go into rehab for the first time. It was spring, 2009.

Paul feels that he was at his worst leading up to this period in terms of his excessive drink and drug-taking and his blatant criminality and that he was destined to hit the skids at some stage. So, in the end, he ran out of alternative options and finally made the long overdue commitment.

The day Paul was due to go in, Denise and another friend, Linda Hamill, had agreed to take him to Kings Cross Station to get the train to the residential rehab centre in Weston-super-Mare. Before the trip to the station, Paul went round to Linda's house and both women were there drinking lager, so he joined in as well.

By the time they went to the station they were all so inebriated that they were spinning each other round on the luggage trolleys in the station! On the train, the staff brought the drinks cart round so Paul bought more beer.

When he finally arrived at the Weston-super-Mare station it was early evening, even though he had meant to be there in the afternoon. Paul got a taxi to the centre and staggered to the front door but he was so drunk that the staff wouldn't accept him. Paul didn't realise how serious an issue this was - he thought as it was rehab surely everyone turned up pissed. What he failed to acknowledge early on was how much seeing other people drunk or even the smell of alcohol could trigger the other residents and set them back on their own recovery.

Paul was eventually allowed in but sent straight to his room and told not to reappear until he was sober the following morning. But an hour later, bored out of his head, he wandered out of his room, off down the corridor and started talking to everyone he met.

The next day, his first ever day in rehab, he was read the 'Riot Act' and had to listen to everyone else's feedback of how his turning up in that state had made them all feel. One client though was sympathetic and said, "he was just saying goodbye to drink and drugs, that's what it was", which was a relief to Paul as in his mind, that was exactly what it was - a send-off. He hadn't realised for one moment that he could be putting other people in jeopardy.

Paul would go on to spend the next five months of his life at the residential centre in Weston-super-Mare.

The procedure for rehab is that for the large majority of people attending, they need to have been to detox first. Paul didn't need to do this though as, through his DRR, it was assessed that he wasn't addicted to the same thing every day. Had he been involved in the detox prior to the rehab he would have probably understood the process of rehab better.

In rehab, everyone engaged in the same daily routine. The clients would get up and eat breakfast and then have a series of chores to do. Their role was to run the house for themselves. The set rota would include washing up, cleaning the toilets and tidying the lounge and meeting rooms. Clients would also help to cook the daily meals. If a client couldn't cook, they'd get paired up with someone else who could. People in active addictions benefit from structure, and many of the clients didn't have this in their life, living instead in a world of spiralling chaos.

After the chores were finished, there would be group activities and reflections at the end of the day which would then be discussed during the following day's group sessions.

Each client would be asked to keep a daily diary and during breakfast, there would be a group 'check-in' where each person would describe how they were feeling and where everyone was encouraged to expand on their emotions. It wasn't enough to just say, "I'm all right" - each person would need to elaborate on what was really going on for them, by describing their present feelings and emotions.

Growing up throughout his life and until he went to rehab, Paul associated himself with only a handful of feelings – happiness, sadness, anger and aggression – he didn't realise there were so many more ways in which an individual could express themselves.

In the residential rehab setting there were normally up to nine clients, along with the staff, but the numbers of clients fluctuated as people came and went. As well as the daytime staff, of whom there were usually three each day, there were key workers who were on site from 6pm onwards for a sleepover. There was usually one staff member assigned to deal with any problems or arguments and document everything that had happened. These would be discussed and dealt with the following day so that all issues were resolved quickly and efficiently.

Unsurprisingly, Paul found rehab very challenging and this was especially true when he had to open up and disclose things about his past. It wasn't until he felt like he was 'finding himself' during his stint in rehab where his true lack of awareness of himself suddenly became very apparent, none more so when the other residents questioned his attitude towards the Michael Lupo relationship during group discussions. Paul told the circle of about nine or ten of his peers and staff members about the serial killer who had become a major part of his life, and he did so as a catalogue of events in a matter-of-fact recollection. During these group sessions, the format is that one person speaks, and then the others provide their feedback and each one has the chance to speak. In turn, everyone said that the way Paul spoke about it was so disconnected that it was almost as if it hadn't happened to him and that he sounded like he was describing the situation as if someone else had been the potential victim.

It was only then that Paul realised the severity of the situation and just how close he had come to potentially losing his life. He had made himself so disconnected from it, not only in the sense of how serious the whole episode was, but moreover in his ability to discuss it as if it wasn't part of his own emotional background. This was indicative of Paul's default way of not dealing with things, but in rehab, his peers "stripped him bare". As a result, Paul found himself being faced more graphically than ever before with the question of who he really was.

Paul admits he didn't even know what the word 'disconnected' meant, although he had become sublimely adept at behaving in a disconnected way throughout his whole life. The ongoing therapeutic work at rehab meant that for the first time Paul had to deal with the experiences that had shaped his existence to date. He would also be faced with other realities such as having to accept that he was deemed to be a "prolific shoplifter and thief", among other things.

During rehab, Paul was also supported to address many of the gaps in his life and to aid this process he wrote a 'no-send' letter to his beloved nan. This process encourages the client to write a letter as if it was to be given to the addressee but it is never actually delivered. In this case, delivery would have been futile as his nan had passed away many years previously, but it was the cathartic, healing nature of the process that helped Paul to finally say a proper goodbye to someone who had been so significant in his life for so many years.

He wrote the letter, bought some flowers and then threw everything into the sea, near the centre. This process, whilst difficult and emotional, was nevertheless very beneficial in many ways and none more so than reinforcing the feeling that his nan was somewhere on a higher plane, looking down and continuing to protect him from beyond the grave. Although he accepts this is a romanticised idea he takes great comfort that she is watching over him and guiding him. It is with a sense of irony though that he queries some of her guidance as he feels she could've perhaps steered him in a more positive direction during some of the more ill-judged decisions he made throughout his life!

As an adult, Paul takes ownership of his own actions but he

recognises that as a child, he was often encouraged into devious ways of living and that this has been a factor in his life since early childhood. In one way or another, in one shape or form, there has been an element of manipulation and ducking and diving throughout his life. Paul has always been aware of it, but only recently has he really felt it, describing it as, "smacking me in the face".

Paul could easily blame this on his alcohol-induced states, but now older and more aware, he accepts that it is a combination of things – he feels a bit shameful, unhappy and not proud - looking back through a more mature set of eyes at some of the things he has done and how he has managed to manipulate himself out of them. Paul doesn't use the word 'manipulation' as him being manipulated by others, but more in the sense of how he has manipulated situations, particularly when caught in criminal acts, and this is something that, on reflection, he clearly carries a sense of immense shame about.

It could be argued that you might say to someone with a criminal record that they should have been able to say no when faced with certain options around their criminal behaviour. Instead, and looking at it more sympathetically, an individual's actions could be blamed on their upbringing and other external factors that are, to a large extent, beyond their control.

Paul doesn't think for him personally the issue is being able to say yes or no to situations, but more of him being able to manipulate it when caught. This makes him feel emotional and carries with it the great sense of shame. A counter argument would be that if a man is faced with prison, he will do pretty much anything to get out of it.

Paul feels conflicted and his feelings of shame are heightened by the fact that he knows he is not stupid, so how could an intelligent man so regularly get into situations that are, on reflection, obviously foolish? He knows the difference between right and wrong. In one sense, he feels that maybe he should have had the book thrown at him and that that might have fixed him up in one way or another.

Paul's underlying intelligence, or if viewed in a more cynical way, deviousness, has meant he has always known what he is doing. When he was shoplifting or stealing he always made sure he had alcohol and drugs in his system because then he could blame the situations he found himself in on his consumption of substances, as opposed to a sober choice being made. Although it could be argued that it would have been rare for Paul not to have drink and drugs in his system anyway, such was the extent of his various addictions.

Paul completed the rehab programme and left in August, five months after he had entered. During his prolonged stay at Weston-super-Mare, Paul would become only the second person to complete the programme in that calendar year. This gives an indication of how difficult it is to succeed and conquer the addictions that people attending rehab are struggling with. Further evidence of how hard this process is to complete can be found in the number of people who use residential rehab to get an earlier release from prison but then discover that rehab is actually even harder than prison life.

In rehab, one of the things Paul learnt to consider was 'little Paul', his inner-child, and how to nurture him. Through this process he was taught how to tap into mindfulness and well-being.

Undoubtedly much of Paul's childhood was, as he describes it, "fucked up", but that doesn't mean that in adulthood he had to always retain his inner-child as just a fucked-up entity. Later and now with the understanding and awareness that only truly comes with experience and a greater holistic acceptance of the world, can he nurture, protect and see the positive side of little Paul's life and how it enabled him to survive and thrive as the adult he became.

The older, understanding, adult Paul feels he can now go back and nurture the young child who didn't have anyone at the time to fulfil that role. Older Paul tells younger Paul to have understanding and not to beat himself up or to sell himself short. Paul attributes a lot of this positive development to his time in Weston-super-Mare where ultimately he didn't go on to cease his addictions completely but nevertheless found a place for his present, for his future, and most notably, for his past.

Finally, Paul had found a peaceful space where he began to allow himself to love himself in a way that countless other people had done throughout his life.

Chapter 30 – No Chance to say Goodbye

In rehab no-one is allowed to make any phone calls for the first two or three weeks to make sure they settle in, without distractions. After this period, the clients are allowed to contact the outside world and while in rehab, Paul would've had regular contact with his mum. During these calls, she constantly told him how unhappy she was.

Paul's mum wasn't a drinker and never went out to bingo or did other things that women her age tended to do in London, so had become increasingly isolated. Like Paul, she never had any money and anything she did have, she would have spent on her family. Paul never knew why she didn't have more money as she rarely had the opportunity to spend much.

Especially in later life, Linda was extremely unhappy and she had said to Paul many times on the phone that she "wanted to end it all" and just "wished that she could die". He had heard her say this so many times over the years, so usually he didn't take any notice.

But these times, while he was struggling so hard with his own demons in rehab, left him fuming to hear this over and over again. He thought it was so selfish and was annoyed that she clearly didn't understand what the rehab treatment was like. He was outraged that she was putting the extra emotional strain on him when he was engaged in his own acute recovery process. The worst thing about it all was that Paul knew his mum meant what she said about wanting to die and in many ways, Paul was powerless to do anything about it.

It was 13th August 2009. Paul had finally completed his five-month rehabilitation process and left Weston-super-Mare, feeling positive about himself as an individual and about his future direction in life.

When he came out of rehab, Paul didn't go to see his mother straight away as he knew he needed time to readjust to his own life first and to get back into his own environment, his own house and his own state of positive emotional well-being. Seeing his mother too early could have set back a lot of the positive efforts he had worked so hard on over the preceding months, such was her propensity for misery and negativity. Paul decided he would wait for a period, secure his own life situation, and then re-engage with his mother when he felt strong enough to cope with her feelings of 'life not worth living'.

A month after he had left Weston-super-Mare, he got a part-time job as a security worker for the setting up of the famous two-day Proms in the Park event. Paul's job was to make sure there were no security breaches during set-up as first the fencing, and then the main stage, were erected.

During the event itself, he was assigned to provide security for the dressing rooms of some of the star performers and presenters including Chaka Khan, Kylie Minogue and Terry Wogan. His job was to keep unwanted press and fans away from the celebrity areas. Paul got a buzz out of the excitement associated with the delivery of the event and the high profile names it attracted.

As a thank you, particularly for keeping the intrusive media at arm's length, Kylie Minogue's manager had handed Paul a bottle of champagne with an almost full glass in her dressing room. Paul, faced with the dilemma of his abstention from alcohol since his stint in rehab and the once-in-a-lifetime opportunity to sip champagne from a glass previously in the hands of one of pop's biggest goddesses, took the middle ground and helped himself to just a small sip!

Following the event and during the takedown process, out of the blue Paul received a phone call. It was his brother, Gary, and he was calling to say that their mother had died the night before. The family had tried unsuccessfully to get hold of Paul as they had an old number for him and had thought he was probably unavailable as he was still in rehab.

The next day, Gary had managed to locate Paul's new number and had called him with the sad news. Paul immediately asked to leave his post and got the bus from Hyde Park to Shepherd's Bush, sitting there, staring out of the window, with floods of tears running down his cheeks. Denise was away in India at the time so Paul called his other close friend, Linda Hamill, who met him and Paul is still so grateful to this day for the support she gave him during this terrible time in his life.

The sudden death of his mother left Paul in a complete state of mixed emotions – he was angry, annoyed, upset and frustrated all at once. His mum had often 'cried wolf' about wanting to die but had never gone through with it. And now, she was dead. She hadn't killed herself, but Paul is adamant that she had given up on life, long before she died. The actual cause of death was pneumonia, dehydration and some other conditions that Paul doesn't fully know about.

What made the pain even more unbearable was that all his brothers and sisters were there as his mum breathed her last, but there he was, the child and adult that had had the closest bond, completely unaware and enjoying his brief role as support to the stars in Hyde Park.

The whole experience felt surreal as Paul hadn't spoken to his sister or brothers for a few years before his mother's passing, one of the many results his twenty-six years of poly-drug use had handed him. His agony was compounded as he was haunted by the memory of his last phone call while in rehab, when his mum again reiterated her wish to die. Now one month after he was out, she was gone.

Paul's mum hadn't been outdoors for nearly all of the last ten years of her life, choosing instead to sit on the sofa in her flat watching TV or reading the paper, instead of socialising or meeting other people. She never had anything much to say, usually just chatting about the weather and other small talk. Paul managed to get more out of his mum than anyone else, as they were in many ways similar and had spent so much time together in Paul's early life, albeit sometimes smotheringly, but even he found it hard to drum up a cheerful conversation with her towards the end.

His mother's funeral was extremely difficult for Paul. The fact that he would have to see his siblings at the funeral was really bothering him. He expressed his concerns to one of the professionals that he was seeing as part of his rehab aftercare, Robert, who supported him with Emotional Freedom Techniques to help him deal with his anxiety around attending the funeral.

For moral support, Denise came along. She had met Paul's mum a couple of times but was really there to support him. He remembers it clearly – he didn't break down or cry at the funeral even when he was carrying his mum's coffin. He managed instead to find a way to detach himself from the occasion and went through the process of going to a funeral, as one would but not for a special loved one.

He was profoundly emotional but he didn't translate this into tears.

It could be that Paul, as an accomplished performer in many ways, has the ability to put up 'a front' and act in a certain way for a certain time, to fit with the required situation. This was a learnt behaviour he picked up from a very early age – whether talking to the school absentee officials, the gasman or the ability to combine the gay man with the hetero-male as the situation dictated, before later in life playing the required role when faced with police, magistrates or the judiciary.

It has very much been the case that Paul's life is his practice and the world is his stage. He can easily slip into an automatic role play mode and this was a method he employed on the day of his mother's funeral. Facing up to his true inner emotions of the occasion would surely have been too much for him or anyone else to cope with. But regardless of how he appeared on the outside, the feelings surrounding his mum's death were, inwardly, tremendously raw and coarse and took many years to subside.

While this ability to fit with the requirements of the situation and to act or be a certain way has certainly served him well throughout his life, Paul also sees the negative side of this in that it has led him to constantly struggle with the question of "who the fuck am I?" He has battled for many years to identify with who he is and most of the time he has seen himself as a misfit, which has led to him being alienated and left him feeling just like an actual alien.

This learnt behaviour was gathered from many years of being around his mum and nan who both found solace in shutting themselves away from the world and from the real sense of themselves. This self-alienation has some pluses in that it may enable the individual to hide away from some element of life's more difficult issues but it also has clear detrimental negative effects. Paul attributes this partly to why he self-medicated so much as it helped him to avoid having to constantly ask himself the real soul-searching questions about his existence.

Throughout his life, Paul has become so many things, and has taken so many drugs alongside. But rehab, although extremely hard and emotionally draining, was about spending five months to try to discover his real self – looking at, and for, his inner child.

The process wasn't just about recovery from alcohol and drugs, moreover it was about Paul, or 'Little Paul' as he was encouraged to describe himself when talking about his past experiences, nurturing that child within.

Latterly, this has led Paul to an understanding and a mindfulness that he can access by using the tools he was given in rehab. He can now tap into himself and is able to look after his own emotions by having the strength to know who he should be with and what behaviours he should be engaged in. This has given him a new maturity with a sense of "it's all about me", not in his previous pretentious, selfish way, but in a healthy awareness of one's self. As a result, Paul finds himself in a place where he feels far more at ease with himself than perhaps he has ever been.

To the lay person, if you were to hear that someone had gone into rehab for drink and drug problems, but that following this they still drank alcohol and took drugs, you would assume that the process had been a failure. But it would seem that in Paul's case, the real issue is less about the consumption of illicit substances and alcohol and is more about Paul discovering himself as a person to support his onward life journey.

The process for Paul was about how he could be better at being himself. It struck Paul that many of his peers in rehab had obvious signs of serious drug abuse like abscesses and dents in their legs, whereas Paul didn't display any of these physical abuses. Perhaps in line with the lack of external signs, internally he saw himself as a functioning addict who could handle it, whereas it seemed many of the other clients around him could not.

Though he empathised with his peers in rehab and understood their experiences, Paul's reason for being there was perhaps somewhat different from the majority of the others. These addicts were controlled by their drugs but in a lot of ways Paul was the opposite and found a way to control the drugs to take him to the place he wanted to be. Even at the height of his drug-taking and alcohol use, Paul nearly always knew what was happening and rarely got to the point where he was completely out of control. It was as if he chose each next step, having his array of uppers and downers and using these to facilitate his chosen emotional state, while always in control of what he was doing.

Paul's addictions were not conventional, he didn't use drugs to numb his life experiences and because he was necessarily hooked, it was more a case of his decision of what emotion he wanted to feel and then using the necessary concoction to get him to that place.

Shortly after he was released from rehab, Paul took control of Bruise who had been housed at Mayhew Animal Centre during his time away. He was delighted to be reunited with his old companion and was soon to add to the family when another offer came his way.

Paul's sister's friend's daughter had a six-month old dog called Betsy. The girl had Betsy in a studio flat but then became pregnant and as she also had a kitten, decided that she would have to rehome Betsy. Paul's sister put her in touch with Paul. Soon she had arranged to meet him and told him that Betsy was an American Staff and had papers. Paul agreed to pay her £100 but never got the papers so ended up not paying as he was doing her a favour anyway by rehoming the dog.

When Paul brought the dog home to Holland Road she began to jump over the back walls in the garden like a show-jumping horse and so he renamed her Horse. She needed a new name anyway as Paul was sure that as a gay man, he wasn't going to call out "Betsy" every time she ran off in the park!

Chapter 31 – From User to Worker

After his experiences in rehab, Paul made a decision that he wanted to use his addictions and lifelong issues to help others. This was something that Paul had always wanted to do and he had begun the process many years previously, ironically at the height of his own drug-taking. During his sober moments, he would have talked with close friends and disclosed that he harboured dreams to become a support worker as opposed to being the one that was supported. In reality though, he had known that there was no real possibility of him moving into this sort of work until he had successfully addressed all of his own addiction issues.

But now, Paul had been mostly clean for nine months following his residential rehab programme and his life was starting to get back on track. He committed to training as a substance misuse practitioner and key worker and embarked on an NVQ Level I and II, and latterly Level III, course in Health and Social Care.

His training began to give him a new air of confidence, he had Bruise and Horse, and he was feeling motivated and settled about the future. What he didn't know, however, was that life was about to force him into yet another major change.

The Holland Road property where he lived was an old Victorian house that had been converted into flats. Paul's was the basement one and there were three flats above his. The lady who owned the flat directly above Paul's invited him up to her flat one day. She gave him some wine and then announced that she wanted her daughter to have the flat downstairs and offered Paul money to leave. She couldn't buy it outright as tenants had to live in a council property for two or more years to enable them to buy the property and avail of a council discount.

The proposal was to give Paul the money for the discounted flat, for him to buy it, then move out and give the flat to the lady and her daughter. For his service, they would pay Paul a few thousand pounds. Paul refused though as he didn't feel comfortable being drawn into the arrangement and didn't want the hassle of all the legal responsibilities.

As a consequence, the lady upstairs made life increasingly difficult, and her and her family became the clichéd 'neighbours from hell'. There was no sound-proofing in the flats and there was constant noise from above Paul's living room, which was where their bedroom was, and vice-versa.

Despite requests, the Council wouldn't do anything about it as it would cost too much to sort out the noise issue. While this had always been a bit of a problem, it ramped up after Paul's refusal to engage in their scheme and the lady upstairs soon began doing provokingly irritating things like endlessly dragging chairs across the marble floor, which was directly above Paul's bedroom.

Eventually it all became too much for Paul to bear. He went on the Council swap site for like-for-like exchanges and saw an available flat in Bloemfontein Road. Much as he wanted to escape the tormentor upstairs, it wasn't easy for Paul to leave Holland Road with its large expanse and the garden which he was, by now, using to grow vegetables in a small allotment.

Paul arranged to meet the current occupant at Bloemfontein and see the new place. Immediately, he saw that it needed work and closer examination left Paul with the assessment that it was a "shit-hole".

He said no to the exchange but several months later, he went past and saw that the tenant had done some repairs and tidied the property up, so he went back and had a chat with the occupant. He told her the situation with his current flat and the problems with the lady upstairs but as she was new, she felt it wouldn't be an issue. She was very keen to move and so also agreed to pay £300 off Paul's rent arrears, which sweetened the deal.

So in 2010, Paul moved from Holland Road to his present home in Bloemfontein Road, Shepherd's Bush. Bloemfontein means Flower Fountain and is from South African derivation. This is a theme for the locality and nearby there are roads including South Africa Road and Nelson Mandela Road. The flat is also a two-minute walk from Loftus Road Stadium, the home of Queen's Park Rangers football club.

Once he had settled in, Paul continued with his training courses and would go on to win the Adult Learner of the Year Award for the whole of the London region in May 2012 – a phenomenal feat for the man who, as a young boy, hardly went to school and had left before he had the chance to take any exams.

But while Paul was committed to forging forward with his work career, an unexpected incident would force him onto the back foot once more. Just before Christmas, Paul and Denise were at the Pavilion, near the BBC building in Wood Lane, for a karaoke night. As it was Christmas, Paul had allowed himself to have a few drinks and true to form, he had ended up having more then he planned to. Shortly after, they left and went to a nearby Chinese take-away along with a man that they had met in the pub.

Completely out of the blue and for a reason Paul still has no understanding of, the man suddenly and viciously hit him from behind. The next thing Paul remembers is waking up in hospital with CID officers asking him questions. The police informed him that he had a fractured skull. They also told him that the CCTV images of the attack were poor so they couldn't make out the assailant. Paul couldn't remember the man as he had been so drunk and was obviously disorientated following the attack, so unfortunately it looked like the perpetrator would get away with it.

Following a brain scan, Paul was told he could leave the hospital. He had a blood clot but it was hoped this would settle down and wouldn't require an operation. Paul was bandaged up and sent on his way. It took a fortnight's rest before the pain from the swelling on his brain had subsided and he began to feel normal. He would have to return to the hospital several times to attend cognitive tests to ensure the pituitary gland was continuing to operate normally as brain injury can occasionally damage this gland and lead to severe complications for the victim.

He would later get compensation of £400 from the Criminal Justice Victim's Fund, although it took over a year for it to come through. Unfortunately the police never traced the man who had hit him during the random assault.

Although it took him a while to recover from the attack, Paul was keen not to let it upset his plans to become a fully-trained support worker. To further his aims, he became involved in carrying out voluntary work with a series of local substance abuse organisations.

This, coupled with his learning achievements, led to him soon getting his first paid position, in a role as a substance abuse practitioner.

Paul had set out to achieve something substantial and had

completed it. As a result, he was now earning a legitimate wage for doing something he loved, and in a role that was making a huge contribution to those he was tasked with supporting. He had achieved a major life aim and was loving life.

This first job as a substance worker was a six-month contract covering for someone who was on a short-term sabbatical. This involved planning and delivering structural stabilisation programmes for people caught up in the criminal justice system. In this role, the clients would be ordered by the courts to attend and if they didn't, they would be in breach and could be sent to prison. Consequently, the majority of the clients were resentful of being there and would dig their heels in, making it difficult to get them engaged. But half-way through their twelve-week programme, usually most of them would turn it around and would wilfully engage, a challenge which Paul really enjoyed being part of.

Then, just before that contract ended, Paul successfully applied for another position which was slightly different from the job he had been doing. The new post involved open access, needle exchange, prescribing and structured day programmes. It was very challenging but Paul felt it couldn't be any harder than his previous role so he threw himself wholeheartedly into it.

This new job was for a recently developed service that had transferred over from the old Foundation 66 to the new Blenheim Community Drug Project. He was told that he would be thrown in at the deep end and he was. Paul was made prescribing lead, peer mentor lead, GP liaison, shared-needle lead and needle-exchange lead as well as having responsibility for facilitating groups.

Initially, all was going well but it wasn't long before something began troubling Paul greatly. When he finished work, he was finding it difficult to switch off. He would go to bed worrying whether he had completed everything that day and thinking about the things he needed to do the next day. He would worry so much that he would find it hard to get to sleep and when he did, he would wake up before he needed to and then find it difficult to get back to sleep.

Also, as Paul lived just across the road from his workplace, he was finding it hard to leave the flat in Bloemfontein without bumping into a steady stream of his clients, who all lived in the same Borough. He was increasingly finding that the balance between his professionalism and his social activities was becoming harder and harder to manage.

He voiced his concerns in supervision but, initially, this didn't make any positive difference.

Around this already difficult time, Paul wasn't helped by a negative experience during one of his days off. This occurred at the hands of Sean who had come round to visit. Sean had made them both a cup of tea and Paul drank his before popping out to see a friend that he had arranged to meet that day. Paul got as far as the traffic lights at the end of his road and collapsed. He was helped up and managed to stumble back to the flat where Sean was waiting.

Paul told Sean what had happened and Sean confessed that he had spiked his tea with a generous quantity of speed. Paul was livid, especially as he was still recovering from the fractured skull just months earlier.

The incident was symptomatic of many of the problems that Paul had with Sean throughout their relationship, due to the erratic and dangerous behaviour that Sean would frequently display, often in the name of fun or humour.

Eventually, Paul was offered counselling through work and he took it. The counsellor he was given turned out to be the same one that he had when he first came out of rehab so he had a good understanding of Paul and stated that he was being badly managed and that he should look for another job.

So, the hunt was on and Paul started regularly looking for alternative employment, but all the jobs he was interested in were too far away for him to travel to. In addition, he was struggling to decide if he even wanted to carry on with this type of work.

Paul was by now very conflicted – he had experienced the feelings of value and self-worth that accompanied such supportive roles as the ones he had been involved in and was keen to do more. But he was also acutely aware of the pressure that this type of work was placing on him and the stress that this could ultimately cause him.

Paul was starting to follow a well-trodden path for many support and social workers who find themselves in incredibly demanding roles in addition to having their professional and personal lives compromised by the close proximity of their home life to the people they serve on a daily basis. Like many of them, Paul had a want and a need to find a means of detachment from the daily worry that he now found himself dealing with, and he began to find himself craving the occasional drink or other means of escape.

Paul understands this, the fact that many workers love what they do but become drained and need to unwind, so they go to the pub as the best means to switch off. But then their regular clients pop into the same pub as they've just robbed some meat from Tesco and they want to sell it to the first available punter to fund their next hit. Or workers try to avoid situations like this but still feel the need to de-role so instead become reclusive home drinkers.

Clearly, these scenarios do not lend themselves well to working as a professional, supporting others' addictions. But all too often, in an effort to deal with the physical and psychological symptoms of stress in the workplace, many workers attempt to self-medicate with alcohol or drugs.

Stress at work has been shown to contribute to a number of serious health issues, one of which is problem drinking. There is, in fact, 'a significant relationship' between job stress and alcohol consumption, in the words of the Mental Health Foundation.

Someone who works in a stressful environment could also become likely to use drugs, or use them more often or in higher doses, which can also lead to the issue of addiction. This often occurs because a person's ability to cope with stress can shrink based on the severity of their drug abuse. As a result, individuals tend to take more of their chosen crutch to help them cope, thus making addiction all the more probable.

Aside from regularly meeting clients outside of the workplace, Paul's other main problem was that he was getting jaded because of the paperwork, especially when dealing with the reality of tenders, bidding, targets and funding which took him away from his real passion of supporting the clients with their addictions. He felt burnt out by always being in work mode and never being able to switch off, even in his downtime hours.

It was beginning to dawn on Paul that the job wasn't what he thought it was. He realised it was just another business and he felt it wasn't really about people's lives as it should be. However, Paul knew he was good at what he did and he hoped he was making some difference. It was difficult to quantify though as, in this kind of work, the positive results aren't always evident. With the client group involved, where only a few may actually be seen to be making progress, it wasn't giving Paul the sense of job satisfaction that he craved, even though he knew he was in tune with the process of support that he was engaged in.

Paul knew his stuff and while a good substance abuse worker doesn't necessarily have to have experienced addiction, they do have to understand addiction. Paul, through his life tribulations, had both of these elements – the lived experience and the awareness and empathy to support others.

Paul benefited from being able to use his own experiences to support others and he does think that people who just went to university or studied addictions in a book may struggle in the world of work as they perhaps haven't experienced the vital feelings or emotions connected to addictive patterns.

Addiction can be cups of tea, cans of coke or crack cocaine – it's the same thought patterns, but the damage to oneself and others is obviously vastly different.

As well as the difficulties in the workplace, Paul wasn't motivated by the need to earn a high wage. He has never placed much value in money and has never been very good at keeping hold of it – as soon as he gets it, he looks to spend it. He's never been interested in accumulating wealth as many people are. As long as he has the basics – food, heat, light, a roof over his head, his dogs – he's happy. Paul loves gadgets but he's not materialistic so will make do without if needs must and he won't worry about having the latest technology. He doesn't feel the need to earn money so he can have everything in the way that drives some people to work in stressful jobs that they hate. And he's not interested at all in the bigger life expenses, things like a mortgage or a car.

Whenever Paul gets money, he wants to spend it, though not all. He has always managed to retain a thought for the next day and will invariably keep a little something back with his future self thanking his former self for being clever enough to think of him. This is something he assures Sean was never able to do. Sean could have a thousand pounds and would spend it on everything and everyone that night and literally wouldn't have ten pence the next day for anything else that was required, like food or electricity.

So once more, Paul found himself having to make another life-changing decision. Despite all the work he had put in to get to the stage he was at and although he very much enjoyed certain aspects of the roles he now found himself in, he reasoned that the negatives associated with the work-life he was now part of would ultimately consume him. Thus, he made the difficult choice to walk away from the world of work.

Although he knew it was the right thing for him to do, Paul still harboured a lot of guilt and shame about how his fledging career had ended. Having left his position, he would have often found himself sitting in a pub directly across the street from where his ex-work colleagues were gathered, having a cigarette and a chat, and he'd wonder if he'd made the right decision. Or he would walk past ex-clients on the street and get a pang of remorse that he was no longer able to help them.

Now it doesn't bother him so much, but it took literally two and a half years of Paul trying to avoid people before he felt confident enough to get on with his life without worrying who he might see on a daily basis.

Regardless, even with the end of his career and the pain he felt at abandoning it, Paul retained some semblance of pride that he had made it that far. Despite the seemingly endless chaos of his life, Paul has always managed to meet his goals, be that as a horse trainer, professional dancer, drug worker or to write this book.

However, Paul's goals were always things that he had envisaged leading up to the age of fifty and now he has recently reached that milestone and achieved all these things, he now must reassess and discover his new goals for his more mature years.

Chapter 32 – Old Habits Die Hard

In 2013, Paul went to Goa in India for the first time, on a three week holiday. Goa, with its silver sands and sparkling blue waters, is a true tourist paradise. Situated in the coastal Konkan region on the bank of the Arabian Sea, the area is a place people fall in love with at first sight. This was true of Denise who had been here several times before and loved the idyllic surroundings as much as the easy profits to be made with the wide array of prescription drugs on sale.

From her previous visits, Denise knew lots of English and local people and had all the contacts needed to stock up on valium and zopiclone or whatever else was on the shopping list. This time, Denise had asked Paul to come along and he loved everything about the place - how cheap it was, the seafood, the glorious weather, the great clubs, the karaoke and English bars, how it is so laid back, the fact everyone speaks English, the fun you can have by bartering for everything you buy and for the fact that no-one ever pays the full price for anything.

Shortly after their arrival, Denise had taken them to one of her favourite chemists where Paul had bought pure MDMA powder over the counter. Denise knew the right chemists to go to where the general rule is that you go after about 8pm and as long as your face fits, the chemist will pull out a special drawer and you can buy pretty much anything you want.

Paul and Denise each had a little pinch of the white powder and then went out to a karaoke bar, arriving shortly afterwards out of their heads. This was pretty much the norm for the rest of the holiday – enjoying the amazing beaches and natural surroundings during the day, before visiting their chemist friends in the evening and then partying the night away along the endless line of bars and clubs, assisted by their chemical companions.

It was the best holiday Paul had ever had and he was loving the fact that everything had gone so well since he arrived. But, as tends to be the case with Paul, drama was never far away.

In the final week of the vacation, he hired a moped but accidentally grazed his foot while turning the bike round. The cut ended up getting infected and he knew that it was cellulitis. This is a bacterial skin infection where the affected area becomes red and swollen and feels hot and very painful to touch. Paul had had this a few years before at Starcraft when dirt got into his hand so he knew it was the same thing again.

Denise took him to the doctor. Everyone has to pay for medical treatment in India and if you're a westerner in the waiting room, you tend to get seen before everyone else as you're nearly always going to be more affluent than the locals.

The waiting room was full of resident Indians with a whole array of ailments and broken bones but Denise just frog-marched Paul straight in to see the doctor. The doctor contemplated sending him to the nearby hospital but decided instead to treat the now heavily swollen foot himself. He put Iodine on it and then got a Stanley blade and cut into each blister that had formed, to remove the infection. This was agony and Paul was biting down hard on the sleeve of his jumper. Finally when all the blisters had been opened, the doctor bandaged his foot, gave him an antibiotic injection and sent him on his way.

Paul would have to revisit the doctor for the next five days, and the same process would occur with the doctor cutting open the blisters and then injecting another antibiotic.

The treatment was obviously extremely painful but the incident also effectively signalled the end of Paul's holiday. The apartment they had rented had an area with a pool but Paul wasn't allowed to swim and had to sit in the shade with his foot bandaged for the remainder of the holiday.

When he finally returned to London, Paul had to readjust to life without work, and without a steady, decent income. The cellulitis aside, he had really enjoyed his time in India and was already thinking that a return holiday there in the very near future would be most beneficial.

But there was one major problem, he didn't have enough money for the airfare, let alone accommodation and funds for his next trip.

To get around the problem, Paul formulated an idea to generate money by cultivating cannabis. He set up a growing room in a black tent in his bedroom complete with lights and a fan and although the crop he first planted was only a selection of small cuttings, it looked like it would soon yield positive results.

But as often happened, Paul didn't legislate for the unexpected, which regularly manifested in the appearance of his wayward boyfriend. Sean had come round to the flat and Paul was there with his friend. Sean was very drunk and Paul refused to let him in. Before Paul knew what was happening, Sean suddenly appeared in the living room, having broken in through the back window. Paul and his friend managed to throw Sean out but, unknown to them at the time, Sean then called the police and told them that Paul was growing cannabis which he had seen through the back window before his break-in.

Shortly after, the police arrived. They knocked on the front door and Paul went out to talk to them. Paul tried to deflect the situation by telling them that he had been broken into but they insisted on searching the flat. An officer entered and saw the cannabis tent and heard the fan. Paul had been caught for cultivation of cannabis and, as a result, was arrested.

To avoid a court appearance and potential custodial sentence, Paul played up on his recent work issues and declared himself to be a regressive alcohol and drug addict. He was subsequently placed on an alcohol treatment order with a worker at Westminster Drug & Alcohol Project (WDP). To ensure he wasn't in danger of ending up in court again, Paul attended all his appointments as required. During the sessions with his worker Paul discussed the possibility of once more returning to residential rehabilitation, but nothing was finalised.

While Paul had managed to again avoid the clutches of the law, his immediate problem of having no ready cash was still a major difficulty but he was about to be offered a possible solution to his issue.

Paul knew of a guy, Ben, a friend-of-a-friend who was always involved in criminal activities of some description and therefore usually had some surplus cash about him.

Paul approached Ben shortly before Christmas 2013 and asked him if he could see his way to lending him some money so that Paul could get his wish and spend the holiday season in his Asian paradise, far from the stresses of London and the drain of the local drug addicts that he was so desperate to avoid.

Ben though was unable or unwilling to help and even when Paul enquired about gainful employment such as any odd decorating jobs, the response was still a negative.

It appeared that Paul would be spending Christmas in Shepherd's Bush but then about a week later, he happened to unexpectedly run into Ben in a local pub.

Ben asked Paul if he could drive, Paul answered in the affirmative and was then asked if he would be willing to drive a car from their local area to Brighton where he would meet a contact and get paid £200 cash for his efforts. If the plan worked out satisfactorily, Paul would be invited to repeat the feat to the tune of a further £200. Paul initially agreed but soon began to doubt the scheme was ever going to materialise as he hadn't heard from Ben for over a week.

Paul was then having a few drinks down one of his local pubs when suddenly his phone rang. It was Ben. He asked if Paul was ready. Paul said he was and less than ten minutes later, he met Ben around the corner and jumped into his waiting car.

Ben handed him a key, told him the vehicle in question was a Range Rover and gave him the exact location of where the car was parked. As Ben dropped him off close to the target, Paul's stomach was churning and he was aware of his heart beating so fast he felt like it was about to jump right out of his chest.

Earlier, in the pub, Paul had been given a line of very expensive cocaine. Now he wasn't sure if this was helping by giving him the extra bravado he needed or if it was the reason he felt like his heart was about to explode. Either way he had committed to the act and was determined to follow it through.

Paul found the car, got in, started it up and proceeded to drive from Shepherd's Bush to Hammersmith, before turning towards the south-bound motorway. The traffic was busy in Hammersmith as he approached the Flyover and all the vehicles were moving very slowly. This only added to Paul's building sense of panic and paranoia as he realised that the almost new and clearly very expensive Range Rover did not look like it should be being driven by someone matching Paul's description.

Paul's fear was somewhat tempered by the excitement of the level of undoubted luxury that came with this car, mixed with the radio which was pumping out tunes that Paul knew and loved. It began to spit with rain and the windscreen wipers came on automatically and as the exterior light began to dim, the car's headlights effortlessly came into operation. The Range Rover was an automatic and that made it really easy to handle, even despite the fact that Paul had never driven an automatic before.

Slowly, Paul found himself relaxing and starting to overcome the initial anxiety that had beset him earlier. Perhaps relaxing too much, he overshot the exit to turn onto the southbound M23 motorway and instead carried on heading towards the west.

Time was getting on and it was getting darker. Paul turned off at the next exit to try and double back on himself but he instead ended up driving into a built-up residential area. To try and get his bearings, he pulled up at the side of the road but then started panicking. It was all taking too long and he was becoming increasingly worried about where he was and how he must have looked, piloting this £48,000 beast.

He decided the best course of action would be to turn around and retrace his steps until he found a way to rejoin the main carriageway that would take him back to the motorway, and hopefully to the safety of the open road to Brighton. But as he made his way back towards the missed exit, he noticed a police car overtake. He was telling himself to look confident, that it was just a coincidence. But then the police car pulled in, right in front of him, just as a second unmarked car came alongside with a blue light flashing unerringly at him.

Paul had no choice but to stop the car and was then ordered to get out and lie on the floor, face down. The police held him down, before handcuffing him and dragging him into the back of the waiting police car.

Paul was taken to Reading Police Station and booked in. His shoes, belt and the contents of his pockets were taken off him and he was put into a cell. While he awaited the next stage of his incarceration, Paul found comfort by rocking himself backwards and forwards, trying not to think about the dire situation he had found himself in. He didn't have to wait long until an officer appeared at his door to breathalyse him.

Paul then asked for a duty solicitor and he was soon shown into a small cubical room with a phone. Initially the solicitor was unable to help Paul as it was unclear whether the arrest was going to be dealt with by Thames Valley Police or the Metropolitan Police. It was to materialise later that it would indeed be Thames Valley Police dealing with Paul, but at this stage it was late into the night so Paul was returned to his cell for what little sleep he could muster.

Morning came and Paul was given a tasteless, microwaved breakfast and coffee but still no indication of when he might be interviewed. It wasn't until lunchtime came and went that he was instructed out of the cell where he was told to sign for his belongings, handcuffed and escorted out of the station by two plain-clothed policemen.

One of them asked Paul if he smoked and he replied that he did. The officers then put him in the back of a waiting unmarked police car. Paul was confused why he had been asked if he smoked - was it some kind of wind-up or a way of annoying him? But then, one of the officers lit a B&H cigarette and gave it to Paul who smoked it.

Strangely, the officers didn't smoke themselves, they just sat in the front chatting away about mundane things like their shift patterns and other officers, like they didn't have a care in the world. All the while, Paul was freaking out about the ash dropping in the back of the car and what he would do when the cigarette burned down to the tip. Once he had finished the cigarette, the officer took it from Paul, threw it out the window and then they set off for Hammersmith Police Station.

Paul was once again booked in, put into a cell and given another microwaved and tasteless meal. He was then asked to do a saliva test for a covert machine, something Paul knew about as he was trained to use these machines in his role as substance abuse practitioner. The test came back positive for cocaine and Paul was later finger-printed and photographed before being put back into his cell.

By this stage, Paul was feeling frightened and very emotional, partly because of what he had been caught for and partly as he was becoming increasingly worried about his dogs who were home-alone in Shepherd's Bush.

Paul had fucked up again and he felt about as low as he had ever done. As the remorse began to flood over him, Paul heard the cell door hatch open and he saw one of the officers holding up Paul's big bunch of keys. The officer asked which the keys to his house were and Paul told him about the dogs and contacting someone to help. The officer said he would make sure the animals had water and dog food and they agreed to let Denise know what the situation was. Although Paul was relieved that the dogs would be alright, it was clear to him that what they really wanted was access to his house so that they could have a look around for evidence.

Once the police had returned from Paul's house, they finally interviewed him. The solicitor that had helped Paul when he had been at the previous station was unavailable so Paul waived his right to have someone present and pleaded guilty to the theft of the car so that he could get out of there as quickly as possible.

As soon as he could after he was released, Paul got an assessment for residential rehab but was told he would have to wait to see what the outcome of the court case regarding the theft of the Range Rover would be.

Before he was due in court, he was assigned a probation officer who recommended that Paul change his plea from theft to 'Taking Without Owners Consent' (TWOC).

Paul was told that the case would be heard the following February and after he felt like he had been waiting forever, the court date finally appeared. As directed, Paul changed his plea to one of TWOC and was subsequently bailed with no additional conditions.

He was to be brought back for sentencing but Paul found this to be the hardest bit of the ordeal. The waiting was eating away at him and to try and mask his emotions and the stark fear of the potential custodial sentence that awaited him, Paul turned to his old allies. He dabbled in cannabis, cocaine, crack, even heroin – anything to try and keep the horrors at bay.

When the sentencing date finally came around, it didn't put an end to the trauma. Instead the case was referred to be heard at the Crown Court and Paul was bailed for a second time. This time, the wait was even more unbearable and Paul had never been as fearful in his whole life. Every morning began with a waking anxiety, shortly followed by a physical hurting.

His stomach, aligned to the stress of his overactive brain, was suffering by displaying cramps and tightness.

When faced with this level of worry, Paul reverted to type and employed his well-trodden path to coping – he balanced out what he could and couldn't get away with drug-wise and teetered between all out self-destruct and the need to attend his necessary appointments with Westminster Drug & Alcohol Project.

But soon, his order with WDP finished and then Paul had only one course of action to get him through until the court date. He stayed indoors and smoked a lot of cannabis. And when the paranoid thoughts that came with getting too stoned kicked in, he tempered these by drinking heavily. When that didn't work, he found his familiar patterns of cocaine use, mixed with a bit of crack, coming to the fore.

After what seemed like a lifetime, the court date came around. Paul had asked Denise to meet him at the Crown Court and once there, they sat together, awaiting further instructions. Internally Paul was a complete mess, his head spinning with thoughts of what might lie ahead.

Eventually, a court clerk came to summon them into the court room which was a big, intimidating space. Paul was already immensely scared that he was going to be sent down, and this was only amplified by everyone in their black gowns and white wigs and the array of legal personnel, all preparing for his fate.

For the hearing, Paul had been allocated a new probation officer, Scott, as the previous one had left. Scott had provided a reference and this had been supported by a character letter from Pat, a retired police officer. Pat was the family friend of Sean's family, the man who had lent him £30,000 for the limo. Paul knew him through Sean and as Sean understood the situation with courts and how to get the best result from the given circumstances, he had got the letter for Paul. And Barbara, Denise's mum, who treated Paul as would a foster mother, wrote one too.

Despite the letters of support, it looked like the proceedings were going to result in Paul being given an eighteen-month custodial sentence.

But at the last minute, Paul revealed that he was going into rehab again very soon. The judge gave this some consideration and eventually deemed this as a more appropriate option.

Escaping by the skin of his teeth, Paul was extremely fortunate to be handed down an eighteen-month suspended sentence along with one hundred hours of community service, twelve months' probation, a £100 compensation fine and a driving ban for two years.

It was later to materialise that the owner of the Range Rover was in on the job. The key that Paul had been given in Shepherd's Bush was a clone key. The man who owned the car was meant to call the police to report it missing but had done so too soon, therefore activating the Thatcham tracker which resulted in Paul being traced.

Yet again, Paul had escaped without a prison term and given the previous months of turmoil, he left the Crown Court feeling incredibly blessed and so very lucky, but at the same time stupid for having got caught up in the whole mess in the first place.

Chapter 33 – Banged up Abroad & Back to Rehab

Shortly after the court case and while awaiting his impending second stint in rehab, Paul had arranged to go out to Goa where Denise was waiting, having gone out the week before, this time for a four-week vacation. Paul had managed to beg and borrow enough money for the trip and wanted it as a last goodbye before his latest attempt to finally get his life in order.

He was scheduled to fly to Doha in the UAE with Qatar Airlines and then get a connecting flight with Emirates to Goa in India. He boarded the Qatar Airlines flight at Heathrow and settled in for the journey.

Paul had a white Nicorette cigarette-replacement inhalator for the flight and was smoking this on the plane. Suddenly a young stewardess started screaming at him and snatched it out of his mouth. Paul, annoyed at the behaviour of the stewardess and having already helped himself to a large amount of the complimentary in-flight Champagne, became very vocal before the incident settled down and the flight continued.

When the plane arrived in Doha it was night-time, and as Paul departed he was met by a policeman, immediately handcuffed and was then taken to an airport holding cell before being transported to a police station. Paul didn't know what was going on as everyone was either Qatari or Indian and none of them spoke a word of English.

At the police station, he was placed in a dark cell with twenty other men. There were several foam mats for sleeping on, a hole for a toilet, and a shower area. Panicked, he hid in the shadows and waited for morning to come.

Paul managed to fall asleep, and the next day he was told he was going to court that evening, as they weren't sitting any earlier due to the heat of the day. This information was conveyed to him by a prisoner who worked in the main holding cell and had managed to translate for him. For some petty criminals, they have to pay a small fee to be released but if they are unable to do this, they are put to work cleaning the floors and carrying out other chores before they are given a meal of naan bread, eggs and chick peas, and then finally released.

The court where Paul now found himself comprised three Arab

men sitting behind a desk. The stewardess had claimed that Paul had hit her during the altercation, which to this day he strenuously denies. He thinks she made the claim up to justify her initial, erratic behaviour in snatching the inhalator from him.

Paul thought that having been sent to court, he would be able to plead his case but this didn't happen. The men simply talked among themselves and then handed Paul some papers which he couldn't understand as they were in Arabic. It was to materialise that they had fined him one hundred pounds. He was taken back to the cell and then, after four hours, was escorted back to the airport.

Paul was able to get the money for the fine out of a cash machine and he paid the police officers who had accompanied him, before they left him alone in the airport.

By now he had missed his connecting flight to Goa and he was stranded in Doha Airport. Denise, meanwhile, was waiting for him in Goa and had sent someone to collect him from the airport. Paul went to the airline help-desk and was told that due to the incident, he wasn't allowed to fly with Qatar Airlines.

His phone was in his suitcase which was being held by the airline but he managed to use one of the airport desk phones and was able to get hold of Barbara, Denise's mum, who by now was aware of Paul's disappearance as Denise had posted her concerns on Facebook. Paul briefly explained what was going on and after sixteen hours of waiting in Doha Airport, Barbara managed to get him a flight back to Heathrow with Gulf Airlines.

Eventually Paul touched down in London again. He hadn't made it to Goa, and had spent thirty-six hours in three different airports and holding cells, before going home.

Once back, Paul collected Horse from a dog-sitter in Hammersmith and then went to Barbara's to get Bruise. Barbara said she could have got Paul a connecting flight to Goa if she had understood properly what was happening but had thought he just needed to get home after his ordeal. Paul wasn't arguing and was just extremely relieved to have survived his very own 'Banged up Abroad' incident.

The whole troubling episode did however have a happy ending as the day after he got home, Paul decided to dig the garden, which had been on his to-do list for a while. He planned to get the lawn sorted out, having not really utilised the garden since he had moved in.

Unexpectedly, while digging, he unearthed a plastic bag. After he had dug it out, he opened it to reveal various old five, ten and fifty pound banknotes. Most of it had been mashed together with years of moisture in the soil but some of it was able to be dried out.

Paul then took the hoard to the Bank of England. He said he had found the money in an old ornament in his home, in case they queried where it had come from. They sent the notes off to be analysed and three weeks later he received £3,000, transferred directly into his bank account.

A few days later he dug up another part of the garden and found more notes, this time lots of old ten pound banknotes which had been folded over and buried in another plastic bag. He put his new stash out to dry on the living room floor and these notes weren't as tattered as the previous ones so when he went to the bank, they gave him £2,000 there and then.

Paul came to the conclusion that the money had been put there not by the previous owner of the flat, but by an older tenant who must have hidden it, not told anyone, and then died. Philosophically, Paul feels he just wasn't meant to go to Goa and his reward for his ordeal ended up being £5,000.

Paul hasn't been back to India since the near-brush with the foreign jail but he might try and go again, some year, for Christmas and New Year. Flights around this season tend to be only £600 return, although he also needs to find £15 a day for each dog to be looked after while he's away.

Shortly after returning from his botched trip to Goa and the surprise £5,000 find, Paul was given a date for his voluntary stay in rehab. It was a date in early June 2014 but just before he was due to start, he contracted a nasty bug and was laid up for three days.

As soon as he recovered, he drank heavily and consumed a mix of cocaine, cannabis and diazepam. On the Monday, he smoked what was left of his cannabis. He was then clean on the Tuesday and headed off for his second rehab visit, this time at Nelson's Trust in Stroud, Gloucestershire.

When he arrived, he confessed what he had taken and was then tested, which showed up positive for all the drugs he had taken during the previous days. He was placed on a treatment programme and was told what he could expect over the next few months of his rehabilitation.

However, unlike his first time in rehab where he fully committed to the process, he struggled this time to fully engage. In the end, he would only be there for six weeks before deliberately sabotaging it. His intentions, whilst perhaps genuine at the start, weren't to last long.

Shortly after arriving at the Nelson's Trust, he was informed that he had an assessment with the Unemployment Office. It was unheard of for a client to have a medical capability assessment while in rehab so Paul kicked up a big stink. The benefits staff wanted to make sure he was able for work but he said he was in rehab and on medication. However, they insisted he leave to attend an hour-long interview with them.

Paul wasn't happy about his rehab being interrupted but he was being left with little option so he attended the interview as requested, before returning to Stroud. Bizarrely, it was worth it though. Several weeks after the interview, he received a letter informing him that he was due a back payment of almost £2,000 and that they were changing his benefit from Job Seekers Allowance to Incapacity Benefit & Employment Support Extra Allowance.

Paul was understandably over the moon with this unexpected turn of events! The only problem was that the rehab staff had his bank card. When clients enter rehab, usually the rehab staff will take control of their finances to avoid the client being tempted to access cash for drink or drugs. During the programme, if a client wants money, the staff will take them to the bank and supervise the withdrawals.

When Paul heard he had this money, his immediate thought was that he wanted to end his rehab and return home. But he had to find a way to get his bank card back and to be allowed to leave rehab.

Initially when he had entered rehab, Paul had been allocated a big double room. The man he was sharing with was lovely and the pair got on really well. Soon after Paul had started, his room-mate left, so Paul had the room all to himself and was happy to stay there.

But shortly after he had returned from his visit to the Unemployment Office, he was allocated a new room-mate, a man from Luton. This new partner was, as Paul describes, "a nutter" who woke up shouting and screaming most nights.

Paul was already itching to go so he could get access to his newly-acquired money and the new crazed room-mate only heightened his desire to escape.

In rehab, clients are sometimes allowed to return home for a day or two, depending on their circumstances and the terms of their rehabilitation programme. Paul badgered them to be given permission to leave to take care of business at home and eventually managed to convince them that he should be allowed to go home. They finally agreed and gave him his bank card.

Although the staff had initially said he could go home, they then rang Paul halfway into his homeward journey and said that he couldn't go as, quite rightly, they had become concerned about his intentions. One of the staff members, who Paul lovingly describes as "a cunt", had said that he had to go back but Paul told the caller to "tell him to fuck off".

By the time he had got off the tube at Shepherd's Bush, he had rang Denise and asked her to meet him at Café Nero. Any lingering thoughts he had of going back were gone as he was now fuming with the rehab staff so he said, "come on, we're going to Wetherspoons". Upon their arrival, Paul bought a bottle of Champagne and not long after they bought some cocaine to share together.

The next day, a meeting was arranged by the rehab staff for Paul, in Warwick Road, Earls Court, which he attended. Here they asked him for a urine test and he immediately tested positive for cocaine. They told him that as he had sabotaged the rehab programme deliberately, he wouldn't be allowed to go back.

Paul's latest attempt at rehabilitation had come to a shuddering and abrupt end! However, during his short second spell, he did have some clear moments of reflection on his life. To give an indication of his conflicted thoughts and what he felt when he had a sober clarity of desire to change, he wrote:

The realisation is I can't, I don't want to drink, take drugs. I want to create for myself a better life for me, an understanding of me, feeling pain and knowing how to handle it and sometimes ask for help when needed. I need to work the rooms, get a sponsor, meet clean healthy people and be fucking able to be honest to myself and everyone else and chase my dreams. They are achievable, they are realistic, specific and time-bound. I know I can have a good life without material possessions. But I need and am trying to deal with life, abstinent, day by day, not projecting, not beating myself up and slowing down sometimes. All my life it's been hungry work. If I apply some of this to my abstinence like then, I'm getting there. I thank everyone for putting up with me, guiding me, telling me no, pushing me through painful times. I'm truly grateful, blessed, sincere and very importantly tired, fed up and I owe me, my inner child, and those around me in my life, a fucking better break and better things.

Despite him abandoning his rehab programme, there was no follow-up. The system is a bit disjointed. As Paul had volunteered to go into rehab and it wasn't something that had been court-mandated, once probation had signed off on it and transferred it to Nelson's Trust, he was off their books and they no longer had any interest. Similarly, when he left Stroud and tested positive for the cocaine use, they weren't interested in him as a client any longer. Thus, Paul was free to carry on with the rest of his life, provided of course he kept his nose clean from now on.

Through rehab, everything leading up to it and then working with people in the criminal justice system, Paul had gained a real insight into the criminal world and importantly, how addictions can often be used to mitigate the perceived reasons for an offender's activity.

Paul knows his addiction wasn't like the situation of junkies committing crimes to feed their habit, which is perhaps most common. His criminal activity has been more through choice. He self-medicated and he knew what he was doing, in and out of his drug use. Many people do things when they are out of their minds on drink or drugs - either criminal or just life choices – but Paul never felt like any of the substances were controlling his behaviours or courses of action.

This awareness however does not negate the clear negative feelings of shame and remorse surrounding his involvement in the theft of the

Range Rover in 2014 and his subsequent arrest and court proceedings. Paul describes this process in no uncertain terms as a "pure cunty nastiness on myself". Although he has never actually been sent to prison for the crimes he has committed, his sense of shame over the incidents may in some way be punishment enough.

Undoubtedly, Paul knows that if anything happens again, then he will surely go to prison. He accepts that he has had his fair share of "getting away with it", and is now at the end of what he can realistically expect to be allowed off with.

He felt gob-smacked at the time, and still does now, about the shoplifting, the Royal Mail thefts and then the Range Rover and how he managed to get away with it all. He is not alone and many others have asked him things like "how the fuck did you get off with that?"

Perhaps one reason that he did get away with it is that magistrates and judges are constantly faced with hardened criminals who genuinely couldn't care less and would stab their own gran on the street for a few pounds. Maybe the various judges and magistrates have seen what the real Paul is like – the vulnerable, conflicted, addicted man who underneath it all is a decent human being who wouldn't benefit from the harsh world of prison? Paul's crimes haven't robbed innocent people directly and he hasn't stabbed anyone (unless you count Sean!) so maybe there is that sense that he didn't truly deserve to go to prison for what he had done.

Paul isn't naive though, and knows that his criminal days are finished. He has come to realise that he needs to make some better, more resolute life alterations. And he knows he has to be more aware of people that, previously, he was spending too much time with and who were having a negative influence on his life.

One such person is Denise, who was someone Paul had once been very close to. But now, he feels that she was someone who encouraged him to drink excessively and to engage in other negative behaviours. His relationship with Denise has recently become quite strained. It is a direct reflection of a lot of Paul's friendships – they serve a purpose at the time but if he is committed to engaging in a better way of being, then sometimes he has to let go of those people that hold him back from that course.

Chapter 34 - Fifty, What Else?

Paul has reached the age of fifty, a feat which in itself looked unlikely at times. He has survived a multitude of challenges and already faced more life experiences than the average person encounters throughout their whole time on this planet. Yet, in comparison, he is still relatively young and has a lot more living left to do.

So what priorities does Paul now concentrate on and what direction should his future life take?

Good and positive friendships remain one of his chief desires, and female company in particular is very important to him. Women have always played a huge part in Paul's life and he always feels he can trust them more than men. He was brought up by his mum, nan and sister with no father-figure and was always taught not to trust men, and black men in particular.

Paul has very few male friends, and no gay friends at all, to speak of. He doesn't like the whole 'cabaret', promiscuous gay scene with the associated rarity of monogamous, loving relationships. And it's not just other men that he mistrusts. He also thinks that maybe he can't trust himself as much as he mistrusts the next man.

In his heart Paul feels like a dinosaur and fears that the queens would have a field day with him nowadays. He asserts that the gay scene is so good at persecuting their own. Homosexuals want to be integrated and accepted but then they have a tendency to often bully and segregate their own.

Though Paul is clearly gay, he has had straight sex at different points in his life. Not that long ago, as recently as a few years back, he had straight sex with a girl that he was friendly with. Paul fucked his female friend in front of her male partner. It was a fantasy that the couple had and they saw Paul as a safe bet to be the third-party. Paul didn't get direct satisfaction from the sex but he did enjoy the whole buzz of the event, helped by a serious amount of cocaine.

This couple had worked on Paul, doing lots of cocaine with him most Friday nights for a while. They soon started playing strip poker together and after many months, worked Paul into being part of the sex act.

The girl clearly enjoyed being fucked by another man and came during the act. To Paul though it was just a thing to do, and it carried no great satisfaction but no remorse either. For him it was just another different experience.

Paul, having now distanced himself from Denise, has very few close friends, citing Linda Brown and Karen Flynn, who he knew from the Holland Road days and before Denise, as his best friends who remain to this day. They drop in and out and are proper friends who, even if they don't see each other for a long time, can just pick up from where they left off whenever they do come into contact with each other.

This lack of close friendships doesn't really bother Paul, and certainly not in the way it may have done in his past. He doesn't really need anyone now and is very content in his own skin, enjoying his own company more than that of others. It would seem as he turned fifty, that he was happier not to have to engage with anyone as opposed to some people of the same age who seem to have the constant urge to be out and about.

Paul, for many years, felt like he had to be out, to be around people but yet always feeling like he didn't fit in. Now, older and wiser, he has a greater understanding and acceptance of himself and that sense of needing to be accepted by others is diminishing. He now knows himself better than he ever did. The days of self-medicating to try and fit in don't exist anymore. He can go anywhere and be around anyone and not feel awkward or that he doesn't belong. Finally, it seems, he has found his place.

Paul had always intended to complete this book project by the time he was fifty, so now having achieved it, what are his other goals?

He still retains his strong love of horses and one day dreams of having a young horse to train. Preferably he would do it in Ireland, his adopted homeland, a place he has always harboured a desire to move to, and a nation deeply steeped in all things equine. Ideally, he would like to move there before he is sixty. He loves Ireland and he loves Irish horses with their hardiness, due mainly to the weather.

There are many good quality Irish, German and Italian show-jumping horses and his wish would be to find a rough diamond and school it to become a prized beast. His plan is to semi-retire in Ireland, get a part-time job that pays for him to live and then, in his spare time, train a young horse that is already broken. He dreams of having his own jumping horse, an all-rounder, that he can school in an indoor and outdoor ménage and then sell on.

Paul has a vision of working for himself with horses, in beautiful scenery. He already has links with Donegal and the North Coast of Ireland and would also like to explore Waterford, Cork and other areas before deciding where to settle. In Ireland, there are vast swathes of open space, fields and beaches that you can't get in London where the cost of living and options for keeping a horse are also limited. And, in the capital, there are hardly any places where you can open up a horse and really gallop. Bridle paths aren't the same, and as Paul is used to quality settings such as the Priory, LWEC and Queen Anne's ride to Windsor Castle, there would be no compromise – this is the way he knows and this is what he would want to keep doing.

Before that, and while still in London, Paul is keen to put his skills to good use by offering himself as a volunteer, perhaps with the RSPCA or another dog centre. He knows about things like health and safety, bloods and spillages and it would enable him to continue to care for those that he has always loved the most – his canine friends.

And what of love? Having reached a half century in years and in experience, he hopes that he will fall in love again. The thought of finding a loving partner is something that he desires but from past experience he won't go looking for someone as this has caused him endless heartache in the past. When he has strived for love, it has never worked out the way he hoped for. He is also very aware of the fact that as he becomes older, he understands more about what he does and doesn't want. He's become ever-more picky and thus the options have become less. Paul now looks more for the interior, rather than the exterior, of a person and this, more than ever, is what attracts him to other men. As a young man, it was more a case of who was most gorgeous or sexy. Now he can see the beauty within far more clearly.

Paul does romanticise about falling in love and having a nice relationship where each partner works together and is at ease with one another. It is genuine companionship that he seeks more than anything these days. He would love a relationship with someone he gets on really well with and who is kind, sincere and thoughtful. It's not going to define his life but it would be the icing on his cake, he feels.

Paul craves that old-school dating world where you got to know someone first before you got to sleep with them. He went down that road before with Tim, they slept together every night for four weeks before having sex. And with the love of his life, Sean, they didn't have sex for the first three weeks. Looking back on those experiences, that's how Paul wants things to be – getting to know someone before you jump in the sack.

In the gay arena, it can be difficult to achieve this. Sex is like a fast-food takeaway, the availability is there, it's open 24/7, and as soon as you get your leg over, you're getting your head over the mattress. It's a very quick and disposable world and Paul wants better than that, more now than ever before.   He looks for that steady start that he enjoyed with Tim and Sean in his previous existences, to have that mental and inner attraction as much as the physical one.

The initial flirting, getting-to-know-you phase is a wonderful part of the game but having sex can often move the players away from that. Paul doesn't want the easy, meaningless and sometimes damaging, soul-destroying sex which has no value or validation.

In the past he has been a sexual piece of meat, whether that was desired or not. Now he craves to be someone's internal, mental, intellectual companion as much, if not more, than their physical partner.

Paul admits he still loves Sean and acknowledges that he always will, but he knows their relationship wasn't right for many years. After Sean, he has had very few and far between one-night stands and certainly not anything he would call a boyfriend. He felt he needed time off after Sean having spent nearly twenty-five years with him, so isn't on the gay scene at all these days.

Paul has had a few last liaisons with Sean over the past few years but has always regretted it afterwards. Whenever it happens, it's like their relationship is back on and it then quickly becomes a nightmare. Sean would have him back straight away and that's why Paul has to be careful with how he plays the situation. One little bit of affection and Sean thinks they're together again, that all the bad stuff is forgotten, and everything is suddenly rosy. But Paul can't forget about the "cunt" in Sean and how "fucking hideous" much of their time spent together was.

In the bedroom, Paul and Sean never had any problems at all. This probably goes a long way to explaining why they had such longevity, as even when all else was failing around them, they still had the magic intensity of each other's bodies. It was out of the bedroom where everything became fucked up but it was their intimacy and love-making that managed to paint a sexy, hazy cloud over the obvious issues in the rest of their relationship.

Although he clearly carries a soft spot for Sean, Paul thinks the main reason they have always been drawn back to each other is the 'better the devil you know' emotions.

Last year, Paul turned fifty - something that, many times throughout his life, he thought he would never even get close to. His 50th birthday wasn't just a big deal as one of the major milestones in his life, it was far more than that as he has always separated his life, at least in his mind, in terms of what and who he wanted to be up to fifty, and the man he dreamed of becoming beyond this date.

Mixed in with this huge array of feelings was the memory of his life with his mother, whose birthday is the day after Paul's, on the 24th July. This is always a raw month for Paul and the last year was the most emotional yet with the milestone of turning fifty, the memories he has of his mum that resurface at this time of year and the inner turmoil from the huge swell of sensitivities that always accompany such thoughts.

The early chapters of this book contain a large amount of Paul's memories of his upbringing and there is a lot of reference within this to his mum. It would seem that when you look at it in the whole, it was a good, positive relationship that they shared. Paul agrees with this sentiment – in his early years he was spoilt with affection in the opposite way that he feels his other brothers and sister were starved of affection.

It is a strange anomaly that whilst Paul's brothers never experienced the same level of emotional connection to their mother, they were all there at her bedside at the end and were able to have their own sense of closure to their relationship. Paul was undoubtedly held most dear and precious by his troubled mum. He was the only one to experience the unique complexity of the union that they shared. Yet, he was never afforded the opportunity to say goodbye and find for himself that degree of finality that the rest of the family seemed to gain.

Paul, now older and reflecting on his life, knows that, despite his mum and his nan's life issues, they spoilt him and this alienated him from his siblings. He had chosen to leave home aged fifteen. The smothering he received may have had something to do with him being able to leave at such a young age and feeling confident and secure enough that he could go away. The rest of the siblings stayed living close by, almost as if they were hanging on for the attention they never had in childhood.

Paul does have a current link to his past though which is blossoming and from which he takes great pride and joy. His niece, Laura, who had been raised as his little sister, would eventually move back to live with her dad, Peter. After many years of struggling to cope with the death of his young wife, Peter had again settled down, this time with a woman called Leanda who he is still with today.

Laura had gone back to live with her dad and his new partner and later was surprised to learn that they had actually got married without her knowing. The young girl only found out when she asked where a new microwave had come from, to be told it was a wedding present! Laura wasn't used to surprises, as Paul's mum had always told her what had really happened to her as she was growing up.

Paul is very much in Laura's life now and they speak every few weeks. She has recently asked him to be Godfather to her new baby which Paul is over the moon about. He has often fantasised about having his own child, but obviously with the way his life has panned out this is filled with complexity so he sees his role as Godfather to the young child, James (or James Junior to Paul), as the next best thing. Paul says James Junior is the first baby he has ever really liked, given that he is gorgeous and not one of these babies "with the usual crunched-up face!"

Laura has just moved from Canary Wharf to a permanent address which is a two-minute walk from where Paul's mum's ashes were scattered in Wapping, East London. It's also a one-minute walk from her dad but they now don't speak and he hasn't even met the baby. Similarly, Paul doesn't speak to his brother, describing him as a "stubborn bastard" who just goes to work and then goes home to get stoned.

Paul has always tried, where possible, to keep the family together and has maintained contact with them whenever he can. Admittedly, there were several years where he didn't engage with his family at all, but he had his reasons for that and in the main, he has tried to make amends.

His sister, Elaine, once said to Paul during his time in Stroud that she didn't know him, perhaps not uncommon in some modern day families, especially as they had gone to different schools and then had separate lives in their adulthood. This hurt Paul though and as he gets older, he is keen to re-establish those important bonds that he spent years missing out on.

Paul is also making music with his nephew, Wesley, who is Elaine's son. Paul gets on well with Wesley, who he sees occasionally. He finds that he has more in common and enjoys the company more of his younger niece and nephew than he does with his own siblings and puts this down to them knowing him more than Peter or Elaine do. It's a nice development as Paul would've seen the nieces and nephews regularly when they were children as Paul's mum watched them while Peter and Elaine went to work. Paul loves to be called uncle Paul and having lived a childless life, he very much enjoys the paternal feeling he gets with his youthful relations.

Paul has achieved many of his life ambitions, to have got to fifty, and to have accomplished a variety of things before he reached this significant milestone. The documenting of his chaotic life through this book was one of his major aims, as is being in a recording studio. But perhaps his biggest achievement is him finally working out who he wants to be as a person and finding a place where he is genuinely comfortable within himself.

On reflection, Paul remains eternally philosophical and believes everything has happened to him for a reason. He contemplates one of the most important features of his life - his mother - and how that ultimately turned out. He thinks maybe it all evened itself out in the end – Paul had the maternal bond throughout his life while his siblings had the final chance to say their goodbyes and find their inner peace at the end. As Paul puts it, "maybe they needed it more".

Paul did eventually find his own way, in his own time, to finally let his mother go. It wasn't like in 2009 when he wrote the 'no-send' letter to his nan but he did construct a 'no-send' process in his head.

Also, in his home, Paul has two stones which are very precious to him and which he keeps especially safe – one for his mum, and one for his nan. He can't remember exactly where he got them from but he recalls it was when he was at a beach somewhere and whilst there, he found a way to say his goodbyes to his beloved mother.

And has Paul used up all of his nine lives? He's had his fair share of life-threatening experiences and near-death events and undoubtedly, he's been blessed with good luck. He could easily have been fatally drowned as a child when he was pushed into the River Thames. His time with the serial killer might have led to an abrupt and very gruesome ending to his story. The gods were shining on him when they picked so many he knew to contract AIDS but left him alone and healthy. And how he has managed to avoid being sent to prison remains utterly remarkable. All these experiences and many more could have resulted in a very different and tragic outcome, but Paul has managed to make it through.

Fast forward ten years and perhaps Paul will be living in Ireland, engaged in hard work, training horses and being around dogs – he has always loved the idea of owning his own Irish wolfhound, the most majestic of all the canines.

Maybe he will have his projects to keep him interested but be living an otherwise relaxed and wholesome lifestyle. Or conceivably, he'll have a partner that he feels completely at one with.

All of these possibilities would be totally brilliant, according to Paul, although he would also throw in his other great love – music – and would find this combination to be a most pleasing vision of his future life.

On the 23rd July 2017, Paul turned fifty. With so much emphasis on reaching the landmark, he felt as though he should commemorate it properly. He had considered what the most appropriate way for him to celebrate would be and decided that if he was to choose one club that would be more fitting than all the others, it would have to be Heaven, under the arches at Charing Cross, at the legendary G-A-Y club, founded by Jeremy Joseph.

He chose this for the memories but also so he could be sure of finding the right sound with the different music across the various rooms and levels that collectively make up Heaven. Given his previous life experience he admitted that he would probably also have "a dabble" and indulge in a little cocaine for the last time, or at least for a while.

The reality though is that Paul didn't go out for a mad clubbing night on his 50th birthday. Instead, he went for a meal with his good friends, Linda Brown, who coincidentally shares his birthday, and Karen Flynn, along with Linda's daughter, Leigh. This is the clearest indication yet that although Paul still harbours some small desire to go out on the town and to take drugs and get drunk like the good old days, in truth he's happier sitting down for some nice food and quality company.

He didn't put a definitive time frame on it but the day after his birthday, on his mum's birthday, he gave her a present which was for him to be abstinent from all alcohol and drugs. This wasn't necessarily for ever and Paul was keen to not put pressure on himself as he knew that might mean he would end up as the teenage Paul and want to rebel and break his promises to himself.

He was though aiming to be abstinent for the foreseeable future. He had decided that should he be invited to a special event, like a wedding, that he would allow himself to have a glass of champagne as a toast. Also when his great nephew was being christened and Paul was there as godfather for the first time, he'd allow himself a drink or two. He reserved the right to break his abstinence but only on this special occasion, or others like it. Generally, he wanted clarity and a clear mind going forward for his next five year goals and his focus on getting his horse and, perhaps, his Irish wolfhound.

Given Paul's experiences in life, it was suggested to him that he'd do well to last the week! He looked thoughtful, pondering the reality of everything he had been, everything he was at that immediate moment and all the things he wanted to be in the future and said that impression of him wasn't accurate anymore.

Without a flicker of irony and with a deadpan look on his face, Paul insisted, "that's not fair - I'll definitely last at least a week and a half!"

We'll let you decide whether you think he got that far or not......

Printed in Great Britain
by Amazon